INFUSING Diversity & Cultural Competence into TEACHER EDUCATION

Aaron Thompson
Eastern Kentucky University

Joseph B. Cuseo
Emeritus, Marymount College

Kendall Hunt
publishing company

Book Team

Chairman and Chief Executive Officer   Mark C. Falb
President and Chief Operating Officer   Chad M. Chandlee
Vice President, Higher Education   David L. Tart
Director of Publishing Partnerships   Paul B. Carty
Editorial Manager   Georgia Botsford
Senior Editor   Lynnette M. Rogers
Vice President, Operations   Timothy J. Beitzel
Assistant Vice President, Production Services   Christine E. O'Brien
Senior Production Editor   Sheri Hosek
Permissions Editor   Renae Horstman
Cover Designer   Jeni Fensterman

Cover image © Shutterstock, Inc.

www.kendallhunt.com
Send all inquiries to:
4050 Westmark Drive
Dubuque, IA 52004-1840

Copyright © 2012 by Kendall Hunt Publishing Company

ISBN 978-0-7575-9940-8

All rights reserved. No part of this publication may be reproduced, stored in a retrieval system, or transmitted, in any form or by any means, electronic, mechanical, photocopying, recording, or otherwise, without the prior written permission of the copyright owner.

Printed in the United States of America
10 9 8 7 6 5 4 3 2 1

Brief Contents

Chapter 1 → Defining and Describing Diversity   1

Human *variety* and *similarity* coexist and complement one another. Thus, diversity education not only enhances appreciation of human differences, it also promotes awareness of universal aspects of the human experience that are common to all people—whatever their particular social or cultural background happens to be. This chapter defines diversity and explains why it should be a part of the formal educational process.

Chapter 2 → The Benefits of Diversity Education   25

The terms "diversity education" and "multicultural education" often conjure up thoughts of cultural appreciation exercises, such as schools celebrating Black History Month, or students bringing artifacts to school that represent their ethnic group. Although these are useful exercises and should be continued, diversity education means more than annual or celebratory events—it is an ongoing learning process that should take place consistently and pervasively throughout the curriculum.

Chapter 3 → Appreciating Diversity: Avoiding Stereotypes and Overcoming Biases   45

All humans carry bias. However as a part of humanity, educators are responsible for not allowing bias to control them. Overcoming bias and moving toward appreciation of diversity may be viewed as a systematic, sequential process. This chapter provides a model for overcoming and controlling bias, thus increasing our opportunity to appreciate and practice diversity.

Chapter 4 → The Context for Diversity Education: Student, Family, School, and Community   73

A school's ability to promote its students' academic achievement is influenced by its teachers, students, students' families, and the surrounding community. When all four of these influential sources work together in a mutually reinforcing manner, students' level of educational achievement can be elevated dramatically. This chapter focuses on how teachers can use all of a student's essential environmental elements in the learning process.

Chapter 5 → Intercultural Communication and Relationship-Building Skills   97

The objective of this chapter is to provide a blueprint for developing a curriculum that includes such skills. The chapter is written primarily for a student audience. Teachers may also use the information in this chapter for ideas and strategies for increasing their own interpersonal contact with people from diverse cultures, or to enhance their intercultural communication skills.

Chapter 6 → *Teaching* for Diversity: Culturally Inclusive and Responsive Instructional Strategies   119

One way teachers can focus on the individual learner is through differentiated instruction which allows teachers to meet the learning needs of every student. If a student is engaged in his or her learning, the student will place more value in the process of becoming an educated citizen. This chapter focuses on student-centered teaching and learning.

Chapter 7 → Effective Culturally Inclusive Assessment of Student Learning and Academic Performance   151

The goal of this chapter is to equip prospective teachers with skills for improving the quality, validity, and equity of assessing student learning. Good principles and strategies for formative and summative assessment will improve the quality of teaching and promote the academic achievement of students from diverse cultural backgrounds.

Contents

Preface vii
Acknowledgments xi
About the Authors xii

1 → Defining and Describing Diversity 1

Activate Your Thinking 1
What Is Cultural Diversity? 7
What Is Ethnic Diversity? 9
What Is Racial Diversity? 9
Diversity from a Cultural Perspective 11
Diversity from a Societal Perspective: Differences in Socioeconomic Status (a.k.a., Social Class) 14
    Diversity in Income 14
    Diversity in Level of Education 16
Diversity from a National Perspective 16
Diversity from an International Perspective 18
Diversity from a Global Perspective 18
Diversity from the Perspective of the Universe (Cosmos) 19
Summary and Conclusion 20
Exercises 23

2 → The Benefits of Diversity Education 25

1. Diversity Education Develops Self-Knowledge, Self-Awareness, and Self-Insight 26
2. Diversity Education Deepens and Accelerates Learning 27
3. Diversity Education Strengthens Students' Ability to Think Critically from Multiple Perspectives 30
4. Diversity Fosters Creative Thinking 34
5. Diversity Education Promotes Career Preparation for the 21st Century 34
6. Diversity Expands Social Relationships and Emotional Intelligence 36
7. Diversity Education Reduces Prejudice and Discrimination in Society 37
8. Diversity Education Preserves Democracy 39

Summary and Conclusion 40
Exercise 43

3 → Appreciating Diversity: Avoiding Stereotypes and Overcoming Biases 45

Stereotyping 45
Prejudice 47
Discrimination 48
Segregation 49
Causes of Prejudice and Discrimination 54
    Feeling Comfortable with the Familiar and Uncomfortable with the Unknown or Unfamiliar 54
    Using Selective Perception and Selective Memory 55
    Mentally Categorizing People into "In" and "Out" Groups 56
    Perceiving Members of Other Groups as More Alike than Members of One's Own Group 57
    The Tendency for Majority Group Members to Be More Strongly Influenced by Negative Behaviors Committed by Members of Minority Groups than by Members of Their Own (Majority) Group 58
    Rationalizing Prejudice and Discrimination as Justifiable 58
    Strengthening Self-Esteem through Group Membership and Group Identity 59
A Personal Development Model for Overcoming Bias and Appreciating Student Diversity 60
    Stage 1. Awareness 61
    Stage 2. Acknowledgment 63
    Stage 3. Acceptance 65
    Stage 4. Action 66
Summary and Conclusion 69
Exercises 71

4 → The Context for Diversity Education: Student, Family, School, and Community 73

Student Diversity 74
Family Diversity 77
Community Diversity 80
School Diversity 82
    The Curriculum 83
    Teachers 87
    School Leaders 89
Summary and Conclusion 91
Exercises 95

5 → Intercultural Communication and Relationship-Building Skills 97

Strategies for Interacting with People without Bias or Prejudice 97
Meeting and Interacting with People from Diverse Backgrounds 98
Interpersonal Communication Skills: Speaking and Listening 99
Human Relations Skills (a.k.a., "People Skills") 105
Take a Leadership Role with Respect to Diversity 110
Summary and Conclusion 115
Exercise 117

6 → *Teaching* for Diversity: Culturally Inclusive and Responsive Instructional Strategies 119

Making the Student-*Teacher* Connection: Establishing Rapport with Your Class 123
Making Student-*Student* (Peer) Connections: Promoting Peer Interaction and Creating a Sense of Community among Classmates 128
Engaging Students in *Small* Group Work 129
    When to Use Small Group Work 130
Strategies for Improving the Quality of Small Group Learning 130
Making the Student-*Course* (Subject) Connection: Engaging Students with the Subject Matter 135
Summary and Conclusion 147
Exercise 149

7 → Effective Culturally Inclusive Assessment of Student Learning and Academic Performance 151

Student Learning Is Promoted by *Frequent Assessment* 156
Hold High Expectations for All Students 157
Student Learning Is Promoted by the Delivery of Performance-Improving *Feedback* 165
Student Learning Is Enhanced by Exercises or Assignments That Promote *Self-Assessment* and *Self-Awareness* 169
Summary and Conclusion 172
Exercise 173

Glossary 175

References 179

Index 199

Preface

Research has shown that the quality of teachers has a direct, considerable impact on student achievement (Marzano, 2003; Sanders & Rivers, 1996). Teachers that are considered to be the most effective possess several traits: excellent verbal communication; solid content and pedagogical knowledge; insight into the process of learning and learners; the ability to construct useful curriculum, engaging learning tasks, and assessments that reveal strengths and weaknesses; and the ability to be self-aware with a continual practice of reflecting on and improving teaching practices (Darling-Hammond, 2000; Darling-Hammond & Bransford, 2005; Wilson, Floden, & Ferrini-Mundy, 2001). However, there isn't a wealth of research concerning how teacher education programs can assist future teachers in being better prepared. The Alliance for Excellent Education released a policy brief in 2009 titled "Teaching for a New World: Preparing High School Educators to Deliver College and Career Ready Instruction" which outlines a plan to ensure teacher candidates have the skills necessary to prepare students for entry into postsecondary education or the workforce; it also encourages teacher education programs to focus on the skills, competencies, and knowledge base teacher candidates should possess once they become classroom teachers.

The demographics of American schools are changing. Between 1996 and 2006, the number of minority students enrolled in elementary and secondary public schools increased by 31.3 percent (National Center for Education Statistics [NCES], 2008). The number of students who had limited English proficiency enrolled in K–12 public education increased by 57.2 percent between 1995 and 2005 (National Clearinghouse for English Language Acquisition, n.d.). The number of people in the United States living in poverty increased to 43.6 million (14.3%) in 2009, the largest figure in the history of poverty data collected for the past 51 years. For those under age 18, the poverty rate increased to 20.7 percent in 2009 (DeNavas-Walt, Proctor, & Smith, 2010). The percentage of black children who live in poverty is greater than all other ethnic groups; low socioeconomic status is associated with lower educational performance (Vanneman et al., 2009). National Assessment of Educational Progress (NAEP) scores in 2007 indicate some gains in closing the achievement gap; however, white students scored an average of 26 points higher than black students in each subject tested (NCES 2008, p. 455). In order to successfully educate the children of the future, the National Education Association (n.d.) describes cultural competence as "the key to thriving in culturally diverse classrooms." Adapted from the work of Diller and Moule (2004), the National Education Association (NEA; n.d.) identifies five basic cultural competence skill areas: valuing diversity, cultural self-awareness, dynamics of difference; knowledge of students' cultures; and institutionalizing culture knowledge and adapting to diversity.

Given the national focus on college and career readiness and the adoption of a core curriculum by many states, future teachers will need to provide the same level of instruction and hold the same level of expectations for all students. Previously, it was the tradition to have several tracks of instruction based on student goals: one track for bright, motivated students who wanted to attend college; one track for students who wanted to enter vocational work; and, lastly, a track for students who chose not to do either (Alliance for Excellent Education, 2009). Given that the majority of new jobs that offer a living wage require at least some postsecondary education (U.S. Department of Labor, 2008) and research shows the skills required to enter postsecondary education or the workforce are now very similar (ACT, 2006), teacher candidates have a common goal: educating every student and expecting them to succeed in the world after high school. A survey conducted on behalf of The Association of American Colleges and Universities by Hart Research Associates in 2009 revealed that employers are looking for specific skills when hiring new employees. Employers indicated that the demands placed on employees are greater than in the past, with 91 percent responding that they expect employees to have additional responsibilities and use a wider range of skills. Most of the employers surveyed believe that colleges should place more emphasis on skills, including the following: the role of the United States in a global marketplace, cultural diversity in the United States and other countries, communicating in an efficient manner orally and in writing, critical thinking, teamwork and collaboration, creativity, and applying knowledge and skills to real-life situations (Hart Research Associates, 2009). Imagine the effect teachers can have on instilling many of these skill sets in secondary education, putting students on a path of success for college and the workforce. The more preparation students receive before high school graduation, the greater chance that they will be successful. Additionally, Assessment & Teaching of 21st Century Skills (ACT21S; n.d.) has identified four categories of essential 21st century skills after utilizing 250 researchers across 60 institutions worldwide. They are as follows: ways of thinking (creativity, critical thinking, problem solving, decision making); ways of working (communication and collaboration); tools for working (information and communications technology and information literacy); and skills for living in the world (citizenship, life and career, social and personal responsibility) (ACT21S, n.d.).

As teachers face increasing diversity within their classrooms in learning styles, race, linguistics, and culture, the academic rigor needed to successfully enter college or a career will require them to differentiate instruction in order for all students to succeed (Hitchcock, Meyer, Rose, & Jackson, 2002). Research has demonstrated that students make academic progress when they are exposed to teachers that encourage communication and reasoning, are sympathetic in their interactions with students, and create an atmosphere that is welcoming, respectful, encouraging, and enthusiastic toward learning (Howes et al., 2006).

This focus on college and career readiness for all students has placed an emphasis on changes in how we train teachers (Laine, 2008). Areas considered crucial to the competency and effectiveness of future teachers are:

- Skills necessary to work with diverse learners, including special education and English language learners;
- Competence in teaching adolescent literacy skills regardless of content area;
- Ability to utilize and assessment to improve teaching and learning;
- Ability to teach in specific teaching environments, including urban and rural schools; and
- Capacity to communicate content knowledge to students in a manner they understand, customized for the academic discipline (Alliance for Excellent Education, 2009).

Thus, the focus of this book is to provide educators and future educators with pathways for achieving cultural competence. Placing this crucial competence in the teacher's toolbox will increase their opportunity and the capacity of ensuring success in and out of the classroom. The tools presented in this book will assist the teacher in making gains in closing achievement gaps, building opportunity for all students, building strong pedagogical skills, enhancing curriculum for their diverse students, and constantly assessing all of these areas to ensure they are maintaining their status as the largest contributor to students' success.

diversity

Courtesy of Madison Holly

Acknowledgments

The mere fact that I am the coauthor of this book makes me grateful to all of the teachers in my life that understood that a poor African American kid from Central Appalachia had talents that, although not ascribed by society, could be fully achieved with great instruction and high expectations. I also want to thank my brothers and sisters who did not have the opportunities I had due to racism and classism. I especially want to thank my brother Lawrence who passed this year. He had the ability to see everything good in me even when he was blind. I also want to thank Billy (my father-in-law) who also passed this year. He may have been my second biggest fan behind Lawrence. I will severely miss them both and the confidence they consistently showed they had in me. Indeed, I have leaned on many peers and other community members in my life to grow as a professional and as a person. One of those is my coauthor Joe Cuseo who clearly assisted me in framing many of my current directions. Many call us the twin towers (although somewhat lopsided) of student success. I call us stable peers, solid friends, and pure bluesmen.

Aaron Thompson

I would like to thank the original members of the San Francisco Giants and the original blues musicians who first showed me that I could identify with (and advocate for) people of all colors. Thanks also to my college professors who awakened me to the prevalence of prejudice, the need for tolerance, and the power of diversity. Finally, thanks to my coauthor, Aaron Thompson, for joining with me to form a team characterized by unity in purpose and values despite diversity in race, religiosity, and verticality.

Joe Cuseo

About the Authors

Dr. Aaron Thompson is the Senior Vice President of Academic Affairs at the Kentucky Council on Postsecondary Education and a Professor of Sociology in the Department of Educational Leadership and Policy Studies at Eastern Kentucky University. Thompson has a PhD in Sociology in areas of Organizational Behavior/Race and Gender relations. He is nationally recognized in the areas of educational attainment and academic success, African American fatherhood, divorce in the Black family, and Black and White differences in marital expectations.

His latest coauthored books are *Humanity, Diversity, & the Liberal Arts: Foundation of a College Education, Thriving in the Community College & Beyond: Strategies for Academic Success and Personal Development, Diversity and the College Experience, Thriving in College and Beyond: Research-Based Strategies for Academic Success and Personal Development, Focus on Success,* and *Black Men and Divorce.* His upcoming books are *Infusing Diversity and Cultural Competence into Teacher Education, The Sociological Outlook,* and *Changing Student Culture from the Ground Up.* He has completed more than 30 publications and numerous research and peer-reviewed presentations.

Thompson has traveled across the United States and has given more than 600 workshops, seminars, and invited lectures and/or researched, taught, and/or consulted in areas of assessment, diversity, leadership, ethics, research methodology and social statistics, multicultural families, race, gender and ethnic relations, student success, first-year students, retention, organizational design, closing achievement gaps, living an unbiased life, overcoming obstacles to gain success, creating a school environment for academic success, college readiness, student success, cultural competence, workplace interaction, organizational goal setting, building relationships, the first-year seminar, and a variety of other topics. He has been or is a consultant to educational institutions, corporations, nonprofit organizations, police departments, and other government agencies.

Joe Cuseo holds a doctoral degree in Educational Psychology and Assessment from the University of Iowa. He is Professor Emeritus of Psychology at Marymount College (California) where, for more than 25 years, he directed the first-year seminar (a course required of all new students) and he was a 14-time recipient of the "faculty member of the year award" (a student-driven award based on effective teaching and academic advising). He is also a recent recipient of the American College Personnel Association (ACPA) Diamond Honoree Award (2010) for contributions made to student development and the Student Affairs profession.

Joe has delivered numerous campus workshops and invited presentations across the United States, as well as Canada, Europe, China, and Australia. He has authored articles, monographs, and books on effective teaching, advising, student retention, and student success—the most recent of which are: *Thriving in College and Beyond: Research-Based Strategies for Academic Success & Personal Development* (a textbook for first-year seminars or student success courses) and *Humanity, Diversity, & The Liberal Arts: The Foundation of a College Education* (a common reading for students transitioning from high school to higher education).

Currently, Joe serves as an educational advisor and consultant for AVID—a nonprofit organization whose mission is to promote the college access and success of underserved student populations.

Defining and Describing Diversity

Activate Your Thinking

Please complete the following sentence:

> When I hear the word "diversity," the first thoughts that come to mind are . . .

The primary goal of this chapter is to promote your understanding of the meaning of "diversity" and awareness of its multiple forms or dimensions.

The word *diversity* derives from the Latin root "diversus," meaning various or variation. Thus, human diversity refers to the variety that exists among people who comprise humanity (the human species). As depicted in **Figure 1.1**, the relationship between humanity and diversity is similar to the relationship between

> ❝ We are all brothers and sisters. Each face in the rainbow of color that populates our world is precious and special. Each adds to the rich treasure of humanity. ❞
>
> —Morris Dees, Civil Rights leader and co-founder of the Southern Poverty Law Center

SPECTRUM OF DIVERSITY*

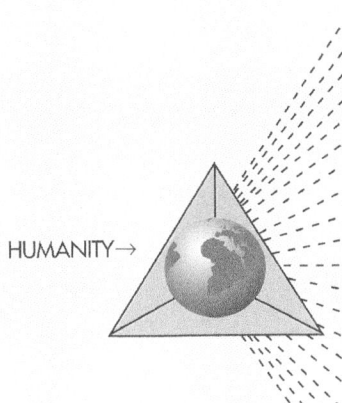

HUMANITY →

- *Gender* (male-female)
- *Age* (stage of life)
- *Race* (e.g., White, Black, Asian)
- *Ethnicity* (cultural background)
- *Socioeconomic status* (educational level/income level)
- *National citizenship* (citizen of U.S. or another country)
- *Native* (first-learned) **language**
- *National origin* (nation of birth)
- *National region* (e.g., raised in north/south)
- *Generation* (historical period when people are born and live)
- *Political ideology* (e.g., liberal/conservative)
- *Religious and Spiritual beliefs* (e.g., Christian/Buddhist/Muslim)
- *Family status* (e.g., single-parent/two-parent family)
- *Marital status* (single/married)
- *Parental status* (with/without children)
- *Sexual orientation* (heterosexual/gay/lesbian/bisexual/transgender)
- *Body type* (e.g., underweight, overweight, obese)
- *Physical ability/disability* (e.g., able to hear/hearing impaired)
- *Mental ability/disability* (e.g., mentally able/challenged)
- *Learning ability/disability* (e.g., absence/presence of dyslexia)
- *Learning styles* (e.g., visual, auditory, kinesthetic)
- *Mental health/illness* (e.g., absence/presence of depression)

FIGURE 1.1

Humanity and Diversity

*This list represents some of the major dimensions of human diversity; it does not represent a complete list of all possible forms of human diversity. Also, disagreement exists about certain dimensions of diversity (e.g., whether certain groups should be considered races or ethnic groups).

sunlight and the spectrum of colors. Just as sunlight passing through a prism disperses into all the different groups of colors that comprise the visual spectrum, the human species occupying planet earth are dispersed into a variety of different groups of people that comprise the human spectrum (humanity).

As you can see in **Figure 1.1**, there's a lot more to diversity than meets the eye. Diversity comes in multiple forms and dimensions, some of which are *hidden or invisible*. Humans differ from each other in a wide variety of ways, including physical features, religious beliefs, mental and physical abilities, national origins, social backgrounds, gender, sexual orientation, and a variety of other dimensions. Although diversity is often thought exclusively in terms of ethnic (cultural) or racial diversity, persons who are members of the same ethnic or racial group may still be diverse with respect to gender, social class (socioeconomic status), religion, and national origin. As a future teacher, the particular forms of diversity that you want to emphasize and capitalize on will depend on the particular composition of your school's student population and its surrounding community.

> " People who would never dream of using an ethnic or racial slur talk about nutcases, wackos, loony tunes, and people all the time say, 'Oh, he's crazy' and it's hurtful, it really is hurtful. "
>
> —Elyn Saks, lawyer, law professor, and author of *The Center Cannot Hold: My Journey Through Madness*—a book about her life as a schizophrenic

---

Reflection 1.1 Look over the list of groups that comprise the diversity spectrum in Figure 1.1. Do you notice any groups missing from the list that should be added, either because they have distinctive characteristics or because they have been targets of prejudice and discrimination?

1.

2.

3.

> " Diversity is a value that is shown in mutual respect and appreciation of similarities and differences. "
>
> —Public Service Enterprise Group

It's important to keep in mind that human *variety* and *similarity* coexist and complement one another. Thus, diversity education not only enhances appreciation of human differences, it also promotes awareness of universal aspects of the human experience that are common to all people—whatever their particular social or cultural background happens to be. For example, despite our racial and ethnic differences, all humans experience the same emotions and communicate them with the same facial expressions (see **Figure 1.2**).

FIGURE 1.2 Humans all over the world display the same facial expressions when experiencing certain emotions. See if you can detect the emotions being expressed in the following faces.
(To find the answers, turn your book upside down.)

  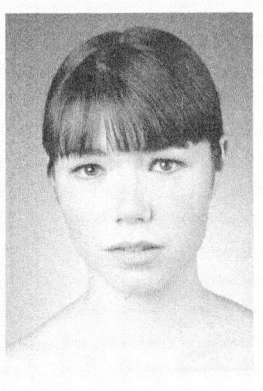
  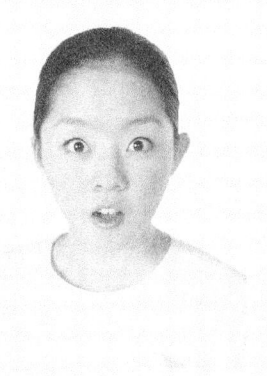

Answers: The emotions shown. Top, left to right: anger, fear, and sadness. Bottom, left to right: disgust, happiness, and surprise.

All images © JupiterImages Corporation.

Reflection 1.2 List three human experiences that you think are universal (i.e., which are experienced by all humans in all cultures).

1.

2.

3.

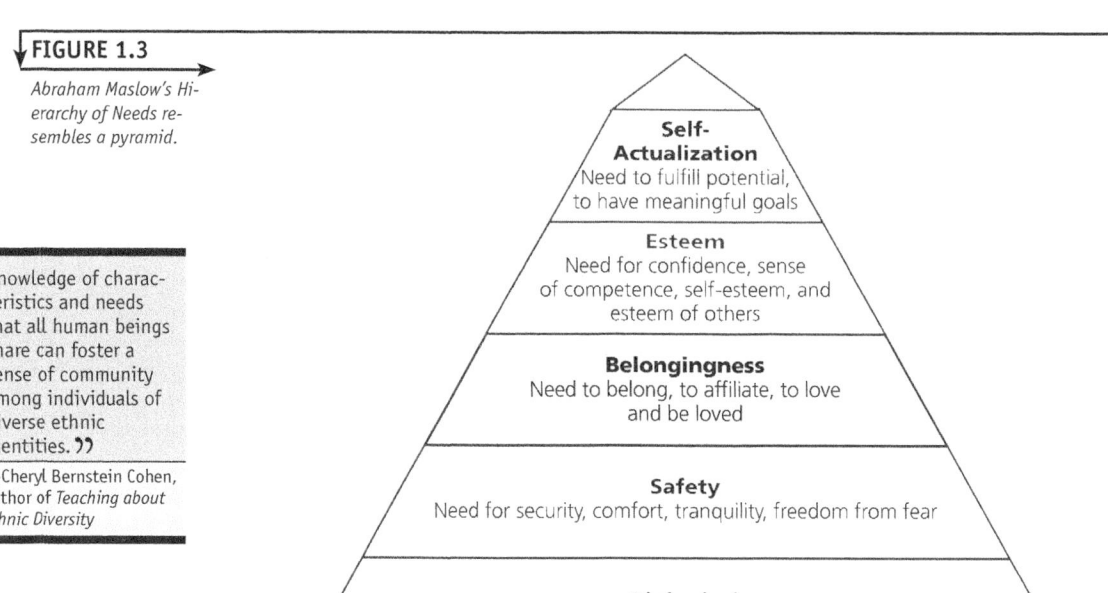

FIGURE 1.3

Abraham Maslow's Hierarchy of Needs resembles a pyramid.

> Knowledge of characteristics and needs that all human beings share can foster a sense of community among individuals of diverse ethnic identities.
>
> —Cheryl Bernstein Cohen, author of *Teaching about Ethnic Diversity*

Human characteristics that anthropologists have found to be shared by all groups of people in every corner of the world include storytelling, poetry, bodily adornment, music and dance, creation and decoration of artifacts, families and socialization of children by elders, a sense of right and wrong, supernatural beliefs, and mourning of the dead (Pinker, 1994). Although different ethnic groups may express these attitudes, beliefs, and practices in different ways, they are universal experiences that are common to all human groups.

Furthermore, humans from all ethnic groups have the same, basic human needs—such as those depicted in **Figure 1.3**—which represents psychologist Abraham Maslow's famous hierarchy (pyramid) of human needs.

PERSONAL INSIGHT

I was born and reared in rural southeastern Kentucky. After many years of teaching about race being more than skin deep but our history has been so heavily ingrained in our psyche that it is all about biology, I had the opportunity to display an example of this in front of a distinguished class of future professionals several years ago. I was a guest lecturer and had asked several people to enter center stage with me to allow the students to ask questions of us. It just so happened that there were four males (including me), two of which were black and two of which were white. The questions could be anything and they had a total of five minutes to ask them. As you can imagine, the questions ranged from the type of employment we were involved in to the type of car we drove. After the time reached its limit on the questions, I asked my three friends to exit stage left. I then asked the students to choose who they thought were the most similar and who were the most different. As you probably guessed, it was reported from the class that the two African-Americans and the two European Americans were the similar pairs. After the three gentlemen rejoined me on stage, I instructed the students to ask several specific cultural questions of the group—specifically on likes, dislikes, upbringing, food, etc. You probably guessed by now that it was found that the African-American from East Kentucky was most similar to the European American from East Tennessee and the Caucasian male from Washington, DC, was most similar to the black male from New York City. First impressions matter but make sure it is not only skin deep.

Aaron Thompson

Consider This...

> Diversity represents variations on the common theme of humanity. Although human groups acquire different cultural differences, those differences are cultivated from the same soil—they are all grounded in the common experience of being human.

The relationship between humanity and diversity is well illustrated by the development of language in children. Although humans across the world speak different languages, when all newborns enter the world, they babble with the same language sounds, which allow them to speak the sounds of any human language. However, they will continue to use only those language sounds they hear spoken in their particular culture—the other babbling sounds they used as newborns will drop out of their oral repertoire (Oller, 1981). The same set of sounds humans use at birth (our "universal language") reflects our common humanity, whereas the distinctive set of sounds different groups of humans use to express themselves in their "native language" reflects our cultural diversity.

Thus, the cultures associated with different groups may be viewed simply as variations on the same theme: being human. You may have heard people say: "We're all human, aren't we?" The answer to this important question is, "yes and no." We are all the same, but not in the same way. A good metaphor for understanding this apparent contradiction is to visualize humanity as a quilt in which different cultural groups are joined together by the common thread of humanity—the common bond of being human. The different patches that comprise the quilt represent diversity—the distinctive cultures that comprise our common humanity. The quilt metaphor acknowledges the identity and beauty of all cultures and differs radically from the original American "melting pot" metaphor, which viewed differences as something that should be melted down or eliminated. The quilt metaphor also differs from the later "salad bowl" metaphor, which suggested that America is a hodgepodge or mishmash of different cultures thrown together without any common connection. In contrast, the quilt metaphor represents the philosophy of cultural pluralism and suggests that the unique identity of different cultural groups should be maintained, recognized, and celebrated; yet, at the same time, these cultural differences are interweaved into a larger, commonly

> ❝ We all live with the objective of being happy; our lives are all different and yet the same. ❞
>
> —Anne Frank, victim of the Holocaust and renowned author of *Anne Frank: The Diary of a Young Girl*, written while she was in hiding for two years with her family during the Nazi occupation of the Netherlands

> ❝ We are all the same, and we are all unique. ❞
>
> —Georgia Dunston, African American biologist and research specialist in human genetics

© steven r. hendricks. Used under license from Shutterstock, Inc.

shared national tapestry (Banks, 2006). On a global level, cultural differences within and across nations join together to form an even larger, unified whole: our shared humanity.

PERSONAL INSIGHT

When I was 12 years old and living in New York City, I returned from school one Friday afternoon and my mother asked me if anything interesting happened at school that day. I mentioned to her that the teacher went around the room, asking us what we had for dinner last night. At that moment, my mother began to become a bit concerned and nervously asked me: "What did you tell the teacher?" I said: "I told her and the rest of the class that I had pasta last night because my family always eats pasta on Thursdays and Sundays." My mother exploded and fired back at me: "Why couldn't you tell her that we had steak or roast beef!" For a moment, I was stunned and couldn't figure out what I had done wrong or why I should have lied about eating pasta. Then it suddenly dawned on me: My mother was embarrassed about being an Italian American. She wanted me to hide our family's ethnic background and make it sound like we were very "American." I never forgot this experience. For the first time in my life, I became aware that my mother was ashamed about being a member of the same group to which every member of my family belonged (including me). After her outburst, I felt a combined rush of astonishment and embarrassment. These feelings eventually faded and my mother's reaction ended up having the opposite effect on me. Instead of making me feel inferior or ashamed about being Italian American, her reaction that day caused me to become more conscious of, and take more pride in, my Italian heritage.

As I grew older, I also grew to understand and sympathize with my mother for feeling the way she did. She had grown up during the era of America's "melting pot"—a time when different American ethnic groups were expected to melt down and melt away their ethnicity. They were not to celebrate diversity, they were to eliminate it.

> "We have become not a melting pot but a beautiful mosaic."
> —Jimmy Carter, 39th President of the United States and winner of the Nobel Peace Prize

Joe Cuseo

Consider This...
When we appreciate diversity and humanity simultaneously, we capitalize on the power of our differences while preserving our collective strength through unity.

As you proceed through this book, keep in mind the following distinctions among humanity, diversity, and individuality:

▶ **Humanity:** All humans are members of the *same group* (the human species).
▶ **Diversity:** All humans are members of *different groups* (e.g., different cultural and gender groups).
▶ **Cultural Competence:** Assessing the effectiveness of diversity outcomes.
▶ **Individuality:** Each human is a *unique individual* who differs from all other humans and all other members of any group to which that individual may belong.

> Every human is, at the same time, like all other humans, like some humans, and like no other human.
> —Clyde Kluckholn, American anthropologist

Looking at a student's group membership should not mean that we overlook the student's individuality. Understanding a person's group membership is just one way of helping us better understand how that person's individuality may be influenced by the cultural group(s) to which that individual belongs.

Consider This...
Appreciating human diversity should not come at the expense of depreciating our commonality (humanity) or individuality. Although it's valuable to learn about different cultures and common characteristics shared by all members of the same culture, the fact remains that significant differences exist among individuals who share the same culture. Don't assume that each individual from the same cultural background has the same personal characteristics.

> I realize that I'm black, but I like to be viewed as a person, and this is everybody's wish.
> —Michael Jordan, Hall of Fame basketball player

What Is Cultural Diversity?

Culture can be broadly defined as a distinctive pattern of beliefs and values that are learned by a group of people who share the same social heritage and traditions. In short, culture is the whole way in which a group of people has learned to live (Peoples & Bailey, 2008); this includes their way of speaking (language), dressing (fashion), eating (cuisine), and expressing themselves artistically. (See **Box 1.1** for a summary of the key components of culture). Even more significant than visible differences in the physical artifacts of different cultures are invisible, deeply held differences in cultural beliefs, values, and world views (National Council for the Social Studies, 1991; Valenzuela, 1999).

> Culture shapes mind . . . it provides us with a tool kit by which we construct not only our worlds but our very conceptions of ourselves and our powers.
> —Jerome Bruner, *The Culture of Education*

Sometimes, the terms "culture" and "society" are used interchangeably as if they were synonymous; however, each of these terms refers to a different aspect of humanity. Society is a group of people organized under the same social system. For example, all members of American society are organized under the same system of government, justice, and education. In contrast, culture is what members of a certain group of people share with respect to their past traditions and current ways of living—regardless of the particular society or social system in which they currently live (Nicholas, 1991). For example, cultural differences can exist within the same society, thus resulting in a "multicultural" society.

Box 1.1 Key Components of Culture

Diversity across cultural groups is expressed in a wide variety of ways, but the following list contains some of the more critical components of culture.

- *Language:* how a cultural group communicates verbally and nonverbally (e.g., the nature of body language its members use while communicating).
- *Space (Distance):* how members of a cultural group arrange or distance themselves in space or place (e.g., how closely they position themselves while engaging in conversation).
- *Time:* how a cultural group conceives of, divides up, and makes use of time (e.g., the speed or pace at which they move and conduct their daily business).
- *Aesthetics:* how a cultural group appreciates and expresses artistic beauty and creativity (e.g., its visual art, culinary art, music, theater, literature, and dance).
- *Family:* cultural attitudes and habits with respect to raising children and treating elderly relatives (e.g., its customary style of parenting children and caring for aging parents).
- *Finances:* how much economic capital the cultural group has to meet its members' material needs (e.g., socioeconomic status), and the values they hold about the acquisition of wealth and consumption of material goods (e.g., amount of emphasis placed on material possessions and the extent to which their possessions should be flaunted publically).
- *Science and Technology:* the culture's attitude toward science and the use of modern technology (e.g., whether or not the culture is technologically "advanced").
- *Philosophy:* the culture's view about what constitutes wisdom, truth, goodness, and the meaning or purpose of life (e.g., the group's predominant ethical viewpoints and moral standards).
- *Religion:* the culture's beliefs about the existence of a supreme being and an afterlife (e.g., heaven, hell, or reincarnation).

Reflection 1.3 Look back at the key components of culture cited in Box 1.1. Think of another component of culture that you think is important or influential and add it to the list. Explain why you think this is an important element of a group's culture.

What Is Ethnic Diversity?

A group of people who share the same culture is referred to as an *ethnic group*. Thus, ethnicity (ethnic group) refers to a group of people *who* share the same culture, and culture refers to *what* an ethnic group shares in common. An ethnic group's common cultural characteristics are not inherited or passed on genetically, they are passed on through *socialization*—that is, they are *learned* and transmitted through the group members' shared social environment and experiences. (Note how this environmental influence on culture is consistent with the use of the term "culture" in such phrases as "becoming cultured" or "cultivating crops.")

It's important for teachers to realize that students from different cultural backgrounds may respond to exactly the same curriculum in very different ways. Consider the following math problem, which was presented to a class of students from different socioeconomic backgrounds: "It costs $1.50 to travel each way on the city bus. A transit system 'fast pass' costs $65 a month. Which is the more economical way to get to work, the daily faire or the fast pass?" Students from higher income suburban families assumed that the individual in the problem was commuting to work five days per week at a rate of $3 per day. However, lower income, inner city students were more likely to respond to the problem with questions such as: "How many jobs are we talking about?" and "Is it a part-time job?" (Ladson-Billings, 1995).

What Is Racial Diversity?

Members of an *ethnic* group share common *cultural* characteristics that have been acquired through shared social-learning experiences. In contrast, members of a *racial* group share common *physical* characteristics (e.g., skin color or facial features) that have been acquired biologically (inherited). It must be remembered, however, that racial categories are not scientifically based concepts, they are social constructs—that is, social-group categories constructed (created) by humans (Anderson & Fienberg, 2000). Human societies have simply decided to organize or categorize themselves into different groups based on certain external differences in their appearance—particularly the color of their outer layer of skin—and then decided to coin the term "race" as a way of labeling groups of people based on differences in their physical appearance. The Census Bureau could have divided people into categories based on other physical characteristics, such as their eye color (blue, brown, green), hair color (brown, blonde, red), or hair texture (straight, wavy, curly, frizzy).

It should be noted that the concept of race emerged late in human history. The ancient Greeks didn't divide people into groups based on differences in physical appearance, but categorized them on the basis of differences in their social status, religion, and language. In fact, the word "race" does not appear anywhere in the English language until 1508, when it was used in an English poem to refer to a line of kings (California Newsreel, 2003).

> "Most variation is within, not between, 'races.' That means two random Koreans may be as genetically different as a Korean and an Italian."
>
> —California Newsreel, *Race: The Power of an Illusion*

Furthermore, scholars still disagree about what human groups actually constitute a biological "race" and whether totally distinctive races truly exist (Wheelright, 2005). There are no specific genes that differentiate one race from another, so there's no way a blood test or any type of "internal" genetic test could be run to determine a person's race. The truth is that no single gene or set of genes are shared by all members of the same race, which would distinguish them from members of other races.

PERSONAL INSIGHT

My father stood approximately six feet and had light brown straight hair. His skin color was that of a Western European with a very slight suntan. My mother was from Alabama and she was dark in skin color with high cheek bones and long curly black hair. In fact, if you did not know that my father was of African-American descent, you would not have thought of him as black.

All of my life I have thought of myself as African-American and all of the people who are familiar with me thought of me as African-American. I have lived half of a century with that as my racial identity. However, several years ago, after carefully looking through available records on births in my family history, I discovered that less than 50% of my lineage was African. Biologically, I am not black. Socially and emotionally, I am. Clearly, race is more of a socially constructed concept than a biologically based fact.

Aaron Thompson

Although humans display diversity in skin color or tone, the reality is that all members of the human species share remarkably similar physical features. Despite differences in the surface appearance of our skin, members of our species are more similar biologically than any other living species (California Newsreel, 2003); over 98 percent of the genes that make up humans from different racial groups are exactly the same (Bridgeman, 2003; Molnar, 1991). This extraordinary amount of genetic overlap across human beings accounts for the many similarities that exist among us—despite superficial differences in color that exist at the surface of our skin. For example, all humans have similar external features that give us a "human" appearance and clearly distinguish us from other animal species. All humans also have internal organs that are similar in structure and function, and no matter what the color of our outer layer of skin, when it's cut, we all bleed in the same color.

The differences in skin color that exist among humans we see today is largely due to environmental adaptations that evolved over thousands of years among human groups that lived in very different climatic regions of the world. Darker skin tones likely developed among humans who inhabited and reproduced in hotter regions nearer the equator (e.g., Africans), where their darker skin evolved to help them adapt and survived by providing their bodies with better protection from the potentially damaging effects of the sun (Bridgeman, 2003). In contrast, lighter skin tones developed over time among humans inhabiting colder geographical regions that were farther from the equator (e.g., Scandinavia), where lighter skin enabled their bodies to absorb greater amounts of sunlight, making more efficient use of the vitamin D supplied by the sun (Jablonski & Chaplin, 2002).

PERSONAL INSIGHT | I was proofreading the material found in this chapter while sitting in a coffee shop at Chicago O'Hare airport. I looked up from my work for a second and saw what appeared to be a white girl about 18 years old. As I lowered my head to return to my work, I did a double-take to look at her again because my first glance left me with the feeling that something about her was different or unusual. When I looked at her more closely the second time, I noticed that although she had white skin, the features of her face and hair appeared to be those of an African-American. After a couple of seconds of puzzlement, I figured it out: she was an *albino* African-American. That satisfied me for the moment and I returned to my work; however, I later began to wonder whether it would still be accurate to say that she was "black" because her skin was actually white. Would her hair and facial features be sufficient for her to be considered (or classified) as black? If yes, then what about someone who had black skin tone, but did not have the typical hair and facial features of black people? Is skin color the physical feature that truly defines an African-American, or are other features equally important? I was unable to answer these questions, but I found it ironic that all of these thoughts were running through my mind at the exact same time I was writing a book about diversity.

Later, on the plane ride home, I thought again about that albino African-American girl and realized that she was a perfect example of how classifying people into "races" is not based on objective, scientifically determined evidence, but on subjective, socially constructed categories.

Joe Cuseo

Reflection 1.4 What race do you consider yourself to be? Would you say you identify strongly with your race, or are you rarely conscious of it? Why?

Diversity from a Cultural Perspective

Cultural differences can exist within the same society (a multicultural society), within the same nation (domestic diversity), and across different nations (international diversity). The major cultural (ethnic) groups found within the United States include:

- Native Americans (American Indians)
  - Cherokee, Navaho, Hopi, Alaskan natives, Blackfoot, etc.

- African-Americans (blacks)
  - Americans whose cultural roots lie in the continent of Africa (e.g., Ethiopia, Kenya, Nigeria) and the Caribbean Islands (e.g., Bahamas, Cuba, Jamaica), etc.
- Hispanic Americans (Latinos)
  - Americans with cultural roots in Mexico, Puerto Rico, Central America (e.g., El Salvador, Guatemala, Nicaragua), and South America (e.g., Brazil, Columbia, Venezuela), etc.
- Asian Americans
  - Americans who are cultural descendents of East Asia (e.g., Japan, China, Korea), Southeast Asia (e.g., Vietnam, Thailand, Cambodia), and South Asia (e.g., India, Pakistan, Bangladesh), etc.
- Middle Eastern Americans
  - Americans with cultural roots in Iraq, Iran, Israel, etc.
- European Americans (whites)
  - Descendents from Western Europe (e.g., United Kingdom, Ireland, Netherlands), Eastern Europe (e.g., Hungary, Romania, Bulgaria), Southern Europe (e.g., Italy, Greece, Portugal), and Northern Europe/Scandinavia (e.g., Denmark, Sweden, Norway), etc.

Currently, European Americans represent the *majority* ethnic group in the United States because they account for more than one-half of the American population. Native Americans, African-Americans, Hispanic Americans, and Asian Americans are considered to be ethnic *minority* groups because each of these groups represents less than 50 percent of the American population.

Ethnic groups can be comprised of whites or people of color. For people of color, their ethnicity is immediately visible to other people; in contrast, members of white ethnic groups have the option of choosing whether they want to identify with or share their ethnicity with others because it is not visible to the naked eye. Members of ethnic minority groups with European ancestry can more easily "blend into" or become assimilated into the majority (dominant) culture because their minority status can't be visibly detected. Minority white immigrants of European ancestry have even changed their last names to appear to be Americans of English descent. In contrast, the immediately detectable minority status of African-Americans, or darker skinned Hispanics and Native Americans, doesn't allow them the option of presenting themselves as members of an already assimilated majority group (National Council for the Social Studies, 1991).

PERSONAL INSIGHT

My mother's family changed their name from the very Italian-sounding "DeVigilio" to the more American-sounding "Vigilis," and my mother's first name was changed from the Italian-sounding Carmella to Mildred. My father's first name was also changed from Biaggio to Blase; he chose to list his first name, not his last name (Cuseo), on the sign outside his watch repair cubicle in New York City because he feared that would reveal his Italian ethnicity and people would not bring him their business.

Thus, my parents were able to minimize their risk of appearing "different" and encountering discrimination, while maximizing their chances of being assimilated (absorbed) into American culture. If my parents were members of a nonwhite ethnic group, they would not have been able to "hide" their ethnicity and reduce their risk of encountering prejudice or discrimination. I learned later that some Jewish Americans used the same name-changing strategies as my parents and grandparents; for example, changing their last name from Greenbaum to Green in order to avoid anti-Semitic treatment.

Joe Cuseo

As with racial grouping, classifying humans into different ethnic groups can also be very arbitrary and subject to different interpretations by different groups of people. Hispanics are not defined as a race, but are classified as an ethnic group by the U.S. Census Bureau. However, among those who checked "some other race" in the 2000 Census, 97 percent were Hispanic. This finding suggests that Hispanic Americans consider themselves to be a racial group, probably because this is how they feel they're perceived and treated by non-Hispanics (Cianciotto, 2005). Supporting the Hispanic viewpoint that others perceive them as a race, rather than an ethnic group, is the recent use of the term "racial profiling" in the American media to describe Arizona's controversial 2010 law that allows police to target people who "look" like illegal aliens from Mexico, Central America, and South America. Again, this illustrates how race and ethnicity are subjective, socially constructed concepts that depend on how society perceives and treats certain social groups, which, in turn, affect how these groups perceive themselves.

STUDENT PERSPECTIVE

"I'm the only person from my 'race' in class."

Hispanic student commenting on why he felt uncomfortable being the only Latino in his class on Race, Ethnicity, & Gender

America will continue to struggle with the issue of racial and ethnic group classification because the nation's racial and ethnic diversity is growing, and members of different ethnic and racial groups are increasingly forming cross-ethnic and interracial families. By 2050, the number of Americans who will identify themselves as being of two or more races is projected to more than triple—from 5.2 million to 16.2 million (U.S. Census Bureau, 2008a). Thus, it will become even more difficult to place Americans into distinct racial or ethnic categories.

PERSONAL INSIGHT

As the child of a black man and a white woman, and as someone born in the racial melting pot of Hawaii, with a sister who's half Indonesian but who's usually mistaken for Mexican or Puerto Rican, and a brother-in-law and niece of Chinese descent, with some blood relatives who resemble Margaret Thatcher and others who could pass for Bernie Mac, family get-togethers over Christmas take on the appearance of a UN General Assembly meeting. I've never had the option of restricting my loyalties on the basis of race, or measuring my worth on the basis of tribe.

Barack Obama (2006)

Reflection 1.5 What ethnic group(s) are you a member of, or do you identify with? What cultural values do you think are shared by members your ethnic group(s)?

Diversity from a Societal Perspective: Differences in Socioeconomic Status (a.k.a., Social Class)

Diversity also appears in the form of socioeconomic status or social classes, which are typically stratified (divided) into lower, middle, or upper class, depending on its members' level of education and income. Groups occupying lower social strata have significantly fewer social and economic opportunities or privileges (Feagin & Feagin, 2003).

Diversity in Income

According to U.S. Census figures, the wealthiest 20 percent of the American population controls approximately 50 percent of the country's total income, and the 20 percent of Americans with the lowest income control only 4 percent of the nation's income. Sharp discrepancies also exist in income level among different racial, ethnic, and gender groups. In 2007, black households had the lowest median income ($33,916) as compared to a median income of $54,920 for non-Hispanic white households (U.S. Census Bureau, 2008b).

Poverty continues to be a problem in America. In 2007, 12.5 percent of Americans (37.3 million people) lived below the poverty line, making the United States one of the most impoverished of all developed countries in the world (Shah, 2008). Although all ethnic and racial groups experience poverty, minority groups experience poverty at significantly higher rates than the white majority. In 2007, poverty rates for different ethnic and racial groups were as follows:

Whites: 8.2%
Asians: 10.2%
Hispanics: 21.5%
Blacks: 24.5% (U.S. Census Bureau, 2008b)

It's estimated that 600,000 families and 1.25 million children are now homeless, accounting for roughly 50 percent of the homeless population. Typically, these families are comprised of a mother and two children under the age of five (National Alliance to End Homelessness, 2007).

Reflection 1.6 What do you think is the factor that is most responsible for poverty in:

(a) the United States?

(b) the world?

PERSONAL INSIGHT When I was a four-year-old boy living in the mountains of Kentucky, it was safe for a young lad to walk the railroad tracks and roads alone. Knowing this, my mother would send me to the general store to buy a variety of small items we needed for our household. Since we had very little money, she was aware of the fact that we had to be cautious and only spend money on the staples we needed to survive. I could only purchase items from the general store that my mother strictly ordered me to buy. Most of these items cost less than a dollar and many times you could buy multiple items for a dollar in the early 1960s. At the store's checkout counter there were jars with different kinds of candy or gum. You could buy two pieces for one cent. I didn't think there would be any harm in rewarding myself with two pieces of candy after doing a good deed. After all, I could devour the evidence of my disobedience on my slow walk home. When I returned home from the store, my mother—being the protector of the vault and the sergeant-of-arms in our household—would count each item I bought to make sure I had been charged correctly. My mother never failed to notice if I was even one cent short!

Growing up in poverty wasn't fun but we managed to eat. What we ate had to be reasonable in price and bought in bulk. Every morning my mother fixed rice or oatmeal for breakfast along with wonderful buttermilk biscuits. Every night she fixed pinto beans and cornbread for dinner. We also had fresh vegetables from the garden and apples, hickory nuts, and walnuts from surrounding trees. Meat was not readily available and was only eaten when we killed a chicken or hog that we had raised.

Aaron Thompson

Diversity in Level of Education

Differences in social class also reflect differences in level of education. Discrepancies continue to exist in the level of education attained between members of majority and minority groups. The high school completion rate for white majority students is significantly higher than it is for students from minority ethnic and racial groups. In 2008, the high school dropout rate for white students was 4.8 percent, compared to 9.9 percent for black students and 18.3 percent for Hispanic students (Chapman, Laird, & KewalRamani, 2010).

College enrollment and graduation rates for minority students are also consistently lower than those for majority students. In 2009, 71 percent of majority students who graduated from high school enrolled in college—compared to 62 percent of Hispanic high school graduates and 63 percent of black high school graduates (Aud et al., 2011). Socioeconomic status also has an effect as to whether students immediately enroll in college after high school. In 2009, the immediate college enrollment rate for students from low income families was 55 percent compared to 85 percent of students from high income families and 67 percent of students from middle income families who immediately enrolled in college after high school (Aud et al., 2011). The percentage of Americans from different ethnic and racial groups who have attained a bachelor's degree is as follows:

Asians (52%)
non-Hispanic whites (33%),
Blacks (20%)
Hispanics (13%) (Aud, Fox, & KewalRamani, 2010)

> "The underlying goal of multicultural education is to effect social change. The pathway toward this goal incorporates of three strands of transformation: the transformation of self, the transformation of schools, and the transformation of society."
> —EdChange Organization, 1995–2009

Diversity from a National Perspective

The United States is home to the largest number of immigrants from the widest variety of countries around the world. America is a nation that has been built and developed by diverse immigrant groups, many of whom came to our shores with the intent of escaping prejudice or discrimination in their native nations and with the hope of gaining equal opportunity to build a better life for themselves and their families (Levine & Levine, 1996).

America's emphasis on the importance of combining diversity with unity is reflected in its national motto: *E pluribus Unum* ("Out of many, one"), which appears on the back of all its coins. The motto stresses the nation's belief that, in a free society, diversity is a source of strength. Providing our students with a multicultural education grounded in the context of national unity serves to put America's motto into practice (National Council for the Social Sciences, 1991).

Because America is rapidly becoming a more racially and ethnically diverse nation, the importance of reinforcing the idea of diversity and unity is probably greater today than at any other time in U.S. history. In 2008, the minority population in the United States reached an all-time high of 34 percent. The population of ethnic minorities is currently growing at a much faster rate than the white majority and this trend is expected to continue. By the middle of the 21st century, the minority population will grow from one-third of the U.S. population to more than one-half (54%), more than 60 percent of the nation's children are expected to be members of minority groups (U.S. Census Bureau, 2008a).

The rise in ethnic and racial diversity in the United States is mirrored by student diversity throughout its educational system—from kindergarten through college. The rising diversity in America's schools is particularly noteworthy when viewed in light of the historical discrimination toward minority groups in the United States. In the early 19th century, education was not a right, it was a privilege available only to those who could afford to attend private schools. Members of certain minority groups were left out of the educational process altogether, or were forced to be educated in inferior, racially segregated schools. This separate and unequal system of American education continued until the groundbreaking Supreme Court decision in *Brown v. Board of Education* (1954), which changed the face of education for people of color by ruling that "separate educational facilities are inherently unequal." The judicial decision made it illegal for Kansas and 20 other states to deliver education in segregated classrooms.

> Of all the civil rights for which the world has struggled and fought for 5,000 years, the right to learn is undoubtedly the most fundamental.
>
> —W. E. B. Du Bois, African American sociologist, historian, and Civil Rights activist

Each American ethnic group has a unique historical experience that contributed to the development of its particular culture. Thus, by incorporating ethnic diversity into our students' historical perspective, they learn about the diverse multicultural histories layered within our national history and the unique struggles that different groups of Americans endured to secure personal freedoms, human rights, and social justice. For instance, a multicultural historical perspective provides students with a clearer understanding of current-day concepts of race and racism. The expression "white race" did not make its historical appearance until it was introduced by Americans in the 18th and 19th centuries. Up to that point in time, the term was not used anywhere else in the world. America became a race-conscious nation in large part because of the expanding cotton industry needing more land—on which Native Americans were settled, and a greater labor force—which could be obtained inexpensively by using African American slaves. To meet their needs for land and labor, the white Anglo-Protestant upper class created and disseminated the idea of a privileged "white race" that was entitled to enslave people of color. Thus, the concept of a white race was originally devised by English settlers to gain socioeconomic advantages and to justify enslavement of African and Native Americans—who were deemed to be "uncivilized savages." Subsequent waves of American immigrants who initially defined themselves as German, Irish, or Italian, gradually began to refer to themselves as "white" as they began to move up to higher levels of socioeconomic and political status (Feagin & Feagin, 2003).

> The Constitution of the United States knows no distinction between citizens on account of color.
>
> —Frederick Douglass, abolitionist, author, advocate for equal rights for all people, and former slave

Diversity from an International Perspective

International communication and interdependence among nations is growing as a result of advances in technology, international travel, and multinational corporations. As a result, acquiring an international perspective and developing intercultural competencies have become essential for career success in today's world and to effectively address our world's most pressing problems (e.g., global warming and international terrorism). Thus, the need for students to acquire an international perspective, cross-cultural awareness, and intercultural communication skills are probably more important today than at any other time in the history of American education. Unfortunately, much work needs to be done because American students lag behind students from other industrialized nations in international knowledge and skills (Bok, 2006). For instance, only 5 to 10 percent of American college graduates have basic competence in any language other than English, and approximately two-thirds of them have not taken a single course in international studies (Adelman, 2004).

Diversity from a Global Perspective

The diversity of humankind becomes strikingly apparent when viewed from a global perspective. If it were possible to reduce the world's population to a "village" of precisely 100 people, while keeping its ethnic and racial proportions exactly the same, this global village would have the following characteristics:

- 82 nonwhites and 18 whites
- 67 non-Christians and 33 Christians
- 60 Asians, 14 Africans, 12 Europeans, 8 Latin Americans, 5 Americans and Canadians, and 1 from the South Pacific
- 51 males and 49 females
- 80 live in substandard housing
- 67 unable to read
- 50 malnourished and 1 dying of starvation
- 39 without access to sufficient sanitation
- 33 without access to a safe water supply
- 24 without any electricity; and, among the 76 with electricity, most would only be able to use it for light at night
- 7 with access to the Internet
- 1 with a college education
- 1 with HIV
- 5 in control of 32 percent of the entire world's wealth; all 5 are citizens of the United States
- 33 attempt to live on just 3 percent of the world's total income

(Meadows, 2005)

Reflection 1.7 Look back at the characteristics of the "global village." Which of its characteristic(s) most surprised you?

Why?

A global perspective on diversity goes beyond just human diversity to include *biodiversity*—variations among all life forms that inhabit planet earth. Biodiversity exists because of *ecosystem* diversity—that is, all biological, climatic, geological, and chemical ingredients in the environment combine to maintain the life of plants and animals, whose life needs are met by interacting with all parts of the environmental system (Norse, 1990). Thus, the contemporary issue of environmental sustainability is actually a diversity issue that embraces both ecosystem diversity and, ultimately, biodiversity. The global significance of this issue is highlighted by the fact that the United Nations declared 2010 to be the "International Year of Biodiversity" (IYB) in order to raise global awareness that preservation of biodiversity requires the collective effort of every nation and all humankind (UNEP News Centre, 2010).

> "Nature models interdependence in marvelous ways. The symbiotic processes of people taking in oxygen and releasing carbon dioxide, which is taken in by plants, which release oxygen. It seems that the world is trying to tell us something."
>
> —Komives, Lucas, & McMahon (2007)

Diversity from the Perspective of the Universe (Cosmos)

Human diversity on planet earth is mirrored by the cosmic diversity of the universe. Let us not forget earth is just one planet (the "third stone from the sun"), sharing a solar system with seven other planets—and it's only one celestial body,

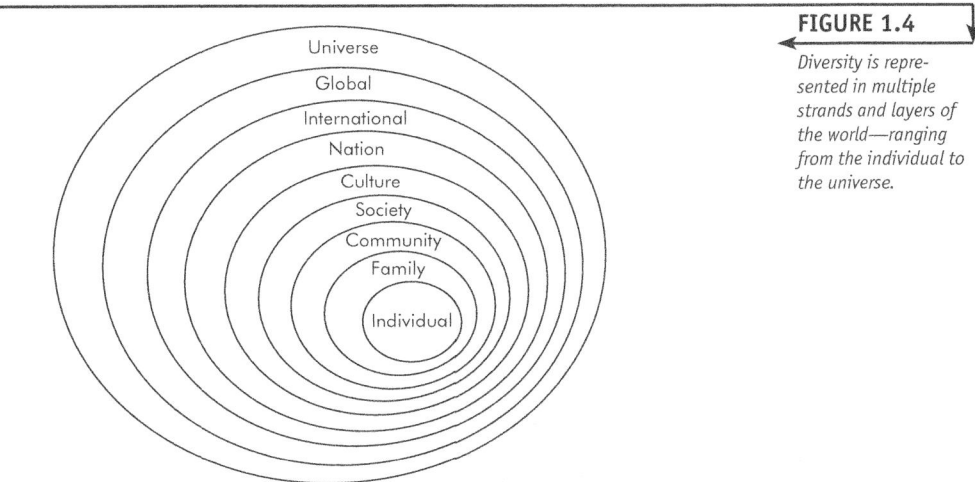

FIGURE 1.4

Diversity is represented in multiple strands and layers of the world—ranging from the individual to the universe.

sharing a galaxy with millions of other celestial bodies that include stars, moons, meteorites, and asteroids (Encrenaz et al., 2004). Thus, diversity is a natural and integral component of both our social and physical world.

Summary and Conclusion

Diversity refers to the wide variety of differences that exist among individuals and groups who comprise humanity (the human species). Humans can and do differ from one another in multiple ways, including physical features, religious beliefs, mental and physical abilities, national origins, social backgrounds, gender, and sexual orientation.

It's important to keep in mind that human *variety* and *similarity* coexist and complement one another. Thus, diversity education not only enhances appreciation of human differences; it also promotes awareness of universal aspects of the human condition that are common to all people—whatever their particular social or cultural background may be.

Racial diversity involves grouping humans into categories that are not scientifically based, but socially determined. There are no specific genes that differentiate one race from another; there is no "blood test" or genetic marker that can be used to detect a person's race. Humans have simply decided to classify themselves into "racial" categories on the basis of certain external differences in physical appearance, particularly the shade of their outer layer of skin.

An ethnic group is a group of people who share a distinctive culture (i.e., a particular set of shared traditions, customs, and social heritage). Unlike a racial group, whose members share physical characteristics that they are born with, the shared characteristics of an ethnic group are *learned* through shared social experiences. Thus, *ethnic diversity* refers to different groups of people with different cultural characteristics. Cultural differences can exist within the same society (multicultural society), within the same nation (domestic diversity), and across different nations (international diversity).

As with racial grouping, classifying groups of people into different ethnic groups can be very subjective and interpreted differently by different groups of people. Both race and ethnicity are arbitrary, socially constructed concepts that depend on how society perceives and treats certain social groups, which, in turn, affect how these groups perceive themselves. America will continue to struggle with this racial and ethnic group classification issue because, as its racial and ethnic diversity grows, members of different ethnic and racial groups will increasingly form cross-ethnic and interracial families.

Diversity also appears in the form of socioeconomic statuses (social class) that are typically stratified (divided) into lower, middle, or upper class, depending on its members' level of education and income. Discrepancies continue to exist in the level of income and education attained between members of majority and minority groups.

When diversity is viewed from an international perspective, the burgeoning "global economy" is creating a greater demand for workers with cross-cultural awareness and intercultural communication skills than at any other time in our nation's history. Viewed from more than a strictly economic perspective, collaboration among diverse nations and cultures is now essential for preserving the planet (e.g., combating global warming or irreversible climate change) and protecting all people from the threat of international terrorism. America's students lag behind students from other industrialized nations in international knowledge and foreign language skills, so much work needs to be done with our students to prepare them for these global challenges.

Exercises

Create a Cultural Autobiography

Write a concise cultural autobiography based on your level of exposure to those who differ from you, how your cultural background has affected your values and beliefs, and whether you faced discrimination, stereotyping, or prejudice as a child. If you can think of a situation where you were not as tolerant as you should have been, note that as well.

Adapted from Baylor University's Community Mentoring for Adolescent Development.

NAME _____ DATE _____

Match the Face with the Background

Form groups of fellow future educators now (and students in your classroom later) to conduct this exercise. Cut out pictures of faces from different sources (not recognizable or famous) that represent different cultures and ethnicities. Group members should study the faces and then offer a description of the person based on their perception.

Name

Age

Occupation

Family background

Friends

Education

Religion

Socioeconomic status

Political viewpoint

The Benefits of Diversity Education

Diversity education may be defined as an intentional instructional process designed to promote positive change in students' attitudes and knowledge through encounters with ideas and people from different cultures or experiential backgrounds. The terms "diversity education" and "multicultural education" often conjure up thoughts of cultural appreciation exercises, such as schools celebrating Black History Month, or students bringing artifacts to school that represent their ethnic group. Although these are useful exercises and should be continued, diversity education means more than annual or celebratory events—it is an ongoing learning process that should take place consistently and pervasively throughout the curriculum.

Diversity education not only ensures equal access to learning, but also empowers students to detect biases and their sources in the information they're exposed to, and actively involves students in learning experiences that encourage interpersonal interaction with individuals from diverse groups, both inside and outside the classroom (Banks et al., 2001). Although one major goal of diversity education is to promote appreciation and more equitable treatment of particular groups of people who have experienced discrimination, it's also a *learning* experience that strengthens the quality of all students' education, career preparation, and leadership potential. The quality of education is enriched by exposure to diverse people who bring multiple perspectives and different approaches to the content of what is being learned and to the process of learning it. When college students across the country were interviewed about their diversity experiences in college, many reported that these experiences enabled them to learn more about themselves. They said that interactions with students of different races and ethnic backgrounds produced "unexpected" or "jarring" self-insights (Light, 2001).

This chapter integrates and documents the major benefits of diversity education for both student and teachers. Eight major benefits (positive learning outcomes) of experiencing diversity are discussed:

1. Acquiring greater self-knowledge, self-awareness, and self-insight
2. Deepening and accelerating learning

3. Strengthening one's ability to think critically from multiple perspectives
4. Fostering creative thinking
5. Promoting career preparation for the 21st century
6. Expanding social relationships and emotional intelligence
7. Reducing prejudice and discrimination in society
8. Preserving democracy

When we become aware of the benefits of diversity and develop an intentional plan to experience them, both teachers and students become more motivated to capitalize on diversity and are better positioned to articulate its advantages.

1. Diversity Education Develops Self-Knowledge, Self-Awareness, and Self-Insight

A multicultural curriculum should provide students with continuous opportunities to develop a better sense of self. Students must ask questions such as Who am I? and What am I? in order to reach conclusions about their own identities. Students should develop more sophisticated understandings of why they are the way they are, why their ethnic and cultural groups are the way they are, and what ethnicity and culture mean in their daily lives (National Council for the Social Studies, 1991).

One of the most frequently cited outcomes of education is to "know thyself" (Cross, 1982). The ability to turn inward and introspect (inspect and examine oneself) and gain self-awareness is considered to an important form of human intelligence—referred to as "intrapersonal intelligence" (Gardner, 1999).

As a member of a human community, our personal identity is shaped and formed in relation to other humans who comprise our surrounding social community (Tatum, 2007). When teachers gain greater awareness of how their own beliefs have been influenced by and contrast with students from different backgrounds (Chisholm, 1994), they gain self-knowledge that can be used to make more informed decisions about their teaching practices and curricular choices.

"When we meet others whose family or community norms vary from our own, it is akin to holding up a mirror, provoking questions we might not otherwise think to ask. Contrast and dissonance can be disturbing in spite of the opportunity they present to examine assumptions, making it possible to more deeply understand who we are in relation to one another" (Ginsberg & Wlodkowski, 2009, p. 7).

When students learn about and from people with diverse backgrounds, it also sharpens their self-knowledge and self-insight by contrasting their life experi-

> " The unexamined life is not worth living. "
> —Socrates, classic Greek philosopher and a founding father of Western philosophy

> " A comparison of American cultural products, practices, and perspectives to those of another culture will lead to a more profound understanding of what it means to be an American. "
> —David Conley, Director of the Center for Educational Policy Research at the University of Oregon, and author of *College Knowledge*

ences with those whose life experiences differ sharply from their own. By stepping outside themselves to see how they compare with other members of diverse groups, students simultaneously step inside themselves and gain a new self-perspective. They move beyond an egocentric perspective and gain access to the multiple perspectives representing different people, places, and cultures. This comparative perspective gives students a new reference point for viewing their own lives by placing them in a better position to see how their particular cultural background has influenced their personal beliefs, values, and lifestyle.

Gaining self-awareness is one of the most important learning outcomes of education.

Know Thyself

When students see what is distinctive about their background experiences, they're also more likely to see how they may be uniquely advantaged or disadvantaged relative to others. For instance, by learning about the limited educational opportunities there are for people to attend college in many countries today, and the limited opportunities there were for certain groups of people in our own country some time ago, students become more aware of the golden opportunity they have today to continue their education through college and to improve their quality of life—regardless of their race, ethnicity, gender, or family history.

Consider This . . .

> The more opportunities we create for students to learn about and from cultures that differ from their own, the more opportunities we create for them to learn about themselves.

Gaining greater self-awareness through diversity experiences is also the first step to overcoming personal biases that may interfere with culturally sensitive and culturally responsive teaching. Just like their students, when teachers contrast their experiences with the experiences of others from diverse backgrounds, they gain self-insight into how they may be uniquely advantaged or disadvantaged relative to the students they teach.

2. Diversity Education Deepens and Accelerates Learning

Learning takes place when the brain makes a physical (neurological) connection between the concept that it is trying to learn and something that it already knows—that is, something that's already been stored in the brain (see **Figure 2.1**). Experiencing diversity broadens students' base of knowledge and facilitates the brain's capacity for making connections. In other words, it's easier for students to assimilate new information and integrate it with their prior knowledge when more

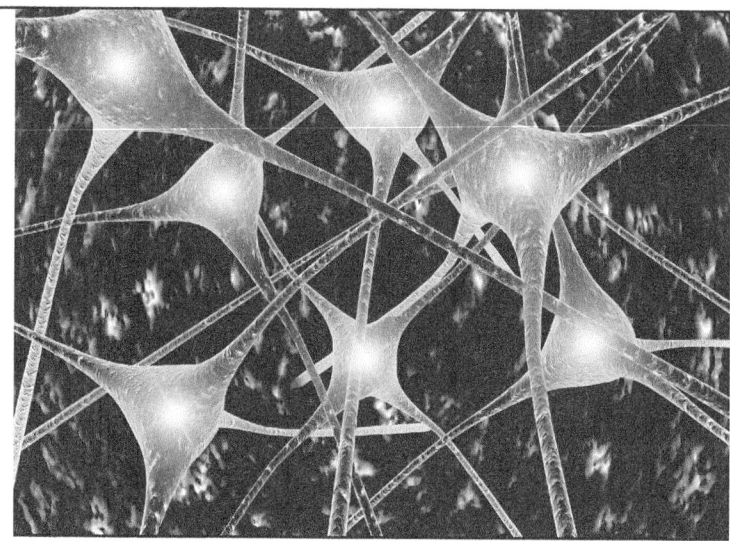

FIGURE 2.1

Learning derives from the Latin root "lira," meaning furrow or track. When we learn, a neurological track or path is created in our brain that connects what we are trying to learn to what we already know. When a variety or multiplicity of connections have already been made in the brain, the more "hooks" there are available onto which new ideas may be connected (learned). This enables learning to occur more efficiently and become more deeply rooted.

© Jurgen Ziewe, 2009. Used under license from Shutterstock, Inc.

interconnections have already been formed in their brain (Rosenshine, 1997). Diversity education adds to the multiplicity and variety of these interconnections, thereby providing the brain with more routes or pathways through which to connect new ideas to, thereby accelerating and deepening learning.

Experiencing diversity also deepens learning because the brain must stretch beyond its "mental comfort zone" and work harder to understand something different or unfamiliar. To make this mental "stretch," the brain needs to expend extra psychological energy, which serves to strengthen and deepen learning. The only way we can learn something new or different is by making the extra mental effort to compare and contrast it to what we already know (Acredolo & O'Connor, 1991; Nagda, Gurin, & Johnson, 2005). This is probably why research consistently shows that we learn more from people who are different from us than we do from people similar to us (Pascarella, 2001; Pascarella & Terenzini, 2005).

When students compare, contrast, and make connections between what they are learning and what they already know, it promotes storage of knowledge in long-term memory (Rosenshine, 1997). Research shows that encouraging students to compare and contrast ideas is an instructional practice of those K–12 teachers who generate the greatest gains in student achievement (Marzano, Pickering, & Pollock, 2001).

> **Consider This . . .**
> Simply stated, humans learn more from diversity than they do from similarity or familiarity.

A large body of research also indicates that students learn more deeply when their learning takes place in a *social* context that involves interpersonal *interaction* and *collaboration* (Cuseo, 1996; 2002). As some scholars put it, human knowledge is "socially constructed"—it's built up from interpersonal interaction and dialogue with others (Bruffee, 1993). According to this social constructivist theory of human learning, our thinking consists largely of "internal" (mental) representations of conversations that we've had with other people (Vygotsky, 1978). Thus, the quality and variety of our conversations with others improves the quality and complexity of our own thinking. If we have multiple conversations with humans from a rich diversity of backgrounds, the nature of our thinking becomes more diverse and nuanced.

Americans have learned from Buddhists about the power of meditation as an effective, drug-free, stress-management strategy (Bodian, 2006). We also learned from Eskimos that their extraordinarily low rate of cardiovascular disease was related to the natural oil contained in their fish-rich diet, which contained a type of unsaturated fat that flushes out and washes away cholesterol-forming fats from the bloodstream (Feskens & Kromhout, 1994; Khoshaba & Maddi, 1999). We can thank the Eskimos for the American Heart Association's current recommendation to adopt a diet high in unsaturated fats (and low in saturated fats) to reduce the risk for nongenetic forms of cardiovascular disease, such as high blood pressure, heart attacks, and strokes (American Heart Association, 2006).

Just as the level of our physical performance is elevated by exposing the body to a varied and balanced diet of foods from different food groups, the level of our mental performance is elevated when our brain is exposed to a diverse and balanced diet of ideas acquired from different groups of people. In contrast, when students restrict the diversity of people with whom they interact because of stereotypes or prejudices, they restrict the variety and balance of their social diet and, in so doing, restrict the breadth and depth of their learning.

Consider This . . .

Holding a negative stereotype and not gaining exposure to diverse experiences that may challenge that stereotype is not just a poor social skill, it's also a poor learning strategy.

When students expand their circle of social interaction to include peers from diverse cultures, they enrich the quality of their education.

© Monkey Business Images, 2009. Used under license from Shutterstock, Inc.

PERSONAL INSIGHT

When I entered the public education system my first teacher was a sharply dressed, highly intellectual African American woman by the name of Helena Mays. The school I attended was a four-room school that housed K–8 African American students. These were the days when schools were segregated in many parts of the South. I attended this school for four years and all of my teachers were African American. I quickly learned that the differentiation that I experienced in that school was based on income and geography. I was the kid that was from the share cropper's farm and did not live within the city limits. I had the blue jeans and holes in the shoes. I also quickly learned that my level of status and acceptance would be one gained through achievement and not what status I was ascribed to. That philosophy quickly changed when the schools were integrated. I understood then that not only was I poor and rural (which did not take on uniqueness because most of the white kids were poor and rural in that district school), I was also now different because I was black. I did not have another teacher of color until I attended graduate school. However, I did have many teachers (many of whom were white) who spent their time understanding all of my uniqueness and helped me to value those while they helped me to learn. Those teachers (e.g., Ms. Ruby Lois Hibbard) are the ones I will always remember and are the ones that inspired me to write this book.

Aaron Thompson

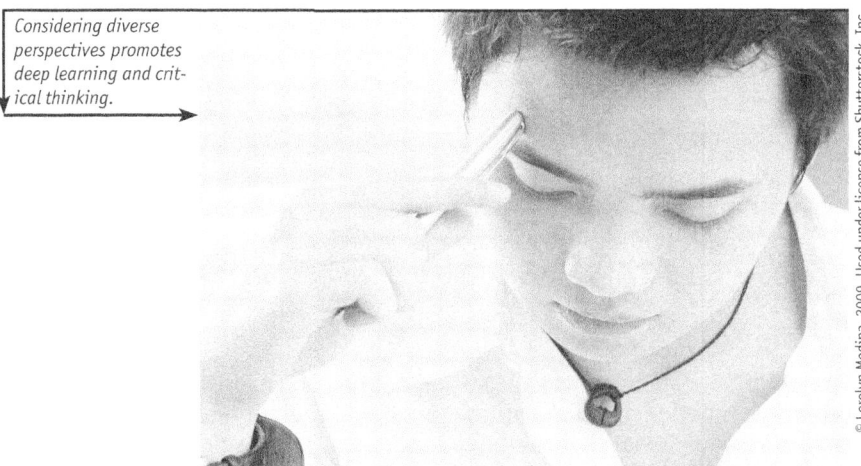

Considering diverse perspectives promotes deep learning and critical thinking.

3. Diversity Education Strengthens Students' Ability to Think Critically from Multiple Perspectives

> Mono-perspective analyses of complex ethnic and cultural issues can produce skewed, distorted interpretations and evaluations.
>
> —National Council for the Social Studies (1991)

A major advantage of culture is that it helps bind its members together into a tight-knit, socially supportive community; however, it can also blind its members from other cultural perspectives. Because culture shapes the way we think, it can cause groups of people to view the world solely through their own cultural lens or frame of reference (Colombo, Cullen, & Lisle, 1995). When the world is viewed through the lens of a single cultural perspective, it provides a one-dimensional and incomplete picture of any issue because it's biased by our own (ethnocentric) vantage point (Paul & Elder, 2002).

Optical illusions provide an excellent example of how our particular cultural perspective can bias us and lead us to make inaccurate judgments. Compare the length of the two lines in **Figure 2.2.**

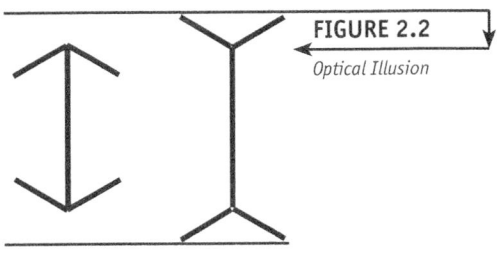

FIGURE 2.2

Optical Illusion

If you perceive the line on the right to be longer than the line on the left, welcome to the club. Virtually all Americans and people from Western cultures perceive the line on the right to be longer. Actually, both lines are equal in length. (If you don't believe it, take out a ruler and check it out.) Interestingly, this perceptual error is *not* made by people from non-Western cultures who live in environments dominated by circular structures (see Figure below), rather than structures with straight lines and angled corners—like the rectangular houses and buildings that characterize Western cultures (Segall, Campbell, & Herskovits, 1966).

This optical illusion illustrates that our cultural experiences—which are stored in our brain—shape and sometimes distort our perceptions of reality. We think we're seeing things objectively (as they really are), but we're seeing them subjectively—from a perspective that has been determined by our own cultural experiences and that has shaped how our mind (brain) interprets what we see. Being open to the viewpoints of diverse people who perceive the world from different cultural vantage points serves to widen our range of perception and helps us overcome our own "cultural blind spots." As a result, we tend to perceive the world with better balance, clarity, and objectivity.

> ❝ We see what is behind our eyes. ❞
> —Chinese proverb

The people who live in these circular huts would not be fooled by the optical illusion in Figure 2.2

© JupiterImages Corporation.

> " It is difficult to see the picture when you are inside the frame. "
>
> —As an old saying (author unknown)

Consider This . . .

Our reality is not everyone's reality—our perception of the external world is shaped (and sometimes distorted) by our prior cultural experiences. When we step outside the boundaries of our own culture and view issues from a broader "world view," we're able to perceive "reality" and evaluate "truth" from a wider range of vantage points. This makes our thinking more comprehensive and less culture-centered (ethnocentric).

Diversity serves to diversify our thinking by liberating us from the tunnel vision created by viewing the world through the narrow focus of just our own cultural viewpoint, and substitutes a wider-focus lens that gives us a broader, multicultural or cross-cultural perspective. This broadened perspective reduces our risk of slipping into *group think*—the tendency for tight, like-minded groups of people to think so much alike that they overlook flaws in their own thinking, which can lead to poor choices and faulty decisions (Janis, 1982). For example, groupthink led American doctors to erroneously conclude that acupuncture was quackery (International Wellness Directory, 2009), until its eventual approval of this Chinese method of pain relief as an effective alternative to pain-killing drugs.

Research demonstrates that when discussion takes place among diverse people with different perspectives, group decision-making becomes less polarized (one-sided) and less susceptible the limitations of group think (Janis, 1982).

> " When all men think alike, no one thinks very much. "
>
> —Walter Lippmann, distinguished journalist and originator of the term, "stereotype"

A good example of how "group think" can lead to ethnocentric decisions that are ineffective (and unjust).

Consider This...

Students' views are shaped, limited, and often biased by their particular cultural perspective. By exposing students to multiple perspectives and diverse viewpoints, a teacher creates opportunities for students to expand their point of view, which leads to more open-minded, multidimensional thinking.

> "The more eyes, different eyes, we can use to observe one thing, the more complete will our concept of this thing, our objectivity, be."
> —Friedrich Nietzsche, German philosopher

Research on educational programs designed to develop critical thinking indicates that the most successful programs are those in which "divergent views are aggressively sought" (Kurfiss, 1988, p. 2). Research also indicates that students who experience high levels of exposure to different dimensions of diversity in college (e.g., students who participate in multicultural courses and events on campus, or who interact and form friendships with peers of different ethnic backgrounds) are more likely to report the greatest gains in:

1. Thinking *complexity*—the ability to think about all parts and all sides of an issue (Gurin, 1999)
2. *Reflective* thinking—the ability to think deeply about personal and global issues (Kitchener, Wood, & Jensen, 2000)
3. *Critical* thinking—the ability to evaluate the validity of their own reasoning and the reasoning of others (Pascarella et al., 2001), encouraging students to ask questions about why different viewpoints are held and how cultural experiences can influence an individual's perceptions or interpretations of events

When students are exposed to different perspectives on the same topic at the same time, it promotes critical thinking by inducing "cognitive dissonance"—a state of cognitive (mental) disequilibrium or discomfort that "forces" the mind to process different perspectives simultaneously (Brookfield, 1987; Kurfiss, 1988).

Covering subject matter from diverse cultural perspectives also helps students critically examine how the knowledge that's acquired and portrayed in different subject areas is not necessarily objective or absolute; instead, knowledge is constructed from the scholar's particular standpoint or viewpoint and may be challenged (Banks, 1995). For example, students learn to question what they read in print and see in the visual media by asking questions such as: "Whose voice is speaking and whose voice am I not hearing?" and "What cultural perspective (or bias) is the author or producer bringing to their book, website, or movie?" (Gorski, 1995; 2009).

Lastly, encouraging critical thinking from multiple perspectives also allows multicultural education to be integrated seamlessly into the traditional (mainstream) curriculum, thus ensuring that both curricula are covered simultaneously and are viewed as being equally important (McKay School of Education, 2010).

> "For optimum effectiveness, the study of ethnic and cultural group experiences must be interwoven into the total curriculum. It should not be reserved for special occasions, units, or courses, nor should it be considered supplementary to the existing curriculum or relegated to a marginal position in the curriculum."
> —National Council for the Social Studies (1991)

4. Diversity Fosters Creative Thinking

Studies indicate that creative thinkers have a wide range of knowledge and interests, and their creative products often reflect combinations of ideas drawn from multiple sources (Riquelme, 2002). Diversity education can stimulate creative thinking by supplying students with a broader band of knowledge and a wider variety of thinking styles that can empower them to think outside the box of a single cultural framework. People who approach problems from diverse perspectives are more likely to look for and discover "multiple partial solutions" (Kelly, 1994). Diversity expands students' capacity for viewing issues or problems from multiple vantage points, equipping them with a wider variety of approaches to solving unfamiliar problems they may encounter in different contexts and situations.

Furthermore, ideas acquired from diverse people and diverse cultures may combine or "cross-fertilize," giving birth to new approaches for solving old problems. When ideas are generated openly and freely in groups comprised of people from diverse backgrounds, powerful "cross-stimulation" effects can occur, whereby one group member's idea can trigger different ideas from other group members (Brown, Dane, Durham, 1998). Drawing on different ideas from people of diverse backgrounds and bouncing ideas off them serves to stimulate divergent (expansive) thinking, which can lead to synergy (idea multiplication) and serendipity (unexpected discoveries of innovative solutions).

In contrast, when different cultural perspectives are not sought out or tolerated, the variety of lenses available to students for viewing new problems is reduced, which, in turn, limits or shrinks one's capacity for creative thinking. Creativity tends to be replaced by conformity or rigidity because ideas do not flow freely and divergently (in different directions); instead, ideas tend to converge and merge into the same cultural channel—the one shared by the homogeneous group of people doing the thinking.

> "When the only tool you have is a hammer, you tend to see every problem as a nail."
> —Abraham Maslow, psychologist, best known for his theory of human self-actualization

> "What I look for in musicians is generosity. There is so much to learn from each other and about each other's culture. Great creativity begins with tolerance."
> —Yo-Yo Ma, French-born, Chinese-American virtuoso cellist, composer, and winner of multiple Grammy Awards

> "The benefits that accrue to college students who are exposed to racial and ethnic diversity during their education carry over in the work environment. The improved ability to think critically, to understand issues from different points of view, and to collaborate harmoniously with co-workers from a range of cultural backgrounds all enhance a graduate's ability to contribute to his or her company's growth and productivity."
> —Business-Higher Education Forum, 2002

5. Diversity Education Promotes Career Preparation for the 21st Century

Learning about and from diversity has a very practical benefit: It better prepares students for their future work roles. Whatever line of employment students may eventually pursue, they're likely to find themselves working with employers, co-workers, customers, and clients from diverse cultural backgrounds. America's workforce is now more diverse than at any other time in the nation's history and it will grow ever more diverse throughout the 21st century. The proportion of America's working age population comprised of workers from minority ethnic and racial groups will jump from 34 percent in 2008 to 55 percent in 2050 (U.S. Census Bureau, 2008a).

Students' future co-workers are likely to come from diverse cultural backgrounds.

A national survey revealed that policymakers, business leaders, and employers seek college graduates who are more than just "aware" or "tolerant" of diversity—they want graduates who have actual *experience* with diversity (Education Commission of the States, 1995). These findings are reinforced by a national survey of American voters, the overwhelming majority of whom agreed that diversity education helps students learn practical skills that are essential for success in today's world—such as communication skills, teamwork, and problem-solving skills. Almost one-half of the surveyed voters also thought that the American school system should "put more emphasis on teaching students about others' cultures, backgrounds and lifestyles" (National Survey of Voters, 1998). Thus, both employers and the American public agree that diversity education is *career preparation*. Intercultural competence is now a highly valued skill and one that is essential for success in today's work world.

The current "global economy" also requires intercultural skills relating to international diversity. Work in today's global economy is characterized by economic interdependence among nations, international trading (imports/exports), multinational corporations, international travel, and almost instantaneous worldwide communication—due to advances in the World Wide Web (Dryden & Vos, 1999; Smith, 1994). As a result, employers now seek job candidates with the following skills and attributes: sensitivity to human differences, ability to understand and relate to people from different cultural backgrounds, international knowledge, and ability to communicate in a second language (Fixman, 1990; National Association of Colleges & Employers, 2003; Office of Research, 1994; Smith, 1997). Thus, learning about and from diversity is not only good education; it's also good career preparation.

> "Only a well educated, diverse work force, comprised of people who have learned to work productively and creatively with individuals from a multitude of races and ethnic, religious, and cultural backgrounds, can maintain America's competitiveness in the increasingly diverse and interconnected world economy."
>
> —Spokesman for General Motors Corporation, quoted in Chatman (2008)

> "The federal government and private organizations with extensive international interests will require the services of increasing numbers of specialists who are fluent in foreign languages and highly knowledgeable about countries, regions, and international problems."
>
> —Derek Bok, President Emeritus & Research Professor at Harvard University, and author of *Our Underachieving Colleges*

Consider This . . .

The ability to relate to people from diverse cultures is a basic life skill that has two powerful qualities:

1. *Transferability:* it's a portable skill that students can carry with them and transfer (apply) across a wide range of cultures, careers, and life situations; and
2. *Durability:* it's a long-lasting skill with enduring value that students will use throughout their lifetime.

6. Diversity Expands Social Relationships and Emotional Intelligence

When students interact with and acquire knowledge about people from a variety of groups, they widen their social circle by expanding the pool of people with whom they can relate and form relationships. Just as we seek variety in food to stimulate our taste buds, seeking variety in the people with whom they interact stimulates our social life. Research indicates that students who have more diverse relationships in college report higher levels of satisfaction with their college experience (Astin, 1993). Furthermore, by widening the range of people with whom they interact, students gain greater social self-confidence and ability to adapt to new people and new situations (Milville, Molla, & Sedlacek, 1992). In contrast, when students limit their social experiences to members of their own culture, they are left with "few opportunities to acquire more than stereotypes about ethnic and cultural groups other than their own" (National Council for Social Studies, 1991).

> " Viva la difference! "
> (Long live difference!)
> —A famous French saying

> " Variety is the spice of life. "
> —An old American proverb

"WE LIKE EVERYONE TO BE THEMSELVES, AS LONG AS EVERYONE FITS IN!"

Lastly, interaction with diverse people whose life experiences, circumstances, and challenges differ from one's own serves to promote empathy—awareness of and sensitivity to the feelings of others. Empathy is an essential ingredient of *emotional intelligence*—which has been found to be a better predictor of personal and professional success than intellectual ability (Goleman, 1995).

7. Diversity Education Reduces Prejudice and Discrimination in Society

Schools can provide the starting place and stimulus for promoting social justice and equity in the larger society (Gorski, 2010). Studies show that positive interpersonal interactions with diverse peers and open conversations among peers, about diversity-related topics that challenge previously held beliefs, serve to reduce personal prejudice and promote openness to diversity (Pascarella et al., 1996; Whitt et al., 2001). However, these positive outcomes don't happen automatically by simply mixing together minority and majority students in the same school environment. School-integration research strongly indicates that mere exposure to, or incidental contact with, minority students does not automatically improve interracial relations (Stephan, 1978), nor does it even promote interracial interaction because minority and majority students still manage to segregate themselves within the school setting (Gerard & Miller, 1975; Rogers, Hennigan, Bowman, & Miller, 1984). In one comprehensive review of all school-desegregation research conducted over a 30-year period, it was discovered that forced desegregation in schools with a hostile social environment actually increases rather than decreases racial prejudice (Stephan, 1986).

Thus, the benefits of diversity cannot be achieved solely by policy decisions and administrative mandates about school district enrollment policies—it also requires learning experiences that empower students to engage in positive and productive interaction with others from diverse cultural backgrounds. (Specific strategies for doing so are provided in Chapter 6.)

Learning from books and teachers helps students learn *about* diversity; however, firsthand interaction with diverse people enables students to learn directly *from* diversity. The difference is comparable to acquiring knowledge about another country by reading about it, as opposed to actually going to the country and interacting with its natives. Interpersonal interaction with others from diverse groups takes students beyond multicultural or cross-cultural awareness to *intercultural interaction*. It transforms diversity appreciation from an attitude or belief into action and commitment.

When intercultural interaction among students increases, not only do those who are the targets of stereotyping and prejudice benefit, the people holding these prejudices also benefit. Research shows that less-prejudiced people report greater satisfaction with their life (Feagin & McKinney, 2003) probably because they be-

> "The mere presence of persons of other cultures and subcultures [on campus] is primarily a political achievement, not an intellectual or educational achievement. Real educational progress will be made when multiculturalism becomes inter-culturalism."
> —Patrick J. Hill, Professor of Interdisciplinary Studies, Evergreen State College

> "Actual interaction with peers of different races is far superior to merely reading or watching a movie about racial issues."
> —Spokesperson for General Motors Corporation commenting on the company's experience with employees (Chatman, 2008)

come more open to new social experiences and less distrustful or fearful of others (Baron, Byrne, & Branscombe, 2006).

Teachers who remain alert to the power of intercultural interaction and use teaching methods that promote interaction among diverse students during the learning process will not only achieve positive learning outcomes, they will also reduce stereotypes and prejudices among the students involved in the learning process.

Studies show that simply mixing ethnic minority students with majority students in the same school does not automatically result in reduced prejudice and positive interaction between minority and majority group members (Stephan, 1978). In fact, a 30-year review of multiple school-desegregation studies showed that racial prejudice in forcefully desegregated schools actually increased rather than decreased (Stephan, 1980). These results may be explained by the fact that many children come to school with misconceptions or negative views about different racial and ethnic groups (Phinney & Rotheram, 1987), which are maintained or intensified after minority and majority students are simply placed together in the same environment (physically) because they self-segregate and remain separated (socially) (Gerard & Miller, 1975; Rogers, Hennigan, Bowman, & Miller, 1984).

What these findings strongly suggest is that something more than mere exposure of different groups to each other must occur in order to stimulate intercultural contact and multicultural appreciation. As Hill (1991) puts it,

> *Meaningful multi-culturalism transforms the curriculum. While the presence of persons of other cultures and subcultures is a virtual prerequisite to that transformation, their 'mere presence' is primarily a political achievement, not an intellectual or educational achievement. Real educational progress will be made when multi-culturalism becomes* interculturalism (p. 41) (emphasis added).

"*Inter*-culturalism" can be achieved when students from different cultural backgrounds work collaboratively in teams in pursuit of a common goal. This is the essence of good teamwork, and it may explain why interracial friendships form easily among athletes on sports teams, and among soldiers in the military (Putnam, 2007). Similar forms of results may be achieved in an educational setting through the formation of interethnic and interracial learning teams that incorporate the following features of cooperative learning:

1. Intentional formation of learning teams comprised of students from diverse cultural backgrounds, thereby ensuring that students collaborate rather than segregate.
2. Training team members on how to engage in true collaboration, constructive dialogue, and consensus building.
3. Assigning interdependent roles to teammates to ensure that they all have equal status and equal opportunity to participate and contribute to the team effort.

4. Identifying a common learning goal for teammates to pursue, which ensures that students are rewarded for collaborating with each other, rather than competing against each other.

Research strongly suggests that when members of diverse groups engage in cooperative learning activities that involve a common goal, equal status between group members (e.g., equally important, interdependent roles), and support by authorities (e.g., teachers or principals), prejudice declines and interracial friendships increase. These results have been found for elementary and secondary school students (Aronson, 1978; Banks, 1997; Slavin, 1980), college students (Nagda, Gurin, Soresen, & Zúñiga, 2009; Worchel, 1979), and workers in business settings (Blake & Mouton, 1979). (More detailed information on cooperative and collaborative methods of learning is provided in Chapter 6.)

> *Intercultural dialogue is a process that comprises an open and respectful exchange of views between individuals and groups with different ethnic, cultural, religious and linguistic backgrounds and heritage.*
> —Council of Europe

8. Diversity Education Preserves Democracy

As a democratic nation, America is built on the philosophical foundation of equal rights and freedom of opportunity for all citizens. Prejudice and discrimination divide citizens and dislodge the two key cornerstones of democracy: preservation of human freedom and government by the people for the people. When the rights or freedoms of any group of citizens in a democratic nation are threatened by prejudice and discrimination, the rights or freedoms of all its citizens are threatened. America's stability and prosperity in the 21st century will require effective development and deployment of the talents of all its citizens, including those from historically diverse and disadvantaged backgrounds (American Council on Education, 2008).

Thus, diversity education prepares students for citizenship and civic responsibility in a democratic nation. When students gain knowledge and awareness of social justice issues, they're more likely to become advocates and activists for equality, they're more likely to become voting citizens who cast their votes for political leaders committed to ensuring equal rights and social justice. Instructors devoted to cultural pluralism "make a strong, unequivocal commitment to democracy, to basic American values of justice and equality" (Brandt, 1994, p. 31).

> *Injustice anywhere is a threat to justice everywhere.*
> —Martin Luther King Jr., "Letter from the Birmingham Jail"

> *United we stand, divided we fall.*
> —Aesop, Greek slave (620–560 BC) and author of *Aesop's Fables*

> *A progressive society counts individual variations as precious since it finds in them the means of its own growth. A democratic society must, in consistency with its ideal, allow intellectual freedom and the play of diverse gifts and interests.*
> —John Dewey, U.S. educator, philosopher, and psychologist

Consider This . . .

Diversity education promotes students' awareness that diversity and democracy go hand-in-hand—by valuing the former, we preserve the latter.

> "A successful democracy demands tolerance and mutual respect from different groups within its citizenry in order to contain the religious and ethnic tensions that have riven so many countries around the world."
> —Derek Bok, President Emeritus & Research Professor at Harvard University, and author of *Our Underachieving Colleges*

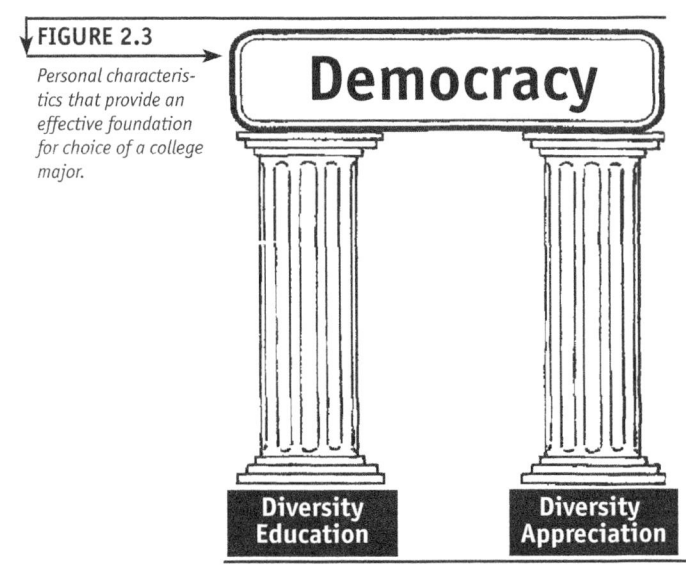

FIGURE 2.3

Personal characteristics that provide an effective foundation for choice of a college major.

> "Democracy and freedom ought to be both the end result of education as well as the means through which education takes place."
> —Bennis & Graves (nd)

In addition to an inclusive curriculum, diversity education also embodies the principles of democratic education (Curran, 2007; Gutmann, 1999b) when student-centered teaching methods are used that empower students to take an active role in the learning process, interact with other students during the learning process, and, ultimately, take more personal responsibility for their own learning. (See Chapter 6 for a detailed discussion of student-centered teaching methods.)

Summary and Conclusion

Diversity education addresses the important political issue of securing equal rights and social justice for all people; however, but it also represents an *educational* issue—it enriches learning and thinking, personal and social development, and career and civic responsibilities. This chapter identifies eight specific benefits or potential learning outcomes of diversity education, each of which is summarized here.

1. **Diversity education enhances self-awareness.**
   Learning from people with diverse backgrounds and experiences sharpens students' self-knowledge and self-insight by encouraging them to compare and contrast their life experiences with others whose life experiences differ sharply from their own.

2. **Diversity education deepens and accelerates learning.**
   Human knowledge is socially constructed—it is built up through interpersonal interaction and dialogue with others. When students converse with a multiplicity and variety of people, their learning is deepened and their think-

ing is broadened. Research consistently shows that students learn more from people who differ from them than they learn from people similar or familiar to them.

3. **Diversity promotes critical thinking from multiple perspectives.**
   Experiencing diversity diversifies students' thinking by liberating them from the tunnel vision of their own culture and empowering them with a broader multicultural or cross-cultural perspective. Being open to the viewpoints of diverse people who perceive the world from different cultural vantage points serves to help students overcome their "cultural blind spots." As a result, they begin to perceive the world with better balance, clarity, and objectivity. This wider perspective reduces their risk of prejudice and *groupthink*—the tendency for tight, like-minded groups of people to think so much alike that they overlook flaws in their own thinking—which can lead to poor choices and faulty decisions.

4. **Diversity education fosters creative thinking.**
   Experiencing diversity supplies students with a broader base of knowledge and a wider variety of thinking styles, both of which serve to enable them to think "outside the box" or boundaries of a single cultural framework. Once diverse perspectives have been acquired, they can be combined or rearranged in ways that result in unique or innovative solutions to problems. Furthermore, drawing different ideas from people of diverse backgrounds and exchanging ideas with them is an effective way to generate collective energy, synergy, and serendipity—the unanticipated discovery of creative ideas.

5. **Diversity education enhances career preparation and career success.**
   Learning about and from diversity better prepares students for today's work world. America's workforce is now more diverse than at any other time in the nation's history and it will grow increasingly diverse throughout the current century. In addition, work now takes place in a global economy characterized by greater economic interdependence among nations, more international trading (imports/exports), more multinational corporations, more international travel, and almost-instantaneous worldwide communication. As a result of these trends, employers now seek job candidates who possess international knowledge, foreign language skills, sensitivity to human differences, and the ability to relate to people from different cultural backgrounds. Both employers and the American public agree that diversity education is *career preparation*.

6. **Diversity education enriches social development and promotes emotional intelligence.**
   Interacting with people from a variety of cultural groups widens students' social circles and, by widening the pool of people with whom they interact, students strengthen their ability to relate and form friendships with a wider range of people with different experiences and interests. Furthermore, learn-

ing about, with, and from diverse people promotes empathy—a hallmark of *emotional intelligence*.

7. **Diversity education reduces societal prejudice and discrimination.**
   The school system is a starting place and stimulus for promoting social justice and equity in the larger society. Studies show that positive interactions with diverse peers, and conversations among peers about diversity-related topics that challenge previously held beliefs, serve to reduce prejudice and promote openness to diversity.

8. **Diversity education preserves democracy.**
   Democratic nations are built on the principles of equal rights and freedom of opportunity for all groups of people. By gaining awareness and knowledge of social justice issues, current students are more likely to become future advocates or activists for equality and future citizens who cast votes for political leaders committed to ensuring equal rights and social justice.

   The case for diversity education is clear and compelling. Its benefits go beyond desirable political outcomes, such as social justice, national stability, and international harmony—a variety of desirable learning outcomes are achieved as well. When teachers utilize instructional materials and methods that capitalize on the power of diversity, students experience a host of educational, vocational, and personal benefits that will last a lifetime.

 **Exercise**

Inclusion/Exclusion

Consider a time when you felt included or excluded from a particular group. Describe how this made you feel.

Adapted from Baylor University's Community Mentoring for Adolescent Development.

Appreciating Diversity
Avoiding Stereotypes and Overcoming Biases

Humans have a long history of displaying prejudice and discrimination toward other members of their own species. Although some of America's more flagrant forms of discrimination have been eliminated (e.g., slavery), a recent panel of national experts reported that the United States still remains a country deeply divided along the lines of culture, class, and religion; these divisions are becoming sharper and more significant due to the increase in the proportion of ethnic and racial minorities in the American population (Brookings Institute, 2008). America's public schools have become more segregated than they were in the late 1960s (Orfield, 1993).

This chapter identifies the common stereotypes, prejudices, and biases that have plagued our society; explores their underlying causes; and proposes a model for overcoming these barriers to effective multicultural education.

Stereotyping

The word "stereotype" derives from a combination of two roots: (a) "stereo," to look at in a fixed way, and (b) "type," to categorize or group together (as in the word "typical"); thus, stereotyping means to *view* individuals of the same type (group) in the same (fixed) way. In effect, stereotyping is rooted in assumptions about the "average characteristics of a group, which are imposed on all members from the group by ignoring or disregarding each member's individuality" (Ginsberg & Wlodkowski, 2009). Thus, all people, or virtually all people who are members of the same group (e.g., race or gender) are viewed as having the same personal characteristics—as in the expression: "You know what they're like; they're all the same."

Stereotypes involve *bias*, which literally means "slant." Bias can be positive or negative; positive bias results in a favorable stereotype (e.g., "Germans are great scientists and engineers"), and negative bias results in an unfavorable stereotype (e.g., "Germans are cold and calculating"). See **Box 3.1** for examples of other group stereotypes.

PERSONAL INSIGHT

When I was six years old, I was told by another six-year-old from a different racial group that all people of my race could not swim. Because I could not swim at that time and she could, I began to think she was right. To be sure, I asked a boy of the same racial group as the little girl if her statement were true; he exclaimed: "Yes, it's true!"

Because I was raised in a geographical area where few other African Americans were around to counteract this belief about blacks, I bought into this stereotype for a long time until I finally took swimming lessons as an adult. I'm now a lousy swimmer after many lessons because I did not even attempt to swim until I was an adult. The moral of this story is that group stereotypes can limit the confidence and potential of individuals who are members of the stereotyped group.

Aaron Thompson

> "Much knowledge about ethnic groups is stereotyped, distorted, and based on distant observations, scattered and superficial contacts, inadequate or imbalanced media treatment, and incomplete factual information."
> —National Council for the Social Studies

Box 3.1 Examples of Common Stereotypes

Muslims are terrorists.
Whites can't jump (or dance).
Blacks are lazy.
Asians are brilliant in math.
Irish drink too much.

Jews are cheap.
Hispanic men are abusive to women.
Men are strong; women are weak.
Gay men are feminine; lesbian women are masculine.

Reflection 3.1

1. Have you ever been stereotyped, based on your appearance or group membership?
   If so,
   (a) how did you feel?
   (b) how did you react?

2. Have you ever unintentionally perceived or treated someone in terms of a group stereotype rather than as an individual? If yes,
   (a) what assumptions did you make about that person?
   (b) was that person aware of or affected by your stereotyping?

Whether you are male or female, don't let gender stereotypes limit your career options

Prejudice

When all members of a stereotyped group are *judged or evaluated* in a negative way, the result is *prejudice*. (The word "prejudice" literally means to "pre-judge.") Technically, prejudice may be either positive or negative; however, the term is most often associated with a negative prejudgment—also known as *stigmatizing*—which involves attributing inferior or unfavorable traits to people who belong to the same group. Thus, prejudice may be defined as a negative judgment, attitude, or belief about another person or group of people that is formed before the facts are known. In effect, it's presuming guilt before allowing an opportunity to prove innocence.

Stereotyping makes prejudice possible because if virtually all members of the group are perceived as being alike, and that perception is negative, the result is a negative prejudgment, or prejudice. Once prejudice is formed toward a group, individuals from that group are typically avoided. This enables the prejudice to continue unchallenged because it allows no chance for the prejudiced person to have positive experiences with members of the stigmatized group that could contradict or disprove the prejudice. Thus, a vicious cycle is established in which the prejudiced person continues to avoid contact with individuals from the stigmatized group, which, in turn, serves to maintain and reinforce the prejudice.

PERSONAL INSIGHT

I was 15 years old when I first became aware that skin color really mattered to some people. I'm a rabid baseball fan and my team is the San Francisco Giants. I grew up in New York during the 1950s and became a fan of the New York Giants baseball team. When I was eight years old, the team left New York to become the San Francisco Giants. Even though the Giants left my hometown, I still considered them to be my team. I got a lot of teasing from members of my extended Italian family about rooting for an out-of-town team and not being loyal to New York. During one teasing episode with my cousins and uncles, I defended my team by saying that they were in first place and that I expected them to win the double-header they were going to play later that day. My 19-year-old cousin, Jimmy, interrupted me to say that the Giants' double-header was going to be cancelled because Malcolm X (black civil rights leader) was holding a meeting! Several of my older cousins and my uncles began laughing, but I couldn't figure out what was so funny. Then I suddenly got the "joke." At that time, the Giants were the team that had more black and Latino players than any other team in baseball. They were the first major league team to have multiple players from the Dominican Republic, and they had players from Puerto Rico and Cuba. I began to realize that all the teasing I received about being a Giants fan had less to do with the fact I was rooting for an out-of-town team and had more to do with the fact that I was rooting for a "colored" team.

Up until the time I heard that joke about Malcolm X at my family get-together, I never thought of the Giants' players as being colored; I just thought they were colorful. They had unique names (Orlando, Willie, and Felipe) and unique playing styles. As a young boy, I saw these players as being refreshingly different and exciting. However, my cousin's wisecrack that day and the reaction it produced among some of my family members, instantly and permanently changed me from being color-blind to color-conscious. It also changed me from being a Giants fan to a Giants fanatic. I was not only rooting for a team; I was rooting for a cause. Later that year, the Giants added a pitcher by the name of Masanori Murakami—the first Asian player ever to play professional baseball in America. I was proud to be rooting for the most diverse team in history. I didn't know it at the time, but I was appreciating and advocating for diversity.

Joe Cuseo

Discrimination

Literally translated, the term discrimination means division or separation. Whereas prejudice involves a belief, attitude, or opinion, discrimination involves an *action* taken toward others. Technically, discrimination can be either negative or positive; for example, a discriminating eater may be careful about eating only healthy foods. However, the term is most often associated with a negative action taken by a prejudiced person that results in unfair treatment or mistreatment of another person, or group of people. Thus, it could be said that discrimination is prejudice put into action. "Hate crimes" exemplify extreme discrimination because they are acts motivated solely by prejudice against members of a stigmatized group (e.g., damaging their property or physically assaulting them).

Other forms of discrimination are more subtle and may be practiced by society's institutional systems rather than particular individuals. These forms of *institutional racism* are less flagrant or visible, and they are rooted in societal policies and practices that discriminate against members of certain ethnic groups. For instance, the term "redlining"—a term coined in the late 1960s—refers to the practice of banks marking a red line on a map to indicate an area where they will not invest or lend money and many of those areas are neighborhoods in which African Americans live (Shapiro, 1993). Studies also show that compared to white patients, black patients of the same socioeconomic status are less likely to receive breast cancer screenings, eye exams if they have diabetes, and follow-up visits after hospitalization for mental illness (Schneider, Zaslavsky, & Epstein, 2002).

Thus, trying to be "race blind" and getting along with people of all colors with whom we interact on an *individual* basis is not all there is to eliminating discrimination. Racism is an issue that goes beyond individual interactions to larger institutional policies and societal systems. One goal of multicultural education is to empower students to eventually change these societal systems by "laying a foundation for the transformation of society and the elimination of oppression and injustice" (Gorski, 2010).

> "I was taught to recognize racism only in individual acts of meanness by members of my group, never as invisible systems. I was taught to think that racism could end if white individuals change their attitude. Individual acts can palliate but cannot end these problems."
>
> —Peggy McIntosh, author of *White Privilege: Unpacking the Invisible Knapsack*

Segregation

Segregation may be defined as a group's decision to separate itself, either socially or physically, from another group. Racial segregation continues to exist in American society (Massey, 2003; Nagda, Gurin, & Johnson, 2005). Research on college campuses reveals that college students, particularly white students, come from highly segregated high schools and neighborhoods (Matlock, 1997). Even with the increasing diversity in our society and our schools, minority students are much more likely than white students to attend schools where minority students are the majority population of the school population. For example, 77 percent of Hispanic students and 73 percent of black students attend schools in which they represent the majority of students at their school; in contrast, just over half of Asian students and only 12 percent of white students attend such schools (Orfield & Lee, 2005). In a long-term study of over 2,500 first-year African American, Asian American, Latino, and white students at the University of Michigan, it was found that white students had the most segregated friendship patterns (Matlock, 1997).

Reflection 3.2 Rate the amount or variety of diversity you have experienced in the following settings.

1.	The high school you attended	High	Moderate	Low
2.	The college or university you now attend	High	Moderate	Low
3.	The neighborhood in which you grew up	High	Moderate	Low
4.	Places where you have worked or been employed	High	Moderate	Low

Which of these settings had the *most* and *least* diversity? What do you think accounts for this difference?

> "Let us all hope that the dark clouds of racial prejudice will soon pass away and the deep fog of misunderstanding will be lifted from our fear-drenched communities, and in some not too distant tomorrow the radiant stars of love and brotherhood will shine over our great nation."
>
> —Martin Luther King, Jr., Civil Rights activist and clergyman

Although segregation itself may not be a blatant, malicious form of discrimination, it leads to reduced contact between the segregated groups. This reduced contact can cause a segregated group to be viewed as "unfamiliar" and this lack of familiarity, in turn, can trigger feelings of uncertainty and anxiety toward the segregated group (Zajonc, 2001). Because anxiety is an unpleasant emotion, if it's repeatedly associated with members of a segregated group, it can lead to avoidance and further dislike of the avoided (segregated) group (Pettigrew, 1998).

Reflection 3.3 Prejudice and discrimination can be subtle and only begin to surface when the social or emotional distance between members of different groups grows closer. Rate your level of comfort (high, medium, low) with the following situations.

Someone from another racial group:

1.	going to your school	high	medium	low
2.	working in your place of employment	high	medium	low
3.	living on your street as a neighbor	high	medium	low
4.	living with you as a roommate	high	medium	low
5.	socializing with you as a personal friend	high	medium	low
6.	being your most intimate friend or romantic partner	high	medium	low
7.	being your partner in marriage	high	medium	low

For any item you rated "low," what do you think accounts for or explains the low rating?

Box 3.2 contains a summary of biased attitudes, prejudicial beliefs, and discriminatory behaviors that must be overcome if humankind is to experience the full benefits of diversity. As you read through the list, place a checkmark next to any form of prejudice that you, a family member, or friend has experienced.

Box 3.2 Blocks to Learning from Diversity:
Biased Attitudes, Prejudicial Beliefs, and Discriminatory Behaviors

- *Stereotyping:* viewing all (or virtually all) individuals of the same group in the same way—as having the same qualities or characteristics.
  Example: If you're Italian, you must be in the Mafia, or have a family member who is.

- *Prejudice*: a negative prejudgment of another group of people.
  Example: Women do not make good leaders because they're too emotional.

- *Discrimination:* unequal and unfair treatment of a person or group of people—prejudice put into action.
  Example: People of color being paid less for performing the same job, even though they have the same level of education and job qualifications as whites performing the same job.

- *Segregation*: a conscious decision made by a group to separate itself (socially or physically) from another group.
  Example: "White flight"—white people moving out of neighborhoods when people of color move in.

- *Racism*: a belief that one's racial group is superior to another group and epressing that belief in the form of an attitude (prejudice) or action (discrimination).
  Example: Cecil Rhodes—Englishman and empire builder of British South Africa—once claimed: "We [the British] are the finest race in the world and the more of the world we inhabit the better it is for the human race."

- *Institutional Racism*: racism rooted in organizational policies and practices that disadvantage certain racial groups.
  Example: Race-based discrimination in mortgage lending, housing, and bank loans.

- *Slavery*: Forced labor in which people are considered to be the property of others, are held against their will, and are deprived of the right to leave, to refuse to work, or to demand wages.
  Example: Enslavement of blacks was legal in the United States until 1865.

- *"Jim Crow" Laws:* Formal and informal laws created by whites after the abolition of slavery to segregate blacks. (The term "Jim Crow" likely derived from a song-and-dance character named "Jump Jim Crow" who was played by a white man in blackface.)
  Example: Laws in the United States that once required blacks and whites to use separate bathrooms and be educated in separate schools.

- *Apartheid*: An institutionalized system of "legal racism" supported by a nation's government. (Apartheid derives from a word in the Afrikaan language, meaning "apartness.")
  Example: The national system of racial segregation and discrimination that existed in South Africa from 1948 to 1994.

> *Hate Crimes*: Criminal action motivated solely by prejudice toward the crime victim.
> Example: Acts of vandalism or assault aimed at members of a particular ethnic group or persons with a particular sexual orientation.

> *Hate Groups*: Organizations whose primary purpose is to stimulate prejudice, discrimination, or aggression toward certain groups of people based on their ethnicity, race, religion, etc.
> Example: The Ku Klux Klan—an American terrorist group that perpetrates hatred toward all nonwhite races.

> *Genocide*: Mass murdering of a particular ethnic or racial group by another group.
> Example: The Holocaust during World War II, during which millions of Jews were systematically murdered. Other examples include the murdering of Cambodians under the Khmer Rouge regime, the murdering of Bosnian Muslims in the former country of Yugoslavia, and the slaughter of the Tutsi minority by the Hutu majority in Rwanda.

> *Classism*: Prejudice or discrimination based on social class, particularly toward people of low socioeconomic status.
> Example: Acknowledging the contributions made by politicians and wealthy industrialists to America, while ignoring the contributions of poor immigrants, farmers, slaves, and pioneer women.

> *Religious Bigotry*: Denying the fundamental human right of people to hold religious beliefs, or to hold religious beliefs that differ from one's own.
> Example: An atheist who forces nonreligious (secular) beliefs on others, or a member of a religious group who believes that people who hold different religious beliefs are immoral "sinners."

> *Anti-Semitism*: Prejudice or discrimination toward Jews or people who practice the religion of Judaism.
> Example: Hating Jews because they're the ones who "killed Christ."

> *Xenophobia*: Extreme fear or hatred of foreigners, outsiders, or strangers.
> Example: Believing that immigrants should be banned from entering the country because they'll increase the crime rate or ruin our economy.

> *Regionalism*: Prejudice or discrimination based on the geographical region in which an individual has been born and raised.
> Example: A northerner thinking that all southerners are racists.

> *Jingoism*: Excessive interest and belief in the superiority of one's own nation without acknowledging its mistakes or weaknesses; it's often accompanied by an aggressive foreign policy that neglects the needs of other nations, or the common needs of all nations.
> Example: "Blind patriotism"—not seeing the shortcomings of one's own nation and viewing any questioning or criticism of their nation as disloyalty or being "unpatriotic." (As in the slogan, "America: right or wrong" or "America: love it or leave it!")

> *Terrorism*: Intentional acts of violence against civilians that are motivated by political or religious prejudice.
> Example: The September 11th attacks on the United States.

"Rivers, ponds, lakes and streams—they all have different names, but they all contain water. Just as religions do—they all contain truths."

—Muhammad Ali, three-time world heavyweight boxing champion, member of the International Boxing Hall of Fame, and recipient of the Spirit of America Award as the most recognized American in the world

STUDENT PERSPECTIVE

"I would like to change the entire world, so that we wouldn't be segregated by continents and territories."

College sophomore

- *Sexism*: Prejudice or discrimination based on sex or gender.
  Example: Believing that women should not pursue careers in fields traditionally filled only by men (e.g., engineering) because they lack the natural qualities or skills to do them.
- *Heterosexism*: Belief that heterosexuality is the only acceptable sexual orientation.
  Example: Using the phrase, "fag" or "queer" as an insult or put down; or believing that gays should not have the same legal rights and opportunities as heterosexuals.
- *Homophobia*: Extreme fear or hatred of homosexuals.
  Example: People who engage in "gay bashing" (acts of violence toward gays), or who create and contribute to anti-gay websites.
- *Ageism*: Prejudice or discrimination based on age, particularly toward the elderly.
  Example: Believing that all "old" people are bad drivers with bad memories who should not be allowed on the road.
- *Ableism*: Prejudice or discrimination toward people who are disabled or handicapped (physically, mentally, or emotionally).
  Example: Avoiding social contact or interaction with people in wheelchairs.

STUDENT PERSPECTIVE

> "Most religions dictate that theirs is the only way, and without believing in it, you cannot enter the mighty kingdom of heaven. Who are we to judge? It makes more sense for God to be the only one mighty enough to make that decision. If other people could understand and see from this perspective, then many religious arguments could be avoided."
>
> —First-year college student

Reflection 3.4 Have you, a family member, or friend experienced any of the form(s) of prejudice in the above list? Why do you think it occurred?

STUDENT PERSPECTIVE

> "I grew up in a very racist family. Even just a year go, I could honestly say 'I hate Asians' with a straight face and mean it. My senior AP language teacher tried hard to teach me not to be judgmental. He got me to be open to others, so much so that my current boyfriend is half Chinese."
>
> —First-year college student

Causes of Prejudice and Discrimination

It's clear that what all forms of prejudice have in common is that they lack deep thought and critical thinking. However, less clear is the answer to the question: What exactly causes people to develop prejudice in the first place? Although there is no single, definitive answer to this question, research has identified the following seven human tendencies as key factors involved in the development of prejudice:

1. Feeling comfortable with the familiar and uncomfortable with the unknown or unfamiliar
2. Using selective perception and selective memory
3. Mentally categorizing people into "in" and "out" groups
4. Perceiving members of other groups as more alike than members of one's own group
5. Majority group members' attitudes being more strongly influenced by negative behaviors committed by members of minority groups than by members of their own (majority) group
6. Rationalizing prejudice and discrimination as justifiable
7. Strengthening self-esteem through group membership and group identity

Feeling Comfortable with the Familiar and Uncomfortable with the Unknown or Unfamiliar

> See that man over there?
> Yes.
> Well, I hate him.
> But you don't know him.
> That's why I hate him.
>
> —Gordon Allport, social psychologist and author of *The Nature of Prejudice*

Studies show that when humans encounter something that is unfamiliar or uncommon, they tend to experience feelings of discomfort or anxiety. In contrast, what's familiar to us tends to become accepted and better liked (Zajonc, 2001). This automatic reaction is likely "wired into" the human body because it has played an important role in the survival and evolution of our species. In our primitive past, when we encountered strangers it was advantageous for ancestors to react with feelings of anxiety and a rush of adrenaline because those strangers may have been potential predators who could harm (or devour) us. Scholars refer to this reaction as the "fight or flight" response (see **Figure 3.1**).

The evolutionary, fight-or-flight response is the likely explanation why infants between about 8 and 18 months of life experience "stranger anxiety"—a stage of development during which they react to strangers by crying, an accelerating heartbeat, and breathing at a faster rate (Papalia & Olds, 1990).

The tendency to fear the unknown or the unfamiliar can contribute to prejudice by causing us to be on guard when encountering members of other groups who are unfamiliar (Aronson, Wilson, & Akert, 2005). Being aware of this biological tendency is an important first step toward preventing it from developing into prejudice. We may not be able to block this subconscious emotional reaction from kicking in; however, we can recognize it and make a conscious effort to prevent it

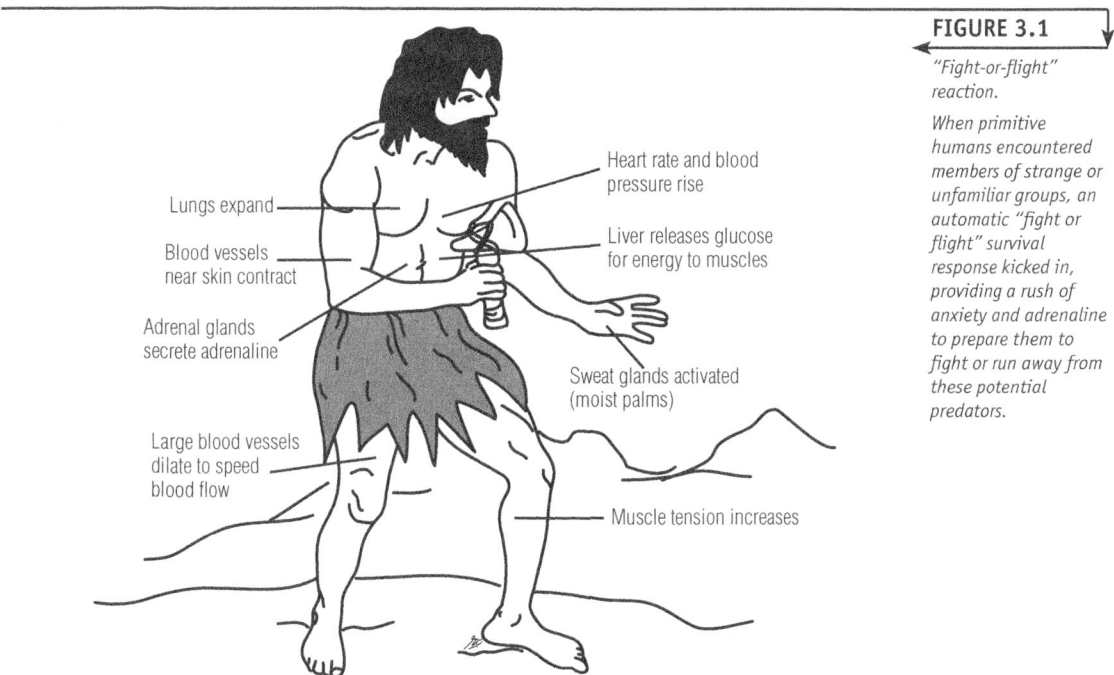

FIGURE 3.1

"Fight-or-flight" reaction.

When primitive humans encountered members of strange or unfamiliar groups, an automatic "fight or flight" survival response kicked in, providing a rush of anxiety and adrenaline to prepare them to fight or run away from these potential predators.

from influencing us conceptually (our opinions) or behaviorally (our actions) toward groups of people who are unfamiliar to us.

Psychological research also indicates that *familiarity* has a powerful effect on human judgment and decision making. This may explain why studies show that we tend to form judgments very quickly (within 40 milliseconds) of others whom are perceived to be emotionally threatening (Bar, Neta, & Linz, 2006; Gladwell, 2005). However, the more exposure humans have to somebody or something, the more familiar it becomes and the more likely that it will be perceived positively and judged favorably. The effect of familiarity is so common and influential that social psychologists refer to it as the "familiarity principle": what is familiar is perceived good (Zajonc, 1968; 1970). The strong influence of familiarity on human judgment may help explain why negative prejudgments (prejudice) can quickly develop toward members of a minority group who are less commonly seen or familiar to members of the majority group. A dominant majority group way of perceiving reality may be so powerful that its view comes to be accepted as common sense or the way things should be, and may even come to be believed by members of the minority group as well (Freire & Macedo, 1987).

Using Selective Perception and Selective Memory

Once prejudice has been formed, it can often remain intact and resistant to change through the psychological process of *selective perception*—the tendency for the biased people to see what they *expect* to see and fail to see what contradicts their bias (Hugenberg & Bodenhausen, 2003). Have you ever noticed how fans rooting for their favorite sports team tend to focus on and "see" the calls or decisions of referees that go against their own team; however, they don't seem to notice or react to as many calls that go against the opposing team? This is a classic, everyday example of selective perception. It could be said that selective perception changes the process of "seeing is believing" into "believing is seeing." This can lead prejudiced people to focus their attention on information that's consistent with the prejudgment, causing them to "see" information that supports or reinforces it, but failing to see or overlooking information that contradicts it. Furthermore, selective perception is often accompanied by *selective memory*—the tendency to remember information that's consistent with the prejudice, beliefs, but forgetting information that's inconsistent with it or contradicts it (Judd, Ryan, & Park, 1991).

The complementary mental processes of selective perception and selective memory often operate *unconsciously*; thus, prejudiced people may not be aware that they're using these biased mental processes or how these processes are working to preserve their prejudice (Baron, Byrne, & Brauscombe, 2006).

Mentally Categorizing People into "In" and "Out" Groups

Humans have a long history of grouping other humans into mental categories, probably for the purpose of making their complex social world simpler (Jones, 1990). Although the tendency to categorize people into groups can help us make sense of, and keep track of, our social world, it can also lead to stereotyping members of human groups and blind us to the uniqueness of individuals who comprise those groups. Classifying people into groups can contribute to prejudice because it may result in the creation of *in*-groups ("us") and *out*-groups ("them"). In-group versus out-group categorization can lead to *ethnocentrism*—viewing one's own cultural group to be the central or "normal" in-group, while viewing other cultures as peripheral or marginal out-groups. Ethnocentrism can, in turn, lead to prejudice and discrimination toward other cultures they deviate from the norm—what's customary and familiar—therefore, they're seen as "abnormal" (deviant or deficient) (National Council for the Social Studies, 1991).

> ### Consider This . . .
> We must consciously remind ourselves and our students not to perceive what's culturally *different* as culturally *deficient*.

Perceiving Members of Other Groups as More Alike than Members of One's Own Group

Research in the field of social psychology demonstrates that humans tend to perceive individuals from different (less familiar) groups as more alike in attitudes and behavior than members of their own (familiar) group (Baron, Byrne, & Brauscombe, 2006). For instance, studies show that members of younger age groups perceive individuals in older age groups to be more alike in their attitudes and beliefs than members of their own age group (Linville, Fischer, & Salovey, 1989).

This tendency may stem from the fact that we have more experience with members of our own group, thus we have more opportunities to observe and interact with a wide variety of individuals within our group. In contrast, we have fewer interactions with individuals from other groups, so we don't have as much contact and personal experience with as wide a variety of people in those groups—which may lead us to conclude that the range of individual differences among them is narrower and their group is more alike in attitudes and behavior than our group.

Lack of contact with individuals from a particular racial group can even lead to difficulties identifying individual members of the segregated group. Studies show that humans recognize members of their own race better than members of other racial groups—a phenomenon known as "own-race bias" (Aronson, Wilson, & Akert, 2007). This bias can be so strong that it becomes more difficult for us to detect differences between the faces of individuals in groups from groups that are unfamiliar to us: "they all seem to look alike" (Levin, 2000). This isn't a genetic or inborn bias because it doesn't occur when members of different races have frequent contact with each other (Sangrigoli et al., 2005). However, when people see faces of individuals from unfamiliar racial groups with whom they have little contact, they fail to detect subtle differences in their personal features that distinguish one group member from another. Instead, these specific features aren't noticed because the viewer's attention tends to be drawn to the general physical features that characterize members of their race—Asian eyes or African lips—which can lead the view that "they all look alike" (Levin, 2000).

Such overgeneralization has resulted in false convictions and imprisonment of innocent members of racial minority groups whom eyewitnesses from majority groups "identified" as committing a crime, but later DNA tests proved the crime was actually committed by a different member of the same racial group (Ramsey & Frank, 2007). This is well illustrated by the case of Lenell Geter, an African American engineer who received a life sentence in prison for a crime he didn't commit. Four of five non-black witnesses misidentified him for another black man who actually committed the crime and was later apprehended.

Such dramatic miscarriages of justice like this make the news. Less newsworthy, but a more common negative consequence of limited contact between members of different racial (and ethnic) groups, is the tendency to view members of unfamiliar groups as more alike in their attitudes and behaviors than they actually are, which can lead to group stereotyping. Even if an individual member of the unfamiliar group doesn't fit the group stereotype, research shows that individual exceptions are likely to be dismissed as an "exception to the rule," or as an exception that "proves" the general rule (Aronson, Wilson, & Akert, 2005).

The Tendency for Majority Group Members to Be More Strongly Influenced by Negative Behaviors Committed by Members of Minority Groups than by Members of Their Own (Majority) Group

Studies show that if negative or unacceptable behavior occurs at the same rate among members of both a majority and minority group (e.g., the rate of criminal behavior in both groups is 10 percent), members of the majority group are more likely to develop negative attitudes (prejudice) toward the minority group than their own group (Baron, Byrne, & Brauscombe, 2006). For example, it's been found that whites in the United States tend to underestimate the crime rate of white men and overestimate the crime rates of African American men (Hamilton & Sherman, 1989). One possible explanation for this estimation error is that minorities are less common and, therefore, more distinctive. Thus, the behavior associated with them is more likely to (a) stand out in the minds of majority group members, (b) be more vividly remembered, and (c) influence their attitudes toward minority groups (McArthur & Friedman, 1980).

Prejudices held by majority groups toward minority groups have led to the most extreme forms of discrimination and domination (Baron, Byrne, & Brauscombe, 2006); however, any group can become a target for prejudice. Members of a minority group can also be prejudiced toward the majority group, as illustrated by the following comment made by the following experience reported by a student of color: "My friend [a student of color] said that he 'hates white people because they try to dominate people of color.' I, on the other hand, feel differently. One should not blame all white people for the mistakes and prejudiced acts that white people have made" (Nagda, Gurin, & Johnson, 2005, p. 102).

Rationalizing Prejudice and Discrimination as Justifiable

Rationalization may be described as a psychological tool that humans use to explain or justify personal behavior that's clearly irrational or unethical. A relevant example of rationalization involves slavery in the United States, a democratic nation built on the principle that all men are created equal and have the right to life, liberty, and the pursuit of happiness. At the time that this principle was enunciated in the Declaration of Independence, slavery was legal and an established feature of the colonial economy. Our nation's first president, George Washington, "owned" more than 300 slaves at the time of his death (Fritz, 1997). Naturally, this practice was a clear contradiction to the democratic ideals upon which this country was being built. To reconcile this contradiction, the concept of different human "races" was introduced: humans of a darker color (race) were not equal to humans of the "white race," therefore they could be enslaved. Thus, the United States continued with its slave-based economy and became the first nation in the world to use a system of slavery that was based entirely on peoples' color. The same rationalization was used to justify extermination of American Indians, forced takeover of Mexican land, and exclusion of Asian immigrants (California Newsreel, 2003).

Strengthening Self-Esteem through Group Membership and Group Identity

Our personal identity is strongly influenced by the group(s) to which we belong and so is our self-esteem—how we feel about ourselves. If people believe that a group they belong to is better or superior, it strengthens their self-image (Tafjel, 1982). The reasoning goes something like this: "My group is superior, and since I'm a member, I'm superior." Self-image building through group identification is even more likely to occur when an individual's self-esteem is threatened by personal frustration or failure. The person whose self-esteem has been lowered by frustration or failure can boost it, stigmatizing members of another group (Rudman & Fairchild, 2004) or using them as a "scapegoat" for their own problems or failure (Gemmil, 1989). Studies show that prejudice and discrimination tends to escalate when times are tough—for example, when the economy is down, unemployment is up, and people are feeling a greater sense of personal threat, frustration, or loss (Aronson, Wilson, & Akert, 2005). The most extreme example of scapegoating in human history took place in Nazi Germany, where Jews were blamed for the country's economic problems and became targets of the Holocaust.

PERSONAL INSIGHT One of the best attended events that ever took place at my college was a presentation made by a guest speaker named Floyd Cochran—a former member and recruiter for the Aryan Nation (a white supremacist hate group) who left the group and went on to become a nationally known Civil Rights activist and educator. He tours the country, speaking out against racist organizations and hate crimes at high schools and universities. After giving his talk on my campus, he asked the jam-packed room if they had any questions. No student raised a hand, probably because the audience was so large and the topic so sensitive. As a faculty member, I thought that maybe if I broke the ice and asked a question, then students would feel comfortable doing the same. I asked him the following question: "Based on your experience with veteran group members and new members you recruited, what would you say was the most common reason why people become members of hate groups in the first place?" Without even the slightest pause, he stated that most members of his hate group had a poor self-image and many came from dysfunctional families where their need for social acceptance was never met. Cochran's answer is a perfect illustration of how extreme prejudice can stem from an attempt to strengthen one's self-image and self-esteem by identification with a "superior" group.

Joe Cuseo

A Personal Development Model for Overcoming Bias and Appreciating Student Diversity

Both students and teachers bring their particular cultural backgrounds, experiences, and potential biases to the classroom. As Bowman (1995) notes, teachers who overlook this reality may "become victims of their own naïve and culture-bound conceptions." Becoming more self-aware of the biases we hold and taking action steps to rid ourselves of these biases are essential preconditions or prerequisites for promoting the success of all students, particularly students from minority cultural backgrounds.

As previously mentioned, bias is a predisposition toward viewing something or someone in a certain way before the facts are known. Thus, bias is built on acceptance of a personal belief without being aware of why that belief is held, or the accuracy of the information on which the belief is based. Only a deep sense of self-awareness can combat the development of bias. We must continually and consciously ask ourselves not only what we believe about a subject, person, or group, but also *why* we hold the belief and what evidence we have to support it. Taking time to introspect and inspect our biases represents the critical first stage in the process of diversity education.

Overcoming bias and moving toward appreciation of diversity may be conceptually viewed as a systematic, sequential process that begins with *awareness* of human differences, followed by *acknowledgment* of any hidden biases we may have toward groups who differ from us, followed by our *acceptance* of group differences, which culminates in our engaging in some *action* or interaction that allows us to capitalize on the power of diversity (Thompson & Cuseo, 2009). Thus, the diversity-appreciation process may be conceived of as a cycle comprised of the following four stages:

1. **Awareness** of our personal beliefs and attitudes toward diverse groups,
2. **Acknowledgment** of how our beliefs and attitudes may be affecting members of diverse groups,
3. **Acceptance** of (empathy for) members of diverse groups, and
4. **Action** taken to reach out and interact with people from diverse groups (see **Figure 3.2**).

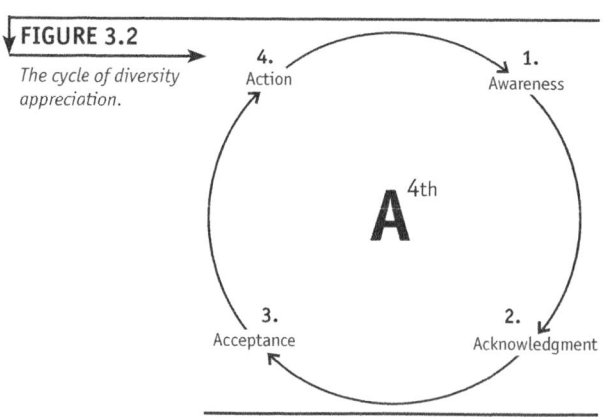

FIGURE 3.2
The cycle of diversity appreciation.

This process is sequential and hierarchical—each stage builds on the stage that precedes it—and we cannot move to a higher next stage until the previous stage has been successfully completed. After the full cycle is completed, we're positioned not only to accept or tolerate diversity, but also to appreciate it and gain from it.

Stage 1. Awareness

From a very young age, our beliefs have been shaped through many years of socialization from a variety of social agents (parents and other family members, peers, media, etc.), often to such a degree that we may no longer question or evaluate them. In fact, to question or challenge long-held beliefs may make us feel as if we're disregarding or disrespecting our upbringing and heritage. However, when we take the time to evaluate how our beliefs have been shaped by our past experiences, we gain greater awareness of both their strengths and limitations. Instead of blindly borrowing or following ideas that have been handed down to us, we should gain insight into them and control over them (Thompson & Cuseo, 2009).

If we're asked to examine our biases, it can easily put us on the defensive because we may feel that we're being wrongfully "accused" or about to be booked for a "guilt trip." Examining our biases is not to admit to being personally responsible for the cases of overt prejudice and blatant discrimination that plague our society, which are clearly unethical, illegal, and punishable. Instead, it is a process of becoming personally aware of more subtle biases, which can lead to less obvious forms of prejudice and discrimination that often take place without full conscious awareness or malicious intent (Butler, 1993). In one famous study, college instructors were totally surprised to discover that they treated students from different groups unequally when shown videotapes of their discussions, or when a colleague visited their class to observe their interactions with students (Sadker & Sadker, 1994). This may happen in part because instructors tend to rely on their own background experiences for examples to illustrate course content, which is more likely to invite participation and interaction from students whose cultural experiences are similar to those of the instructor.

> *The first requisite for culturally responsive teaching [is] a sincere sense of self-scrutiny, not to induce guilt but to deepen sensitivity to the range of ways educators are complicitous with inequitable treatment of others and to open ourselves to knowing the limitations of our own perspectives and our need for those of others. Mindfulness of who we are and what we believe culturally can help us examine the ways in which we may be unknowingly placing our good intentions within a dominant and unyielding framework—in spite of the appearance of openness and receptivity to enhancing motivation to learn among all students. One of the most useful places to begin the exploration of who we are culturally and the relevance of that identity is to ask what values we hold that are consistent with the dominant culture (Ginsberg & Wlodowksi, 2009, pp. 13 & 330).*

Consider This...

Engaging in the process of becoming more aware of our biases and prejudices is not a "guilt trip"—it's a process for lifelong learning, personal development, and professional success.

> We must learn to be vulnerable enough to allow our world to turn upside down in order to allow the realities of others to edge themselves into our consciousness.
>
> —Lisa Delpit, *Harvard Educational Review*, "The Silenced Dialogue: Power and Pedagogy in Educating Other People's Children."

Research indicates that prejudice and discrimination often occur unconsciously or unintentionally (Baron, Byrne, & Branscombe, 2006). Thus, the first stage in the process of appreciating diversity is developing self-awareness about our beliefs and attitudes toward differences, particularly awareness of any stereotypes or prejudices we may have that are biasing our perception of, or behavior toward, different groups of people. At the bare minimum, we want to behave in a way that demonstrates tolerance or acceptance of diversity and avoid conscious or unconscious prejudice that may prevent us from effectively reaching and teaching certain students. When teachers gain greater awareness of their own biases, they gain greater understanding of how preconceived beliefs or attitudes may be unconsciously affecting their relationships with students in their classroom. Becoming aware of subtle, subconscious biases promotes self-awareness and self-transformation, which are key goals of multicultural education (Gorski, 2010)

A procedure that may be used to take a first step toward increasing awareness of your feelings, beliefs, and biases about diverse groups consists of the following steps:

- Take a moment to list all of the things that come to your mind about a group of people that are different than you, or about a group with whom you've had very little interaction. (The diversity spectrum on **p. 1** may be used to identify one such group.)
- Write down all feelings and thoughts you have about them, and write down what you truly believe, rather than what sounds right or seems socially acceptable.
- Be completely honest; don't worry about whether your thoughts and feelings will be judged right or wrong because you will not be asked to share your thoughts with anyone else.
- Go very deep into the thought process to dig up any and all hidden notions you may have about the group you have chosen. Once you have explored your deepest thoughts and feelings, and have recorded them in writing, honestly answer the following questions, probing for reasons and sources of influence or evidence that underlie your answers.

Reflection 3.5 Would you say that any of the beliefs and feelings represents a stereotype, negative bias, or prejudice?

If yes, why do you hold it, and how do you think you acquired it in the first place?

___

Once you have answered the above questions honestly, you're now ready to move on to the next stage in the cycle of diversity appreciation: *Acknowledgment*. A culturally sensitive teacher has an awareness of:

- the effect of communication style on learning
- the individual needs of students within their classroom (e.g., disabilities, learning styles, etc.)
- the cultural backgrounds of their students
- the effect institutional racism has had on society
- the influence of context and culture on behavior

Stage 2. Acknowledgment

To appreciate diversity, we first need to acknowledge the diversity around us and how it can benefit, rather than limit us. Acknowledging the diverse groups that make up our social environment and how their experiences differ from our own involves more than simply saying, "Live and let live" or, "We're all human, so let's come to terms with our differences and move on." Such statements deny students' group identity—which is an important component of their self-concept and self-esteem. Furthermore, they minimize or ignore the fact that different groups of people continue to face different life challenges because they have experienced different degrees of privilege (e.g., unearned access to resources and sources of influence simply because they belong to a certain social group). For example, individuals born into families with greater wealth and socioeconomic status have the privilege of being able to tap into a network of influential people who can help them gain access to employment, loans, educational services, and legal assistance.

Although it is the American ideal that all people are created equally and that socioeconomic prosperity is based entirely on merit, the belief that all Americans have an equal opportunity to rise from "rags to riches" is "rooted in cultural mythology that overlooks the social, political, and economic forces that favor certain groups over others. Thus, achievement has at least as much to do with privilege as to personal desire and effort" (Ginsberg & Wlodkowski, 2009, p. 14). Said in another way, not all people start the race to success at the same starting line—some

> ❝ In my younger and more vulnerable years, my father gave me some advice that I've been turning over in my mind ever since: 'Whenever you feel like criticizing anyone, just remember that all the people in this world haven't had the advantages you've had.' ❞
>
> —F. Scott Fitzgerald, in *The Great Gatsby*, an American literary classic

are born with the advantage of a silver spoon in their mouth, some with a plastic spoon, and others with no spoon at all.

Acknowledgment also involves understanding how our thoughts and feelings may affect others who are different than us, and how they view themselves. George Cooley, famous sociologist, coined the term "looking glass self" to capture the idea that seeing how others act toward us and react to us is like looking in a mirror; their actions and reactions (positive or negative) reflect back on us and affect how we view ourselves (positively or negatively) (Cooley, 1922). Thus, even if children come to the school environment with academic ability and motivation, low teachers' expectations can affect their academic self-image and self-confidence, which, in turn, can adversely affect their behavior and success in school (Bowman, 1995). For instance, the common stereotype that women cannot perform as well in math and science as men has been found to lower teachers' expectations of women in these subject areas (Clewell, Anderson, & Thorpe, 1992; Tobias, 1978).

Not only may low expectations have an adverse effect on students' academic achievement, it can also reduce their level of involvement in the learning process. For example, there is evidence that some white, male college professors tend to treat female students and students from ethnic or racial minority groups differently than they do males and nonminority students. In particular, females and minority students in classes taught by white, male instructors are more likely to:

> A lot of us never asked questions in class before—it just wasn't done, especially by a woman or a girl, so we need to realize that and get into the habit of asking questions and challenging if we want to—regardless of the reactions of the profs and other students.
>
> —Adult female college student, quoted in Wilkie & Thompson (1993)

- receive less eye contact from the instructor,
- be called on less frequently in class,
- be given less time to respond to questions asked by the instructor in class, and
- have less contact with the instructor outside of class (Hall & Sandler, 1982; 1984; Sedlacek, 1987; Wright, 1987).

In the vast majority of these cases, the discriminatory treatment received by these female and minority students received was subtle and not done consciously or deliberately by the instructors (Green, 1989). Nevertheless, these unintended actions are still discriminatory, and they may send a message to minority and female students that their ideas are not worth hearing, or that they are not as capable as other students (Sadker & Sadker, 1994).

Teachers can help guard against unconscious tendencies to interact differently with students of different gender or ethnicity by having their classroom teaching behavior videotaped, or by having a colleague visit class and provide objective "third party" feedback about whether they're treating certain groups of students differently, albeit unknowingly.

Reflection 3.6 Would you say that you have held biased or stereotyped beliefs (positive or negative) toward any group that may have either benefitted or disadvantaged them?

A culturally sensitive teacher *acknowledges* that:

- a teacher's attitudes and actions can affect the self-development of students
- learning is maximized in a classroom environment that is inclusive and personally validating
- the role of a teacher is a bridge builder between the culture of the student, the school, and the surrounding community
- the students' parents have a vested interest in the learning of their students
- the students' language and culture are interrelated
- cultural and linguistic diversity are essential elements of the learning experience
- cultural dialect is a valid expression of language that should not be devalued, but utilized to enhance a student's ability to learn, read, and communicate

After honestly acknowledging how our thoughts, feelings, and actions have affected others who differ from us (particularly if the impact has been negative), we're ready to move on the next stage in the cycle of diversity appreciation: *Acceptance*.

Stage 3. Acceptance

Acceptance involves sensitivity, empathy, and insight into the experiences of others who have been adversely affected by biases or prejudices. In this stage, we accept that although we may never be able to actually feel what others have felt who have been on the receiving end of prejudice, we can still sympathize with them. By so doing, we develop empathy—which is a critical component of emotional intelligence (Goleman, 2006) and a potent predictor of career success (Goleman, 1995).

To increase your understanding and empathy for the experiences of members of another group, imagine yourself as a member of that group and attempt to visualize what the experience might be like. Better yet, see if you can place yourself in the position or situation of someone from that group (e.g., spending a day in a wheelchair to experience what it is like for someone who is physically disabled, or wearing blinders to experience what it's like to be visually impaired.)

> *Instruction begins when you, the teacher, learn from the learner; put yourself in his place so that you understand what he learns and the way he understands.*
>
> —Soren Kierkegaard, 19th-century Danish theologian and philosopher

PERSONAL INSIGHT

As I mentioned earlier in this chapter, one of the best attended events that ever took place at my college was a presentation made by Floyd Cochran, a former member and recruiter for the Aryan Nation (a white supremacist hate group) who left the group and went on to became a nationally known Civil Rights activist and educator. During his talk, he mentioned that the major event in his life that caused him to change his views was an edict issued by Aryan Nation leaders that Cochran's recently conceived son had to be aborted because ultrasound results indicated that the developing boy had cleft palate, which, in the in minds of the supremacist group, meant that he was "defective" and couldn't be a member of their genetically superior group. This left Cochran with two choices: (a) abort his son and remain a member of his supremacist group, or (b) keep his son and be ostracized by the group whose beliefs he passionately endorsed. Cochran chose to quit the supremacist group, to renounce his racist beliefs, and to begin speaking out publicly against the hateful prejudices he once firmly believed and taught. He became a nationally known Civil Rights activist and educator who toured the country, speaking out against racist organizations and hate crimes at high school and universities.

After hearing Cochran's story, it struck me that the key event or turning point in his incredible transformation was really an exercise in role reversal. When his son was deemed "inferior," he was thrust into a reversed role—he became the recipient rather than the perpetrator of hateful discrimination. Cochran's radical reversal from hateful racist to Civil Rights activist is a dramatic example of the power of role reversal for promoting empathy and sensitivity to the rights of others.

Joe Cuseo

Acceptance involves not only realizing how our biases have affected others, but it also involves how bias affects us. Bias not only impedes members of other groups from reaching their full potential, it also impedes the development of the biased person (and our society as a whole).

A culturally sensitive teacher accepts that:

▶ motivation is key to learning
▶ students' self-esteem needs to be increased through classroom expression
▶ different learning styles will require differentiated instruction
▶ all students have the ability to learn and excel

Stage 4. Action

Once we (a) become aware of our biases, (b) acknowledge any effects that our biases may have had on members of other groups, and (c) accept the feelings of others who may have been adversely affected by our biases, we can take action with respect to appreciating and capitalizing on the power of diversity. This stage in the cycle of diversity appreciation involves moving beyond sensitivity to responding effectively to differences in such a way that it allows us to capitalize on diversity to promote our own personal and professional development, as well as the development of the students we teach. Thus, we reach the highest level of diversity appreciation: *cultural competence*. When we attain cultural competence, we move be-

> " I have always felt that the true textbook for the pupil is his teacher. "
> —Ghandi, political and spiritual leader of India during the Indian independence movement

yond mere acceptance or tolerance of diversity to a deeper, more authentic appreciation of diversity, and we model that appreciation for our students to emulate.

Research suggests that when diversity education focuses on differences alone, members of minority groups feel even more isolated. Authentic appreciation of diversity takes place when students from different groups interact, work together, and learn from one another (Smith, 1997). Someone who merely tolerates diversity, or simply coexists with diverse groups, might say things like: "Let's just get along," "live and let live," or "to each his own." Cultural competence moves us beyond diversity tolerance to a higher level of diversity *appreciation*, which involves learning about, with, and from diverse people. Cultural competence empowers teachers to be culturally sensitive and responsive educators who recognize, appreciate, and capitalize on student differences to facilitate the learning process and the achievement of learning outcomes that benefit all students (Etsy, Griffin, & Hirsch, 1995).

Culturally competent teachers acknowledge and accept the cultural identity of their students, and engage in continuous development of that identity through *action*, such as:

- Attending community meetings and activities to gain a deeper understanding of their students' cultural background
- Communicating high expectations for all students
- Employing instructional techniques that allow students to acquaint themselves with one another and learn about each other's backgrounds
- Encouraging students to work independently and interdependently to discover diverse people and perspectives
- Soliciting ideas from family and community members of students from diverse backgrounds for possible inclusion in curricular and instructional decisions
- Involving families in their students' education by offering a variety of ways in which families can participate
- Becoming an advocate for diverse students in the school and their community

At a societal level, achieving cultural competence may be characterized as an ascending stairway of 12 steps that begins at the lowest and most extreme forms of resistance to diversity and escalates to the pinnacle of cultural competence (see **Figure 3.3**).

> " Children are educated by what the grown-up is and not by his talk. "
>
> —Carl Jung, influential Swiss psychiatrist who pioneered understanding of the human mind through dreams, art, mythology, and religion

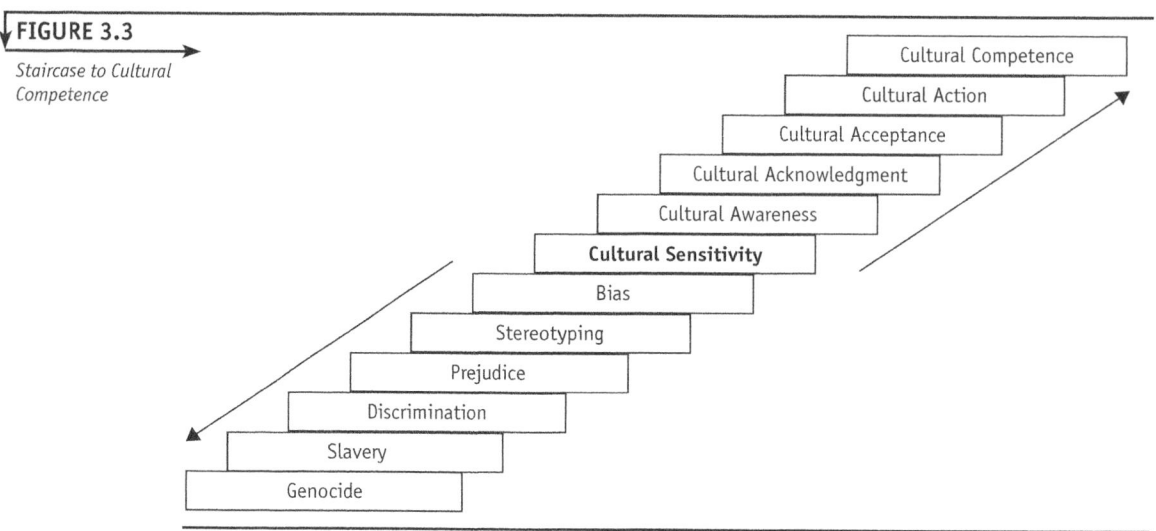

FIGURE 3.3

Staircase to Cultural Competence

Box 3.3 Five Progressively Higher Levels of Cultural Sensitivity

- *Cultural Awareness:* awareness of one's own biases and the effects they've had on ourselves and others.
- *Cultural Acknowledgment:* acknowledging the differences that exist between individuals, races, and cultures, and viewing those existing differences as assets rather than liabilities.
- *Cultural Acceptance:* valuing human differences and commonalities, and seeing how they can serve as a valuable educational resource for learning and personal development. This is a positive force that benefits all people.
- *Cultural Action:* the process of not only recognizing and valuing differences, but actually seeking them out and experiencing their benefits.
- *Cultural Competence:* the capability to appreciate and capitalize on human differences by interacting effectively with people from diverse cultural backgrounds.

Thus, the first step in becoming a culturally competent teacher is to become aware of your own beliefs and recognizing that they are founded in your own cultural identity and history. Teachers should also become aware of any beliefs that may differentiate the expectations of one student from another. Teacher awareness of the key cultural elements of individual students is a critical first step toward developing a meaningful educational experience for diverse students.

Summary and Conclusion

This chapter identifies the major stereotypes, prejudices, and biases that have plagued our society; explores their underlying causes; and proposes a model for overcoming these barriers to effective multicultural education.

Stereotyping involves viewing individuals of the same type (group) in the same (fixed) way. In effect, stereotyping ignores or disregards a person's individuality; instead, all people, or virtually all people, who are members of the same group (e.g., race or gender) are viewed as having the same individual characteristics. When all members of a stereotyped group are judged or evaluated in a negative way, the result is *prejudice*. Stereotyping makes prejudice possible because if virtually all members of a group are perceived to be alike, and that perception is negative, the result is a negative prejudgment, or prejudice.

Whereas prejudice involves a belief, attitude, or opinion, *discrimination* involves action. "Hate crimes" exemplify extreme discrimination because they are acts motivated solely by prejudice against members of a certain group. Other forms of discrimination are more subtle and may be practiced by society's institutional systems rather than particular individuals. These forms of *institutional* discrimination are less flagrant or visible—they are rooted in societal policies and practices that discriminate against members of certain ethnic groups.

Segregation may be defined as a group's decision to separate itself, either socially or physically, from another group. Although segregation itself may not be a blatant, malicious form of discrimination, it leads to reduced contact between the segregated groups. This reduced contact can cause a segregated group to be viewed as "unfamiliar" or "strange"; this lack of familiarity, in turn, can trigger feelings of uncertainty and anxiety toward that group.

Although the causes of prejudice and discrimination are still not completely understood, we can help guard ourselves and our students against prejudice by remaining aware of the five tendencies that can contribute to its development, namely the human tendency to:

1. favor familiarity and fear the unknown or unfamiliar.
2. use selective perception and selective memory.
3. mentally categorize people into "in" and "out" groups.
4. perceive members of other groups as more alike than members of their own group.
5. be more strongly influenced by negative behaviors of minority groups than by negative behaviors exhibited by their own (majority) group.
6. rationalize prejudice and discrimination as justifiable.
7. strengthen their self-image through group membership and group identity.

Overcoming bias and moving toward appreciation of diversity may be viewed as a systematic, sequential process that begins with *awareness* of human differences, followed by *acknowledgment* of any hidden biases toward groups who differ from our own, which leads to *acceptance* of group differences, and culminates in our taking *action* to capitalize on the diversity that surrounds us. Thus, the diversity-appreciation process may be conceived of as a cycle comprised of the following four stages:

1. *Awareness* of our personal beliefs and attitudes toward diverse groups;
2. *Acknowledgment* of how our beliefs and attitudes may be affecting members of diverse groups;
3. *Acceptance* of (empathy for) members of diverse groups; and
4. *Action* taken to reach out and interact with people from diverse groups.

NAME _____ DATE _____

Exercises

Interpreting Quotes

How would you interpret the meaning or message of the following quotes?

"Every human is, at the same time, like all other humans, like some humans, and like no other human."

—*Clyde Kluckholn, American anthropologist*

"The more eyes, different eyes, we can use to observe one thing, the more complete will our concept of this thing, our objectivity, be."

—*Friedrich Nietzsche, German philosopher*

"The mere presence of persons of other cultures and subcultures [on campus] is primarily a political achievement, not an intellectual or educational achievement. Real educational progress will be made when multiculturalism becomes inter-culturalism."

—*Patrick J. Hill, Professor of interdisciplinary studies, Evergreen State College*

Comfort Levels

Racial bias can be subtle and may only begin to surface when the social distance between members of different groups grows closer.

Rate your level of comfort (high, medium, or low) in the following interracial social situations:

1. Going to your school   high   medium   low
2. Working in your place of employment   high   medium   low
3. Living on your street as a neighbor   high   medium   low
4. Living with you as a roommate   high   medium   low
5. Socializing with you as a personal friend   high   medium   low
6. Being your most intimate friend or romantic partner   high   medium   low
7. Being your partner in marriage   high   medium   low

For the item(s) you rated "high," why would you feel comfortable?
For the item(s) you rated "low," why would you feel uncomfortable?

NAME _____ DATE _____

Multi-Group Self Awareness

We can be members of multiple groups at the same time and our membership in these overlapping groups likely has influenced our personal development and identity. In the following figure, consider the shaded center circle to be yourself and the six non shaded circles to be six different groups that you are a member of and that you think have influenced your personal development or personal identity.

Fill in the non shaded circles with the names of groups to which you belong that have had the most influence on your personal development and identity. You can use the diversity spectrum that appears on page 1 to help you identify different groups to which you may belong. Don't feel you have to come up with six groups to fill all six circles. What is more important is to identify those groups that have had a significant influence on your personal development or identity.

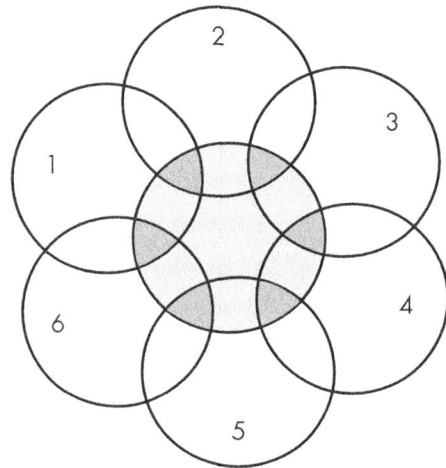

After you identify these groups, take a moment to reflect on the following questions:

1. Which one of your groups has had the greatest influence on your personal development and identity? Why?
2. Have you ever felt limited or disadvantaged by being a member of any group(s)? Why?
3. Have you ever felt that you experienced advantages or privileges because of your membership in any group(s)? Why?

Switching Group Identities

If you were to be born again as a member of a different racial or ethnic group:
What group would you want it to be? Why?
With your new group identity, what aspects of your life do you think would likely change the most? Why?
Despite your new group identity, what aspects of your life do you think would likely remain the same? Why?

(Adapted from the University of New Hampshire, Office of Residential Life, 2001, 153).

The Context for Diversity Education:
Student, Family, School, and Community

A teacher's influence on the academic achievement of diverse students doesn't take place in a vacuum but in a context that includes a number of other influential sources. **Figure 4.1** depicts the four major sources of influence that should be considered and responded to when working with students from diverse backgrounds. As the figure illustrates, student diversity is accompanied by diversity in students' family and community backgrounds; schools are diverse due to site-to-site differences in their curriculum, fiscal resources, teachers, and administrative leaders.

A school's impact on students' academic achievement is influenced by the effectiveness of its teachers, but also by the characteristics of its students, the students' families, and the surrounding community. As the figure suggests, when all

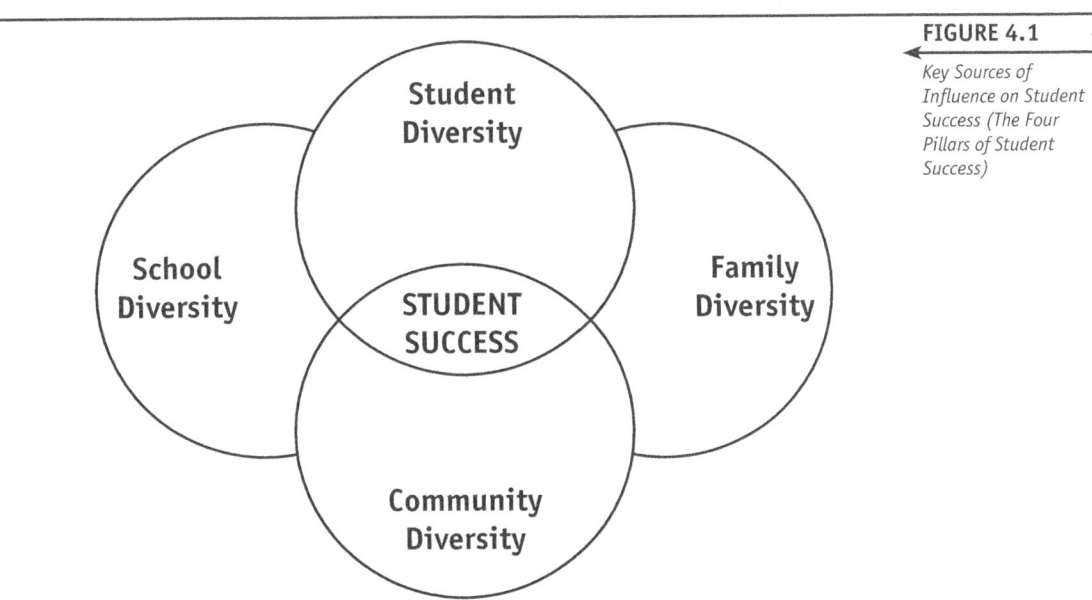

FIGURE 4.1

Key Sources of Influence on Student Success (The Four Pillars of Student Success)

four sources of influence intersect and reinforce one another, student success is likely to take place. However, if each of these influences fail to complement one another, students are less likely to experience success. For instance, Yan (1999) discovered that the academic achievement of African American students depends on the quality of their relationships with their parents, their parents' relationships with the school, and their parents' relationships with parents of other students attending the same school. When these three relationships were mutually supportive and were focused on promoting student learning, higher levels of student achievement took place. Research also shows that if students' perceptions of their family and school environments are positive, they display higher levels of academic performance—this pattern holds true for students of all ethnicities (Chang et al., 2003; Ireson & Hallam, 2005).

Studies also reveal that the academic success of minority students is promoted when schools acknowledge student diversity, family diversity, and the quality of family interaction with school officials (Epstein, 1995; Lareau & Horvat, 1999; Yan, 1999). For instance, it has been shown that parents of African American students who perceive racism to be taking place in their child's school are more likely to report that their child doesn't like school and that the school's teachers don't have high expectations for their child (Thompson, 2003). On the other hand, when African American students are exposed to engaging teaching methods in the classroom and are encouraged to become involved in school activities outside the classroom, they experience significant gains in academic achievement (Wiggan, 2008).

Student Diversity

Student diversity in our nation's schools is greater today than at any other time in U.S. history and it will continue to increase. Minority student enrollment in the American K–12 system jumped from 35 percent in the 1995–96 school year to 43.5 percent in 2006–07. At the same time, the percentage of white, non-Hispanic students declined (National Center for Education Statistics [NCES], 2008). During the 2006–07 school year, the percentages of students from different ethnic and racial backgrounds were as follows:

>   White: 56.5%
>   Hispanic: 20.5 %
>   Black: 17.1 %
>   Asian/Pacific Islander: 4.7 %
>   American Indian/Alaska Native: 1.2%

America's changing demographics make it paramount that its educational system effectively accommodate and educate students from all cultural backgrounds. This poses a challenge because a long-standing gap continues to exist between the academic achievement of white students and students of color. In a study conducted by the National Assessment of Educational Progress (NAEP; 2005), it was discovered that 47 percent of white fourth graders scored at or above proficiency in math—compared to 19 percent of Hispanic students and 13 percent of black students. The NAEP also reported that the following percentages of eighth graders were reading below grade level:

Blacks: 88%
Hispanics: 86%
American Indian/Alaskan Natives: 81%
Whites: 62%

The same report revealed that 74 percent of American Indian/Alaskan native 12th graders read below grade level, compared to 57 percent of white students. Reading scores of African American 12th grade males are also significantly lower than the scores of all other racial and ethnic groups (NAEP, 2005). In addition, 71 percent of English-as-a-second-language (ESL) eighth graders scored below grade level in reading—compared to 25 percent of non-ESL students (NCES, 2007). This is a particularly disappointing finding given the fact that the rate of immigration to the United States in the 1990s was the largest in 70 years; it is estimated that at least one of every four Americans today speak a language other than English at home (Suarez-Orozco & Suarez-Orozco, 2002).

At the high school level, only one-third of American high school students meet the necessary requirements for postsecondary education. In the case of minorities, the situation is even worse. Among all students in America who entered public high schools in 2002, only 23 percent of black students and 20 percent of Hispanic students completed high school with the minimum academic skills needed to be admitted to a four-year college. To make matters worse, only about 50 percent of Native American students successfully completed high school (Orfield et al., 2004). In contrast to students from minority ethnic groups, approximately twice as many white students graduate from high school with the basic academic skills needed to gain entry into four-year colleges and universities (Greene & Winters, 2005). These gaps in the educational attainment level of students from different ethnic and racial groups are associated with gaps in their eventual level of family income. (See **Figure 4.2**.)

Achievement gaps also exist among students from families with different levels of income. Children in high socioeconomic living situations at the preschool age prior to entering kindergarten have cognitive scores that are 60 percent above the average scores of children in the lowest socioeconomic group (Lee & Burkham, 2002). By the third grade, children from middle class families with well-educated parents have a vocabulary of 12,000 words; for children from low income families and uneducated parents, their vocabulary is limited to 4,000 words

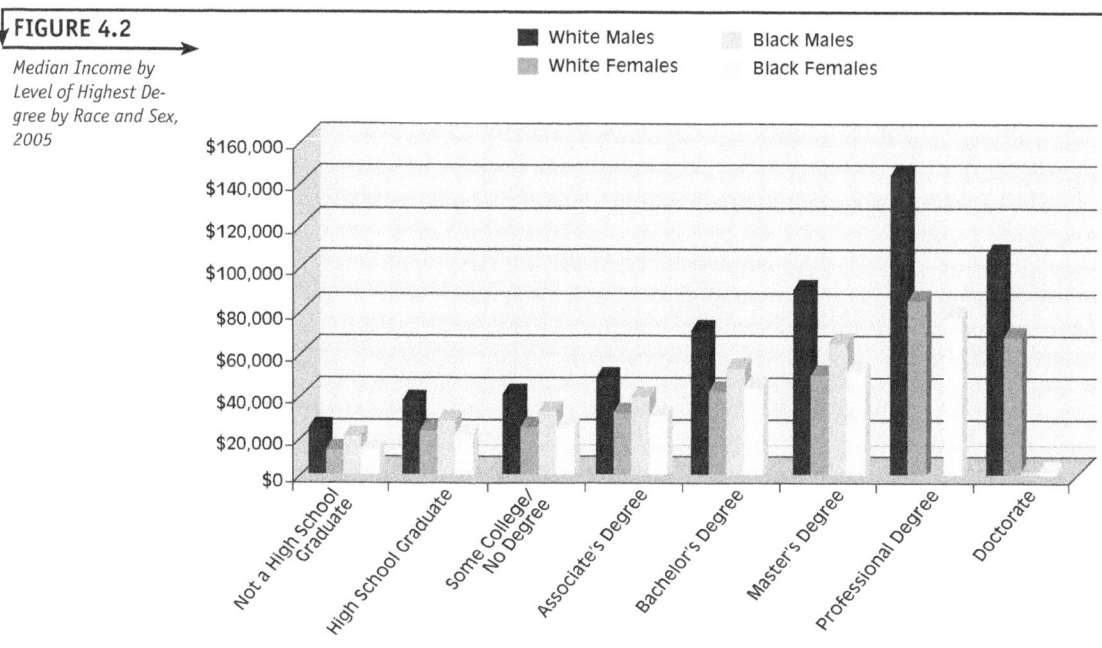

FIGURE 4.2
Median Income by Level of Highest Degree by Race and Sex, 2005

(Snow, 2005). The math achievement gap for fourth graders living below and above the poverty line is 22 points; it grows to 27 points by the eighth grade (Kopkowski, 2006).

Box 4.1 How Do We Close the Achievement Gap for Low Income Students?

- Utilization of an intentional curriculum (research-based, content-driven, emphasizes active learning, attentiveness to social and regulatory skills, responds to cultural diversity and ESL students, promotes positive interactions with teachers and peers, developmentally appropriate)
- Promotion of early literacy and math skills in a nurturing and supportive classroom environment
- Teachers participating in training and education that focuses on how young children grow and learn
- Teachers participating in professional development in the areas of diversity, cultural competence, cultural traditions, and the increasing number of immigrant and limited English-proficient students

Source: Klein & Knitzer, 2007

People of color experience higher rates of poverty (U.S. Census Bureau, 2000); by 2020, almost one-half of the nation's school-age population will be students of color, and about 27 percent of them will be living below the poverty line. Currently, more than 60 percent of black and Hispanic students attend high-poverty schools—schools in which more than 50 percent of the student body lives below the poverty line—compared to 30 percent of Asian students and 18 percent of white students. In the case of extreme-poverty schools (more than 90 percent of the student body living in poverty), only 1 percent of white students attend such schools—compared to 12 percent of black and Hispanic students (Orfield & Lee, 2005).

Ethnic and racial groups with higher income levels and socioeconomic status are privileged with two major forms of capital: (a) *economic* capital—*what* they have (e.g., homes, health benefits, and discretionary income for travel and other educational experiences for their children), and (b) *social* capital—*who* they know (e.g., contacts with employers, college admissions personnel, and "power players" in the legal and political system). Students of higher social class families acquire these privileges without having to earn them and they will benefit from these privileges at all stages of their life. For instance, families with higher socioeconomic status have greater social capital for getting their children into college (Conley, 2005) and greater economic capital to prepare them for college access and success (e.g., financial resources to pay for college admissions test preparation services and to hire independent counselors who help their children get into college or the "best" college possible).

Promoting the educational achievement and academic success of students from low income families represents an opportunity for school systems to create a more level playing field by compensating for the limited economic, social, and educational resources available to these students. Ultimately, success in school is the primary ticket for economically disadvantaged young Americans to overcome their lower socioeconomic status and gain upward social mobility for themselves and their future families.

Family Diversity

To fully understand the family background of students is to appreciate diversity of family arrangements in the United States. American families are formed in diverse ways including the number of parents, children and extended family members in the home, racial makeup of the family, socioeconomic status of the family (e.g., one wage earner), and marital status and sexual orientation of the parents or guardians.

Thus, teachers and administrators need to be mindful of the uniqueness of families and how family influences students' self-perceptions and behavioral patterns.

Reflection 4.1 What did your family arrangement consist of as a child?
In what way(s) do you think your family structure affected your development and the person you are today? Why?

There is a strong relationship between parental involvement with their children and their children's educational achievement. This relationship exists regardless of race/ethnicity, parents' level of education, or socioeconomic status (Thompson & Luhman, 1997). A national survey of 10th grade students conducted by the U.S. Department of Education (2008) revealed that students from black families place a higher value on education than their white peers. Compared to students from white families, black students were more likely to state that getting a good education is important (80 percent vs. 90 percent), getting good grades is very important (47 percent vs. 62 percent), and attending school is important primarily for academics—rather than extracurricular activities or socializing with peers. Seventy-seven percent of black 10th graders also report that they want to earn a bachelor's degree.

PERSONAL INSIGHT

My mother was a direct descendent of slaves and moved with her parents from the deep south at the age of 17. My father lived in an all-black coal mining camp, into which my mother and her family moved in 1938. My father remained illiterate because he was not allowed to attend public schools in eastern Kentucky.

In the early 1960s, I was integrated into the white public schools along with my brother and sister. Physical violence and constant verbal harassment caused many other blacks to quit school at an early age and opt for jobs in the coal mines. But my father remained constant in his advice to me: "It doesn't matter if they call you n____; don't you ever let them beat you by walking out on your education." He'd say to me, "Son, you will have opportunities that I never had. Many people, white and black alike, will tell you that you are no good and that education can never help you. Don't listen to them because soon they will not be able to keep you from getting an education like they did me. Just remember, when you do get that education, you'll never have to go in those coal mines and have them break your back. You can choose what you want to do, and then you can be a free man."

Being poor, black, and Appalachian did not offer me great odds for success, but constant reminders from my parents that I was a good person and that education was the key to my future freedom and happiness enabled me to beat the odds. My parents were not able to provide me with monetary wealth, but they did provide me with the gifts of self-worth, educational motivation, and aspiration for academic achievement.

Aaron Thompson

Despite placing a higher value on education, research also indicates that African American parents are less engaged with their children's school than white parents (Abdul-Adil & Farmer, 2006). The lower level of black parents' engagement has often been interpreted as lack of interest in their children's education (Fields-Smith, 2003). However, teachers and administrators must take into consideration the familial circumstances of black families before concluding that lack of parental involvement reflects a lack of commitment to their child's education. Level of parental involvement in a child's education is influenced by a variety of factors, including family structure and socioeconomic status. For example, non-English-speaking parents, single-parent households, or a parent holding two jobs are all factors that can reduce parents' level of involvement in their children's education.

Teachers and administrators should make an earnest attempt to communicate with families to gain knowledge about circumstances that may interfere with parental involvement, and this knowledge should be used to make scheduling and procedural adjustments that may facilitate their involvement (Archer-Banks, 2008). Regular communication with parents about their student's performance and encouragement of parents to participate in decision making about their student's education are distinguishing features of effective schools, which are schools that promote the highest levels of academic achievement (Marzano, 2003). Some strategies that effective schools have used to promote partnerships with parents are identified in **Box 4.2**.

> *Throughout high school, I was consistently working 25–35 hours a week and had to work two jobs when my mother lost her eyesight due to diabetes and was no longer able to continue working. From a very early age, my parents relied on me to place calls to banks, write letters, fill out checks, translate correspondence, and to do just about anything that involved English.*
>
> —Hispanic female student with non-English-speaking parents

Box 4.2 Strategies for Involving Parents as Educational Partners

Parent Newsletter: periodically during the school year, a family newsletter is sent to the homes of students to provide information on school information and activities and to encourage parental participation at upcoming school events.

School Hotline: at certain times during the day, including after-school hours, parents can call the school and speak with a school representative. The hotline may be used to identify questions that arise in the parents' newsletter, as well as for school self-assessment purposes (e.g., keeping a log of hotline calls to identify recurring parental issues or concerns, which then become target areas for school improvement efforts).

Home Visits: if parents are unable to make school visits to discuss learning or behavioral issues, the teacher (or principal) visits the parents at the student's home. Home visits allow the school official to gain insight into the student's family situation; they also increase family appreciation of the school's interest in their student, and promote parental willingness to partner with the school in efforts to promote their student's success.

Welcoming New Students: when a family with school-age children moves into the school's community, information about the school is sent to the student's home and family members are invited to upcoming school functions. Better yet, the teacher or principal makes a home visit to welcome family members and to encourage their involvement with the school.

Parent Interview: students are given an assignment to interview their parents about issues related to education in general and their school in particular.

Family Guest Speakers: students' parents or other relatives visit the class as guest speakers.

Family Use of School Facilities: for example, the school provides classrooms and personnel for after-school day care.

Community Diversity

A community may be defined as a group of people that share the same environment, interests, beliefs, and values. Communities play a major role in students' socialization process and their development of personal identity; to ignore a school's local community is to ignore "the everyday world in which students live" (National Council for the Social Studies [NCSS], 1991, p. 32). Knowledge of students' communities (and the diversity of those communities) can be capitalized on to promote learning through a wide variety of programs and practices, such as those listed in **Box 4.3**.

Box 4.3 Strategies for Building School-Community Relationships and Learning Opportunities

- The school surveys community needs (e.g., need for child day care), community opinions (e.g., about school dress codes) or community practices (e.g., languages spoken and ethnic traditions), and uses the results to create new programs and policies, or to improve existing ones.
- A school newsletter is sent to board members, business leaders, and other key decision makers in the community.
- News releases about the school are prepared for the local news media.
- Local media are contacted to publicly recognize students for outstanding academic and volunteer service and school or community members who've made special contributions to improving school-community relations.
- Students are regularly assigned articles to read in the local newspaper.
- Students write reports about their community and what the school might do to better meet the community's needs (and vice versa).
- Students take field trips to local museums, outdoor markets, or festivals.
- Students visit community businesses and nonprofit organizations to explore career fields (e.g., observe professionals at work and ask questions about their work).
- Student groups engage in community fundraisers to raise money for class trips or educational resources.
- Community businesses and organizations collaborate with student clubs (e.g., students involved with the school newspaper or journalism club work with an editor for the local newspaper).
- School and organizations in the local community share or pool their resources (e.g., share facilities, equipment, and fundraising or grant-writing ventures).
- Local businesses offer discounts to students who achieve academic excellence (e.g., reduced prices on store items or a free video rental).
- Members of ethnic groups in the community are invited to class as guest speakers or panelists. (In homogeneous communities, the teacher may need to go beyond local boundaries to solicit speakers from different racial and ethnic groups.) In preparation for these visits, students may be asked to submit questions for the guest speaker, which are screened by the teacher and passed on to the speaker.
- Successful members of the community serve as student tutors or mentors.

> "An active contributor to an ethnic neighborhood may be more of a hero to the local community than a famous athlete."
> —National Council for the Social Studies

- Local businesses and organizations provide part-time employment or internship opportunities for students.

(Mitrofanova, 2004; U.S. Department of Health & Human Services, 2003)

Building a strong base of community support can generate significant benefits for the school, such as support from community organizations for after-school programs and increased school funding. Furthermore, students' pride in both their school and community are buoyed when they see their school reaching out to people similar to themselves in the community and recognizing them as role models and honored guests. As Delpit (1995) states, "Teachers cannot hope to begin to understand who sits before them unless they connect with the families and communities from which their children come. To do that it is vital that teachers and teacher educators explore their own beliefs and attitudes about non-white and non-middle class people" (see the Cycle of Diversity Appreciation in Chapter 3).

The local community can also provide students with opportunities for volunteer experience. Research strongly supports the positive impact of community service on multiple outcomes, including diversity appreciation, leadership skills, achievement, motivation, and deep learning (Astin et al., 2000; Eyler & Giles, 1999; Vogelgesang et al., 2002). Students who become involved in service to the local community might also be encouraged to invite diverse members from the community to visit class as guest speakers or panelists. If students reflect about their service experiences via reaction papers or focused discussions, their volunteer service is transformed from volunteerism into *experiential learning*.

> *The multicultural curriculum should make maximum use of experiential learning, especially community resources.*
> —National Council for the Social Studies (1991)

The local community can serve as a source of "community cultural wealth"—a form of social capital that can enable students of color to persist and learn amid disadvantaged or oppressive circumstances (Yosso, 2005).

Lastly, it should be kept in mind that both classrooms and schools are communities in their own right and may be used as vehicles for developing students' civic skills and civic character. The school environment "offers students a place to question, to participate, to develop civic skills, and to respect and understand the pluralistic world in which they live" (Morse, 1989, p. 3). Students can begin to develop civic character by demonstrating civility toward their classmates and by being respectful of, and sensitive to, the rights of other members of their school community, including students and staff from diverse cultural backgrounds.

In a classroom community, students have an experiential opportunity to learn how to exercise expression of their individual rights and freedoms without interfering with the rights and freedoms of others to learn. Students can develop civic character by learning how to treat fellow members of their school community in a humane and compassionate manner, including stepping up to defend others whose rights are violated. Being part of a harmonious and welcoming school community benefits all students, regardless of their race or ethnicity; research indicates that both white students and students of color develop a greater sense of belonging and a stronger social connection with classmates when they perceive their school climate to be civil and hospitable, rather than alienating and hostile (Locks et al., 2008).

School Diversity

Besides the family, schools play a major role in the socialization process of children and adolescents. However, all schools aren't created equally. Diversity exists among schools in terms of their (a) student body, (b) curriculum, (c) teachers and administrators, (d) resources, and (e) facilities.

America has a highly decentralized system of education, with more than 15,000 local school districts making their own decisions about instructional policies, programs, and practices. The positive intent of decentralization is to allow different schools the freedom to be responsive to the unique needs of their local community; however, a negative consequence of decentralization is that it results in wide disparity in the effectiveness of different schools and their commitment to education. Because schools are funded by local property taxes, the amount of fiscal resources available to a school to educate its children will vary depending on the wealth of the local community in which the school is located. The wealth of the community that surrounds the school affects the amount of tax dollars available to support the community's schools. Thus, schools located in poorer communities often have fewer educational resources and poorer physical facilities. For instance, in 2005, school districts serving the highest concentration of poor students received an average of $938 less per-pupil funding than districts serving students with the lowest poverty rates; school districts serving the highest concentration of minority group students received an average of $877 less per-student funding than districts serving the lowest concentration of students from minority groups. Ironically, this school-funding formula should be reversed because minority students attending schools in poor communities have fewer educational resources available to them at home and in their local community. If the estimated cost of providing these compensatory educational resources to schools that serve high concentrations of poor and minority group families is factored into the funding equation, the gap widens further to $1,532 less per pupil in low income school districts and $1,275 per pupil for high minority group districts (The Education Trust, 2008).

Research consistently shows that students in racially segregated schools exhibit lower academic performance, largely because of the fact that racial segregation and poverty go hand in hand (Arum & Roska, 2011). For instance, segregated African American and Hispanic schools enroll a significantly higher percentage of children from very poor families, which reduces funding for school resources, compromises the rigor of the curriculum, and lowers the quality of student support services (Orfield & Eaton, 1996). Thus, America's schools are not immune to the inequalities that exist in its larger society; in fact, they often mirror the nation's societal inequalities (Kozol, 1991; Gorski, 2010). About 12 percent of America's public high schools account for 50 percent of the nation's high school student dropouts. In these "dropout factories," more than 40 percent of 9th graders are enrolled as 12th graders four years later (compared to 90 percent of students at other high schools around the country). Disturbingly, these dropout factories are high schools with a substantial proportion of low income and minority students (Balfanz & Legters, 2004)—the very students for whom education is likely to be their only ticket to socioeconomic prosperity for themselves and for their future children.

Rather than serving as a vehicle for perpetuating existing societal inequities, America's public educational system—originating in the work of Horace Mann in the mid-1800s—was intended to provide all the nation's citizens with equal opportunity for upward social mobility (Groen, 2008). Our nation's schools are still viewed as a vehicle for transforming society by reducing inequities and promoting social justice (Gorski, 2010).

Fortunately, political leaders in some states have found the will and the way to use state dollars to eliminate gross inequities between the educational funds available to schools in poor and rich communities (The Education Trust, 2008). If America really believed in the rhetoric of "no child left behind"—all students in all schools should reach the same educational finish line—its school-funding formulas should ensure that all students start the race from the same starting line.

> Education, then, beyond all other devices of human origin, is the great equalizer of the conditions of men—the balance-wheel of the social machinery. It gives each man the independence and the means by which he can resist the selfishness of other men. It does better than to disarm the poor of their hostility towards the rich: it prevents being poor.
>
> —Horace Mann, abolitionist, educational reformer, and "Father of the Common School"

The Curriculum

A core component of effective multicultural education is an inclusive curriculum that represents and respects diverse cultures. Studies show that a curriculum that recognizes and emphasizes cultural diversity is a distinguishing feature of high-performing schools located in low socioeconomic school districts (Wang, 1998). Transformation of the traditional curriculum into a truly multicultural curriculum that authentically represents the diverse histories and cultures of different ethnic groups typically progresses through the following four stages (Banks, 1993; McIntosh, 2000).

> Democratic education is a process where teachers and student work collaboratively to reconstruct curriculum to include everyone.
>
> —Amy Guttman, author of *Democratic Education*

> School districts with the greatest needs often receive the least funding. In too many communities, students who are poor, minority, or English learners do not get their fair share of education funds. With the right leadership, inequitable funding patterns can be changed. We can unstack the deck.
>
> —The Education Trust, 2008

Stage 1. Mainstream Curriculum

This is the traditional, Eurocentric, male-centered curriculum, which largely ignores the contributions and perspective of nondominant groups. Such a curriculum fails to validate the culture of minority groups, which can further alienate them from a school culture that already differs greatly from their home culture. In addition, it reinforces the dominant group's "false sense of superiority, gives them a misleading conception of their relationship with other racial and ethnic groups, and denies them the opportunity to benefit from the knowledge, perspectives, and frames of reference that can be gained from studying other cultures and groups" (Banks, 1993, p. 195).

STUDENT PERSPECTIVE

> I want to study Asian history and women's history. I'm tired of studying about white people and men.
>
> Overheard comment made by a female high school student to a friend at a coffee shop in California

Stage 2. Heroes and Holidays

At this stage, diversity is "celebrated" by exposing students to cultural information and artifacts from diverse groups (e.g., Black History Month and Women's History

Month). Although this stage represents an advance in curricular reform over the traditional mainstream curriculum, it has two major weaknesses:

1. It covers nondominant groups outside the context of the required curriculum, which reinforces the idea that acquiring knowledge about these "other" groups is supplementary, or a secondary "side show" to the "main event;" and
2. By focusing exclusively on the achievement of heroes or extraordinary people, it fails to cover the common experiences, struggles, and voices of most members of nondominant groups (Gorski, 2010).

> "A national culture or school curriculum that does not reflect the voices, struggles, hopes, and dreams of its many peoples is neither democratic nor cohesive."
> —National Council for the Social Studies (1991)

Stage 3. Integration
This curriculum moves beyond diversity heroes and holidays to include significant information about nondominant groups. For example, a course on women's history or African American history may be added to the history curriculum, or a unit on Latin American music may be added to a music curriculum. This represents a major advance beyond the previous stage because it integrates diversity into the mainstream curriculum; however, its major weakness is that it covers diversity as stand-alone topics or units that are separated from the "meat" of the curriculum covered in the school's textbooks (Banks, 1993).

Stage 4. Structural Reform
At this most advanced stage of curricular transformation, diversity is woven seamlessly into the mainstream curriculum and is presented in the form of multiple perspectives thereby encouraging students to learn to view the curriculum's major ideas and events through different cultural lenses. For example, the curriculum's textbook for American history incorporates the history of women, African Americans, Latinos, and Asian Americans (Gorski, 2010).

Science education researchers have demonstrated that diversity material can be readily and seamlessly infused into the science curriculum by intentionally including both a Western scientific value (e.g., control over nature) and a non-Western value (e.g., harmony with nature) in each lesson plan (Aikenhead, 1997; 2001; Lee & Buxton, 2008). Multiculturalism can be readily effectively infused into the existing curriculum "as long as existing knowledge is not presented as facts and doctrines to be absorbed without question, as long as existing bodies of knowledge are critiqued and balanced from a multicultural perspective, and as long as the students' own themes and idioms are valued along with standard usage" (Shor, 1992, p. 35).

At this stage of curriculum, students learn to consider the diversity implications of any topic discussed in the traditional curriculum. They are prepared to use diversity-related examples to support and illustrate their points and, when they research a topic, they're able to choose and examine it from multiple (i.e., multicultural) perspectives. Coverage of Western civilization in the history curriculum can also be infused with diversity by identifying discrepancies between democratic ideals and social realities. For instance, coverage of American history includes the Indian Removal Act in 1830 that forced Native Americans to leave their reservations and move west, as well as the forced internment of Japanese Americans during World War II. Failure to include such events not only fails to provide a complete and accurate history of the United States, it can also promote cynicism and alienation among minority youth who are often well aware of the gaps between their nation's ideals and realities (NCSS, 1991).

When students see their ethnic identities represented in the curriculum, they see their cultural history is valued, which serves to promote students' sense of political efficacy—that is, their belief that participation in their nation's governance may make a difference for them (Bernstein, 1986). This is an important student-learning outcome of a multicultural curriculum because, historically, people of color have not been empowered to influence political policies and institutions, which often leaves them with a sense of societal helplessness and a lack of political influence over their collective future (Ogbu, 1990).

Although a major goal of education is to enable individual students to better themselves vocationally, education is also about promoting the collective good. Thus, a diversity-responsive curriculum should include current issues relating to social justice. To help students and teachers remain informed about current events relating to the preservation of human rights and the prevention of human rights' violations across the country and around the world, the following two websites are recommended.

> The multicultural curriculum should help students develop political efficacy for effective citizenship in a pluralistic democratic nation.
>
> —National Council for the Social Studies (1991)

> The curriculum should help students understand the significant historical experiences of ethnic groups [and] the critical contemporary issues and social problems confronting each of them.
>
> —National Council for the Social Studies (1991)

www.tolerance.org: This is the site of an educational and public service organization for people interested in fighting bigotry in America and creating communities that value diversity. It tracks hate groups, hate crimes, hate websites, and hate music. It also supplies research-based strategies for promoting social justice on campus and in the community. The site provides access to a free newsletter that provides updates on the latest social, educational, and legal news relating to diversity and bigotry.

www.amnesty.org: This is the website of Amnesty International (AI)—a worldwide organization of people committed to preserving human rights. Whereas Tolerance.org is a national organization, AI is an international movement that includes almost 2 million members from over 150 countries in every region of the world. Many of its members have very different political and religious beliefs, but they all share the same concern and goal: preventing violation of human rights. Its website includes strategies for protecting and promoting human rights, as well as information on how to join the organization and participate in its local volunteer activities. (If you visit this site, read AI's *Universal Declaration of Human Rights*—a powerful document that has been translated into more than 300 different languages for worldwide use.)

An effective multicultural curriculum should also infuse *academic success skills and effective learning strategies* into coverage of its subject matter. Schools with high percentages of language-minority students that also promote high levels of student achievement are typically schools with a curriculum that integrates academic skills and academic content (Pierce, 1991). For instance, schools that promote the greatest gains in academic achievement of both minority and majority students are schools whose curriculum includes teaching students how to take notes on what they are learning and how to summarize what they have learned (Marzano, Pickering, & Pollock, 2001).

When students acquire effective learning strategies in addition to subject matter knowledge, they acquire skills with two powerful qualities:

1. *Transferability*—effective learning strategies are portable skills that "travel well" across different contexts and situations, and which can be transferred (applied) across a wide variety of careers, and life roles.
2. *Durability*—effective learning strategies are enduring skills with long-lasting value that can be used continually throughout life.

> "Give a man a fish and you feed him for a day. Teach a man how to fish and you feed him for a lifetime."
> —Author unknown

Equipping students from economically and educationally disadvantaged backgrounds with effective academic learning strategies is particularly critical to their success because they are less likely to have family members at home who can model these skills for them.

Lastly, an effective multicultural curriculum includes courses that prepare students from all ethnic groups to advance and succeed at the next level of education. For instance, a multicultural high school curriculum should prepare both minority and majority students to succeed in college. However, studies show that there is a wide discrepancy in knowledge of college admissions requirements between families of lower and higher socioeconomic status, one result of which is that less privileged students often experience a precollege curriculum that leaves them unprepared for college entry and college success. By age 24, 75 percent of children from families whose income ranks among the top one-quarter of American families go on to receive a bachelor's degree; in contrast, less than 9 percent of children whose family income lies in the bottom quarter will do so (Postsecondary Education Opportunity, 2005).

> "To close the gap between those who understand how to prepare to succeed in college and those who do not, high schools will have to make sustained efforts to redesign their instructional programs and their information systems"
> —David Conley, Director of the Center for Educational Policy Research at the University of Oregon, and author of *College Knowledge: What It Really Takes for Students to Succeed and What We Can Do To Get Them Ready*

This suggests that the course enrollment patterns of low income students (and other student groups that have been historically underrepresented in college) should be analyzed and closely monitored. Special attention should be paid to the schedules of these student groups to ensure that they are not underrepresented in college preparatory courses (Conley, 2005). Given the fact that the average student-to-counselor ratio in American schools is 457 to 1 (American School Counselor Association, 2010), other members of the school community may need to assume a greater role in monitoring the course-taking patterns of underrepresented students and encourage their enrollment in courses that promote college access and success. For instance, teachers can play a powerful role in the college advising process and school administrators can further empower teachers to fulfill this role by supplying them with key information on requirements for admission to local colleges and state universities (Conley, 2005).

Teachers

The majority of K–12 teachers in the American school system are white and from middle class socioeconomic backgrounds (Coopersmith, 2009). During the 2007–08 school year, 83.5 percent of the teachers in America's K–12 system were white, non-Hispanics. The race or ethnicity of the remaining teachers was as follows:

Blacks: 6.7%
Hispanic: 6%
Asian non-Hispanics: 1.3%
Multiple race non-Hispanic: 0.9%
American Indian/Alaskan Native non-Hispanic: 0.5%
Native Hawaiian or other Pacific Islander non-Hispanic: 0.2%

New teachers typically begin their careers in schools where (a) a high percentage of students are members of minority groups, (b) at least 75 percent of their students receive free or reduced-price lunches, and (c) many are English-language learners with limited English proficiency (NCES, 2009). Schools lack qualified teachers (in terms of both number and preparation) to handle the growing population of Latino students (Menken & Holmes, 2000). During the 1999–2000 school year, 73 percent of students in ESL/bilingual education classes were taught by instructors who did not have a major, minor, or certification in the field of bilingual education. For high school students during the same time period, 71 percent enrolled in ESL/bilingual education courses taught by teachers without qualifications in that field (Seastrom et al., 2002).

Although teachers from nonminority groups can effectively promote the academic achievement of minority students, teachers still bring the perspective of their own cultural and socioeconomic background—either consciously or unconsciously—to their school's culture (National Collaborative on Diversity in the Teaching Force [NCDFJ], 2004; Villegas & Lucas, 2002). If teachers disregard or devalue their students' home culture, students are forced to make an uncomfortable choice: choose to value their family, friends, and community, or choose to adopt the school's culture and face alienation from family, friends, and community (Bowman, 1995).

The academic achievement gap between students from majority and minority groups does not represent a gap in the learning ability or learning potential of these two groups of students. Numerous studies confirm that students' cultural background influences how they respond to classroom learning experiences (Gonzalez & Maez, 1995; Moss & Puma, 1995; Speidel, 1992; Wong-Fillmore, 1991). For example, Rivera and Rodgers-Adkinson (1997) note that children from Asian and Native American cultures are commonly taught that it's important to be obedient and submissive to authority figures (e.g., teachers). This cultural norm may be expressed in the classroom by not speaking up during class discussions, not being comfortable in asking questions, or approaching the teacher (an authority figure) for help. African American children are often taught to be strong, outspoken, and not to follow the rules of authority figures without questioning their validity. Although such behaviors may be acceptable in the family and community, they are not typically acceptable in a school environment (Cartledge, Singh, & Gibson, 2008).

Research indicates that there is a strong relationship between student motivation and educational achievement (Ginsberg, 2005) and that students' motivational response to an educational activity or lesson plan is influenced by their cultural background (Kitayama & Markus, 1994). Thus, teachers should be mindful of the cultural characteristics background that students bring with them to the classroom—such as their racial and ethnic identity, socioeconomic status, and the educational experiences of their family members and peers (Ginsberg, 2005).

It is also important for teachers to be aware that the achievement gap between students of different cultural groups is not exclusively related to their family and community environment, but also to the school environment (Kober, 2001; Smith, 2005). For instance, research has shown that each of the following characteristics of a school's environment contribute to underachievement among minority students: (a) teacher misperceptions or misjudgments of minority students, (b) lack of cultural respect or acceptance, (c) low expectations for success, (d) poor teacher-student relationships, or (e) a privileged attitude displayed by the teacher (Howard, 2002; Gordon, Piana, & Keleher, 2000; Revilla & Sweeney, 1997; Thompson & Luhman, 1997; Weissglass, 2001).

Effective, culturally competent teachers have high expectations of students and believe that they are primarily responsible for promoting student learning (Cawelti, 1999). Research shows that these instructors: (a) believe in themselves, (b) believe that all children can and will succeed, (c) view themselves as engaged members of their school community, and (d) are intrinsically interested in inspiring their students to learn and become engaged members of their own communities (Meaney et al., 2008).

Box 4.4 Strategies for Teachers for Closing the Achievement Gap

- Educate community members
- Provide incentives for parents to attend parent/teacher conferences
- Hold community meetings during evening hours and on weekends; utilize space in minority communities
- Have community leaders speak at school functions
- Identify children with needs early in the educational process
- Provide literacy based instruction (language development, writing, vocabulary)
- Be a representative of the virtues you seek to impart to your students: honesty, tolerance, fairness, respect for and appreciation of diversity and cultural differences
- Examine your teaching practices; expand your knowledge base and incorporate the latest research
- Examine your pedagogical practices and level of cultural competence

> *In the effective school, there is a climate of expectation in which the staff believe and demonstrate that all students can attain mastery of the essential content and school skills, and the staff also believe that they have the capability to help all students achieve that mastery.*
>
> —Association for Effective Schools

Source: National Education Association, 2000

Research repeatedly shows that culturally competent teachers and culturally responsive teaching methods reduces the achievement gap significantly, or can eliminate it altogether. For instance, effective teachers increase the math achievement scores of African American ninth graders by 50 percent beyond the usual gains in learning that take place during this year of school (Aaronson, Barrow, & Sander, 2007). Research also indicates that when economically disadvantaged students are exposed to above-average teachers for four to five consecutive years, the achievement gap is completely eliminated (Hanushek, 2005). Additional studies demonstrate that the academic gains made by students who have effective teachers for three successive years are almost triple that of students taught by ineffective teachers for the same three-year period (Haycock, 1998). In fact, effective teachers have been found to be the leading factor concerning students' educational progress and academic success (Wiggan, 2008).

School Leaders

The cultural and socioeconomic background of America's school leaders looks much the same as America's school teachers. During the same 2007–08 school year, the race/ethnicity of K–12 principals was as follows (U.S. Department of Education, 2008):

White: 82.3%
Black: 9.6%
Hispanic: 5.9%
Other: 2.1%

The shortage of both minority teachers and minority administrators means a shortage of visible role models at school with whom minority students can readily identify. This can cause minority students to perceive their school culture as "foreign," especially if it contains elements that are inconsistent with the culture shared by their family and community (Salinas, 2002). Thus, one major way in which school leaders can help create a diversity-sensitive and diversity-responsive school environment is to develop or implement a plan to recruit qualified minority teachers and staff members.

Effective school administrators can also provide instructional leadership for diversity by equipping their teachers with the tools they need to accommodate and incorporate diversity into their teaching. They provide their teachers with instructional resources (e.g., supplies and materials), professional development opportunities (e.g., in-service development), and personal support (encouragement and recognition). Culturally responsive teaching can only take place in a school culture created by school leaders who (a) seek input from teachers working "in the trenches" with students, (b) collaborate with teachers in a joint effort to improve their students' performance, and (c) provide teachers with adequate support and professional development opportunities (Holmes & Wynne, 1989; Reyes, 1990; Sashkin & Walberg, 1993).

Effective schools that promote the highest levels of learning among all students (regardless of their cultural background) have three distinguishing characteristics—all of which are influenced primarily by the school leader.

1. *Clear School Mission*: there is a shared understanding and commitment among all members of the school community to instructional goals, school priorities, and individual accountability.
2. *Instructional Leadership*: the school's instructional leader articulates the school's mission and communicates it to teachers, support staff, and parents.
3. *Safe and Orderly Environment*: the school's atmosphere is free from threat of physical harm and a campus climate that isn't oppressive, but disciplined and conducive to teaching and learning (Association for Effective Schools, 1996).

School principals are responsible for ensuring that diversity education permeates the entire school culture, which includes not only the content of the classroom curriculum, but also the instructional materials available in the school's learning resource center and library. Similarly, principals provide primary oversight for ensuring that diversity is reflected outside the formal curriculum, such as in school assemblies, hallway decorations, extracurricular programs (e.g., honor societies and athletic teams), cafeteria menus, and school attendance policies pertaining to ethnic and religious holidays.

The National Council for the Social Studies has developed an evaluation checklist to help school leaders assess the quality of their school's overall multicultural education program. The checklist includes the following assessment questions.

Box 4.5 Checklist for Evaluating the Quality of a Multicultural Program

- Do school assemblies, decorations, speakers, holidays, and heroes reflect racial and ethnic group differences?
- Are extracurricular activities multiethnic and multicultural?
- Is the school staff (administrators, instructors, counselors, and support staff) multiethnic and multiracial?
- Does the school have systematic, comprehensive, mandatory, and continuing multicultural staff development programs?
- Do staff development programs provide opportunities for learning how to create and select multiethnic instructional materials and how to incorporate multicultural content into curriculum materials?
- Does the school library and resource center offer a variety of materials on the histories, experiences, and cultures of diverse racial and ethnic groups?
- Does the curriculum reflect ethnic and cultural diversity?
- Are ethnic content and perspectives incorporated into all aspects of the curriculum?
- Do instructional materials treat racial and ethnic differences and groups honestly, realistically, and sensitively?
- Does the curriculum examine the total experiences of groups instead of focusing exclusively on "heroes"?

➢ Does the curriculum include the study of societal problems that different ethnic and racial groups have experienced, such as racism, prejudice, discrimination, and exploitation?
➢ Does the curriculum help students develop a sense of efficacy (i.e., the sense that by taking action they can influence the outcomes of their life and society?)
➢ Does the curriculum help students develop skills necessary for effective interpersonal and intercultural group interactions?
➢ Does the curriculum help students participate in cross-ethnic and cross-cultural experiences and reflect upon them?

Source: National Council for the Social Studies (1991)

In short, a school that provides effective diversity education:

(a) *acknowledges* differences—is aware of the diversity among its students and their distinctive curricular and extracurricular needs;

(b) *accommodates* differences—treats diverse students in a fair, nonprejudicial, and nondiscriminative manner; and

(c) *cultivates* differences—capitalizes on diversity within the school and the surrounding community to advance the learning and personal development of all its students.

Summary and Conclusion

A school's ability to promote its students' academic achievement is influenced by its teachers, students, students' families, and the surrounding community. When all four of these influential sources work together in a mutually reinforcing manner, students' level of educational achievement can be elevated dramatically.

Student diversity in our nation's schools is greater today than at any other time in U.S. history and will continue to increase. America's changing national demographics also make it paramount that its educational system needs to effectively accommodate and educate students from all cultural backgrounds, and reduce the persistent achievement gap that exists between students of color and their white peers.

Supporting the academic success of students from low income families represents a societal opportunity to create a more level playing field by compensating for the fewer economic, social, and educational resources that students have at home and their local community. Ultimately, success in school represents the primary way in which low income students can overcome the disadvantages associated with lower socioeconomic status and gain upward social mobility for themselves and their future families.

There is a strong relationship between family involvement with their children and their children's educational achievement. This relationship exists regardless of the students' race/ethnicity, parents' level of education, or school. Students come to school from a wide variety of family backgrounds and arrangements and teachers and administrators need to be mindful of the uniqueness of families and how students' family backgrounds have influenced their self-perceptions and behavioral patterns. Regular communication with parents about their student's performance and the encouragement of parents to participate in decisions about their student's education are distinguishing features of effective schools that promote the highest levels of academic achievement.

Community plays a major role in a student's socialization and personal identity. To ignore a school's local community is to ignore the world in which they live. Building a strong base of community support can generate significant benefits for the school, such as support from community organizations for after-school programs and increased school funding. Furthermore, student pride in both their school and community is increased when successful members of the local community are invited to school to serve as honorary guest speakers and role models.

Diversity exists among schools in terms of their (a) student body, (b) curriculum, (c) teachers and administrators, and (d) resources and facilities. Schools located in poorer communities typically have fewer educational resources and poorer physical facilities for the children they serve. Thus, America's schools are not immune to the inequalities that exist in its larger society; in fact, they typically mirror societal inequalities. If America really believes in "no child left behind" (i.e., all students in all schools should reach the same educational finish line), then its school-funding formulas should ensure that all students start from the same starting line.

A core component of effective multicultural education is an inclusive curriculum that represents and respects diverse cultures. At its most advanced stage of curricular transformation, diversity is woven seamlessly into the mainstream curriculum and is presented in the form of multiple perspectives, whereby students learn to view the curriculum's major ideas and events through different cultural lenses. A multicultural curriculum should also: (a) include current issues relating to social justice, (b) infuse *academic success skills and effective learning strategies* into coverage of its subject matter, and (c) courses to ensure that minority students enroll in courses that prepare them to advance to and succeed at the next level of education.

Effective teachers have been found to exert greater impact on students' educational progress and academic success than any other factor. Research repeatedly shows that culturally competent teachers and culturally responsive teaching methods can reduce the achievement gap significantly, or eliminate it altogether. Effective, culturally competent teachers believe that they are primarily responsible for promoting student learning and have high expectations of students from all cultural backgrounds.

School leaders also play a pivotal role in promoting effective diversity education. They can help create a diversity-sensitive and diversity-responsive school environment by: (a) recruiting and hiring qualified minority teachers and staff members, (b) empowering teachers to accommodate and incorporate diversity into their teaching, (c) seeking input from teachers who work closely with diverse students on a daily basis, (d) collaborating with teachers in a joint effort to improve the performance of all students, and (e) providing teachers with adequate support and professional development opportunities.

> **Consider This . . .**
>
> Diversity in the United States is here to stay. Student diversity will continue to swell throughout the current century, thus presenting America's schools with an unprecedented challenge (and opportunity) to promote higher levels of educational achievement among students from increasingly diverse backgrounds. Meeting this challenge will require the concerted effort of teachers, school administrators and educational policymakers—as well as families and local communities—working together to foster the future success of our growing multicultural student population.

 Exercises

Family Ties

Answer the following questions to the best of your ability:

1. What is the race or ethnicity of your father, mother, and grandparents?
2. How strongly do your family members identify with their race or ethnicity?
3. How strongly do you identify with your race or ethnicity?
4. How do your views of other racial or ethnic groups differ from those of your parents and grandparents?

(Adapted from *American Public Works Association Diversity Resource Guide*, p. 19)

Community Ties

1. What was the majority ethnic group in the neighborhood where you grew up?
2. How much exposure did you have to other racial or ethnic groups during your elementary and high school years?
3. If you had contact with other racial ethnic or racial groups, where did this contact typically take place?

Personal Idols and Historical Role Models

1. My personal hero is . . .
2. The most important issue facing our country today is . . .
3. For me, the historical figure that has had the most positive influence on America was . . .

Cross-Cultural Curiosity

Write down (in question form) one thing you've always wondered about, or would like to know more about, the following groups of people:

1. Native Americans (American Indians)
2. Hispanic Americans (Latinos)
3. African Americans
4. Asian Americans
5. Elderly
6. Gays and lesbians

Would you feel comfortable approaching a member of each of these groups to ask your question about their culture? Why or why not?

NAME _____ DATE _____

Cross-Cultural Interview

Find a student, faculty member, or an administrator on campus whose cultural background is different than yours, and ask if you could interview that person about his or her culture. Use the following questions in your interview:

1. How is "family" defined in your culture, and what are the traditional roles and responsibilities of different family members?
2. What are the traditional gender (male/female) roles associated with your culture? Are they changing?
3. What is the culture's approach to time (e.g., is there an emphasis on punctuality? is doing things fast valued or frowned upon?)
4. What cultural traditions or rituals are highly valued and commonly practiced?
5. Are there special holidays celebrated by member your culture?

Intercultural Communication and Relationship-Building Skills

The National Council for the Social Studies (1991) recommends that the following question be included among the questions used to assess the quality of a multicultural education program: "Does the curriculum help students develop skills necessary for effective interpersonal and intercultural group interactions?" The objective of this chapter is to provide a blueprint for developing a curriculum that includes such skills. The chapter is written primarily for a student audience. Its content may be used for teacher presentations to students in class or, depending on the students' grade level, it may be given to students as an out-of-class reading assignment or in-class reading exercise. Teachers may also use the information in this chapter for ideas and strategies for increasing their own interpersonal contact with people from diverse cultures, or to enhance their intercultural communication skills.

Strategies for Interacting with People without Bias or Prejudice

Consciously avoid preoccupation with physical appearances. Go deeper and get beneath the superficial surface of appearances to judge people not in terms of how they look, but in terms of *who* they are and how they act. Remember the old proverb: "It's what's inside that counts." Judge others by the quality of their personal character, not by the familiarity of their physical or cultural characteristics.

Form your impressions of each person on an individual, case-by-case basis, rather than by using some general "rule of thumb." Make a conscious effort to perceive each person with whom you interact not merely as a member of a group, but as a unique individual with a unique personal identity. This may seem like an obvious and simple thing to do, but research shows that humans have a natural tendency to perceive individuals who are members of unfamiliar groups as being more alike (or all alike) than members of our own group (Taylor, Peplau, & Sears, 2006). Thus, we have to make a deliberate effort to resist this tendency to over-generalize and "lump together" individuals into homogenous

> *"The common eye sees only the outside of things, and judges by that. But the seeing eye pierces through and reads the heart and the soul, finding there capacities which the outside didn't indicate or promise."*
>
> —Samuel Clemens, a.k.a., Mark Twain, writer, lecturer, and humorist

> "Stop judging by mere appearances, and make a right judgment."
> —*The Bible*, John 7:24

> "You can't judge a book by the cover."
> —Hit record, 1962, by Elias Bates, a.k.a., Bo Diddley (Note: a "bo diddley" is a one-stringed African guitar)

groups by making a conscious attempt to focus on each person as a unique human being.

Consider This . . .

Although it's valuable to learn about different cultures and common characteristics shared by members of the same culture, significant differences exist among individuals who share the same culture. Don't assume that all individuals from the same cultural background share the same personal characteristics.

Meeting and Interacting with People from Diverse Backgrounds

Once we overcome biases or stereotypes about individuals from diverse groups, we are now positioned to proceed to higher levels of interaction, collaboration, and friendship formation. In other words, we're ready to move beyond multicultural awareness to *intercultural interaction*.

> "Mere knowledge is not power; it is only possibility. Action is power."
> —Francis Bacon (1561–1626), English philosopher, lawyer, and champion of modern science

Learning from diversity is enriched when we move beyond acquiring knowledge about diversity *vicariously*—through someone else (e.g., through lectures and readings) to learning from diversity *experientially*—through direct, personal contact with people from diverse groups (Nagda, Gurin, & Lopez, 2003).

Formal courses and programs can help us learn *about* diversity, whereas first-hand interaction with diverse people enables us to learn directly *from* diversity. The latter represents a significant increase in our level of involvement with diversity. The difference would be similar to acquiring knowledge about another country by reading about it, as opposed to actually going to the country and interacting with its natives. Interpersonal contact with individuals from diverse groups takes us beyond multicultural or cross-cultural awareness to *intercultural interaction*. It transforms diversity appreciation from an attitude or belief into action and commitment.

Place yourself in situations and locations where you will come in regular contact with individuals from diverse groups to create opportunities for interaction and conversation with them. Research demonstrates that people tend to form relationships with others whom we share similar prior experiences and cultural background (Uzzi & Dunlap, 2005). Consciously resist the temptation to associate only with people who are similar to you and diversify your social networks by intentionally placing yourself in situations where individuals from diverse groups are nearby and potential relationships can develop. Studies show that meaningful interactions and friendships are more likely to form among people who come in regular contact with one another (Latané et al., 1995). Studies also show that stereotyping and prejudice is sharply reduced when contact between members of different racial or ethnic groups is frequent enough to allow time for the development of friendships (Pettigrew, 1998). You can create this condition in the classroom by sitting near students from different ethnic or racial groups, or by joining them if you are given the choice to select whom you will work with in class discussion groups and group projects.

Join a school club or organization that is devoted to diversity awareness (e.g., multicultural or international student club). Spending time in such venues will enable you to make contact with members of groups other than your own, and it sends a clear message that you value contact with people from diverse cultural backgrounds because you've taken the initiative to go to "their turf."

Take advantage of the Internet to "chat" with students from diverse groups at your school, or with students from different schools. Electronic communication can be a more convenient and more comfortable way to initially interact with members of diverse groups with whom you have had little prior experience. After you've communicated successfully *online*, you may then feel more comfortable about interacting with them *in person*.

Participate in volunteer experiences that allow you to work in diverse communities or neighborhoods. Studies show that people who periodically devote time to doing good things for others report higher levels of personal "happiness" and personal satisfaction with their life (Myers, 1993). This is probably due to feelings of self-satisfaction and pride that the experience of knowing they made a difference in someone's life. Volunteer experiences in communities beyond the borders of your campus may also give you the opportunity to interact with diverse groups of people.

Volunteering also enables you to acquire hands-on work experience in "real-life" settings. You can use volunteer opportunities to network with people in the community who may serve as excellent resources, references, and sources for letters of recommendation. Moreover, volunteer experiences give you the opportunity to gain diversity experience while, at the same time, allow you to explore the world of work and gain inside information on career fields that may interest you.

Interpersonal Communication Skills: Speaking and Listening

Scholars consider the ability to relate effectively with others to be a major form of human intelligence, referred to as *interpersonal intelligence* (Gardner, 1993; 1999) or *social intelligence* (Goleman, 2007). Developing interpersonal and human relations skills is as important as developing academic and intellectual skills because research shows that the ability to relate to others is crucial for personal and professional success in today's world (Goleman, 2006; 2007). Employers place a high value on interpersonal skills in their hiring decisions (Felstead, Gallie, & Green, 2002; National Association of Colleges & Employers, 2003). Furthermore, the ability to effectively communicate with and motivate others is also a key characteristic of effective leadership (Avolio, 2005).

> *"I will pay more for the ability to deal with people than any other ability under the sun."*
> —John D. Rockefeller, American industrialist, philanthropist, and once the richest man in the world

> "Precision of communication is important, more important than ever, in our era of hair-trigger balances, when a false, or misunderstood word may create as much disaster as a sudden thoughtless act."
>
> —James Thurber, author, humorist, and cartoonist

Interpersonal intelligence is especially important when communicating with people from diverse cultures because if our message is unclear or culturally insensitive, it can lead to an immediate communication breakdown and termination of a potentially fruitful relationship. When communicating with others from different cultures, we are often so concerned about saying the "right thing" (what to say), we forget about saying it the "right way" (how to say it) (Du Praw & Axner, 1997).

Listed below are key strategies for strengthening your interpersonal communication skills. Some of these strategies may appear to be very simple and obvious, but it's probably because they're so simple or obvious that they're often overlooked, taken for granted, or used inconsistently. Don't be fooled by the seeming

---

Reflection 5.1 What would you say are the universal important rules or principles of good communication (verbal and nonverbal) that should be used when communicating with anyone from any culture?

---

simplicity of the following suggestions and don't underrate or underestimate the impact they have on the people with whom you interact. Be mindful of using these suggestions when interacting with all people, and particularly when interacting with people from diverse cultures. The more consistently you use these practices, the more automatic they become, and the better you'll become at intercultural communication.

Work hard at being a good listener. Human relations scholars report that we need to improve our listening skills because listening attentively and sensitively is a very demanding mental task (Nichols & Stevens, 1957; Nichols, 1995). We have only one chance to understand words that are spoken to us; if we miss the meaning of a spoken message, we cannot replay it or re-read it like we can a recorded or printed message. Studies show that our listening comprehension for spoken messages is less than 50 percent (Nichols & Stevens, 1957; Wolvin & Coakley, 1993).

> "Chi rispetta sara ripettato." (Respect others and you will be respected.)
>
> —Italian proverb

The capacity to listen well is important for any human interaction, but is especially important when the interaction takes place between people with different cultural backgrounds because the conversationalists may be unfamiliar with each other's verbal and nonverbal styles of communication. If we do not listen well to the ideas expressed by those who are different than us, it can send the unwanted message that we lack interest in, or respect for, their culture.

Since we're not actively "doing" anything while listening, we can easily fall prey to passive listening—we give the impression that we're totally focused on the

Listening closely can be challenging, but it is an important interpersonal skill that lets speakers know they are worthy of your complete and undivided attention.

speaker's words, but our attention is really divided and part of our mind is actually somewhere else. As listeners, we need to remain consciously aware of this tendency toward "attention drift" and make a deliberate attempt to concentrate when listening to others. If we make a deliberate attempt to listen attentively, we also send others the message that they're worthy of our complete and undivided attention. This message is particularly important to send others from diverse groups because they may need more assurance that we accept them and are truly interested in developing relationships with them.

A frequently recommended strategy for becoming an effective listener is to periodically check whether we're following the speaker's message. "I messages" are particularly useful for this purpose, such as: "What I hear you saying is . . ." When the speaker finishes, you can paraphrase what you heard in your own words to be sure the message you received is consistent with the message that the speaker intended to send; for example: "Let me check to be sure that I am following you. Are you saying that . . .?" (Donahue & Siegel, 2005).

This strategy transforms a passive listener to an active listener—who is alert and involved in the conversation, which, in turn, sends the speaker the message that we are genuinely interested in what he or she has to say. This active listening strategy is particularly important to use when listening to spoken messages delivered by people from other cultures because there's a greater risk we may misinterpret the message because of our different cultural backgrounds. Occasionally checking to see if we understand the speaker's message assures us (as listeners) that we're following the meaning of the message, and it assures the speaker that his or her message has been accurately received and interpreted.

> *Seek first to understand, then to be understood.*
>
> —Stephen Covey, author of *The Seven Habits of Highly Effective People*

Box 5.1 Snapshot Summary

Avoiding the Three "Egos":
The Type of Person You Don't Want to Be When Interacting with Others

Good listeners (and good people) are those who get outside themselves and get interested in others. The following types of people are more into themselves than listening well; consequently, they tend to "turn off" people with whom they interact. Don't be one of them.

Egocentric—an egocentric person views the world as if he or she is always at the *center* of it (and every conversation), showing little interest in or empathy for others. The words "me" and "I" appear with relentless frequency when an egocentric person speaks, and you may get the feeling that this person is not talking *with* you but *at* you.

Egotist—an egotistical person is basically *conceited*—a braggart who boasts, shows off in front of others, and spends lots of conversation time talking about his or her outstanding features or personal accomplishments (often to cover up feelings of personal inadequacy or low self-esteem).

Egoist—an egoistic person is basically *selfish* and unwilling to share things with others or do things for others.

> "We have been given two ears and but a single mouth in order that we may hear more and talk less"
> —Zeno of Citium, ancient Greek philosopher and founder of Stoic philosophy

> "Give every man thine ear, but few thy voice."
> —William Shakespeare, English poet, playwright, and most quoted writer in the English-speaking world

An egocentric person wants to be at the "center" of (and the subject of) every conversation.

> "The most important thing in communication is to hear what isn't being said."
> —Peter F. Drucker, Austrian author and founder of the study of "management"

Be aware of the nonverbal messages you send while listening. It's often been said that 90 percent of communication is nonverbal; body language often communicates stronger and truer messages than spoken language (Mehrabian, 1972). Nonverbal communication is especially important in any human interaction, but its importance is multiplied when interaction occurs across different cultures because we're more likely to look for nonverbal cues when verbal messages sent by people whose culture is less familiar to us—particularly if they're attempting to speak in our language, which is not their native tongue (LeBaron, 2003).

The nonverbal signals we silently send others are often the most important signals they receive about whether we're really listening to them. For example, if a person say he's is excited or enthusiastic about some idea you've presented to him, but his nonverbal communication indicates otherwise (e.g., his eyebrows don't raise and he sits motionless), you may have reason to doubt whether the person is really interested in what you're saying.

Similarly, when we are doing the speaking, awareness of our listeners' body language can inform us about whether we're holding or losing their interest; this can inform us about whether or not we should continue talking about the same topic. Nonverbal messages that signal to others that we're not interested in what they are saying include finger tapping, paper shuffling, and rapid head-nodding, all of which send the message that you want the speaker to hurry up and finish. The nonverbal signals we should send others while listening may be remembered by using the acronym "SOFTEN," with each letter standing for a different nonverbal signal:

S = **Smile**—periodically, but not continually because the latter may convey the nonverbal message that your smile is an artificial pose.
Sit Still—don't fidget and squirm because the speaker may interpret this to mean that you're feeling uncomfortable or being put on the spot by what is being said.

O = **Open posture**—as opposed to a "closed posture" (e.g., arms crossed or hands folded together), which may give the impression that you're closed minded or passing judgment on the what the speaker is saying.

F = **Forward leaning**—as opposed to leaning back, which may send the message that you're distancing yourself emotionally from the speaker—as if you're feeling threatened by what's being said or psychoanalyzing the person saying it.
Face the speaker directly—with both shoulders lining up directly with the person who's doing the speaking; in contrast, facing the speaker sideways—with one shoulder turned away from the speaker—may send the message suggesting that you're giving the speaker the "cold shoulder" or turning your attention to something else.

T = **Touch**—a light touch on the arm or hand can be a good way to communicate warmth—but no rubbing, stroking, or touching in ways that could be interpreted as inappropriate by members of a different culture, or as sexual harassment by members of a different gender.

E = **Eye contact**—periodic, but not continuous eye contact, because the latter could be interpreted by members of some cultural groups as staring or glaring. For example, in working-class Hispanic and African American culture, sustained eye contact is considered inappropriate (Taylor, 1990). On the other hand, little or no eye contact can convey the nonverbal message that you're uncomfortable with the speaker or that you'd like the conversation to end (much like a student who avoids eye contact to avoid being called on in class).

N = **Nod your head**—slowly and occasionally, but not repeatedly and rapidly—this can send the message that you want the speaker to hurry up and finish up so you can start talking!

An effective way to gain greater self-awareness of your nonverbal communication habits is to ask someone whose judgment you trust to imitate your body language, particularly someone whose cultural background is different than yours. Observing others mimic us can sometimes reveal nonverbal messages that we're sending without our conscious awareness and which may be misinterpreted by individuals whose nonverbal cultural habits are different from our own.

Sending positive nonverbal signals when listening to members of diverse groups encourages them to become more self-confident and open about sharing their ideas and personal experiences with us. This also benefits us as listeners because the challenging task of listening becomes less difficult (and more interesting) when we're listening to others who are more self-confident and open about sharing their ideas.

Be open to different topics of conversation. Resist the temptation to be a closed-minded or selective listener who listens to others like listening to the radio—changing stations and "tuning into" conversational topics or viewpoints you're instantly interested in, and "tuning out" everything else.

Consider This . . .

> People learn more from others whose interests and viewpoints do not necessarily match their own. Ignoring or blocking out information and ideas about topics that don't immediately interest us or support our particular perspective is not only a poor social skill, it's also a poor learning strategy.

It's likely that people whose background experiences are very different than our own will express viewpoints that we're unfamiliar with that we don't agree with; however, we still owe them the courtesy of listening to what they have to say (rather than shaking our head, frowning, or interrupting them). This is more than just a matter of social etiquette, it's a matter of social ethics. Only after others have finished sharing their perspective or point of view should we then interject our own.

Also, when expressing your views, be sure that the opinions you express are *informed* opinions, rather than opinions rooted in your personal biases or ethnocentric perspectives. Don't express your opinions in an *opinionated* way—stating them so strongly that it sounds like your viewpoint is the only rational or acceptable one while all others are irrelevant or inferior (Gibb, 1961). Expressing opinions in such a cocky and condescending fashion is likely to put an immediate end to a potentially positive exchange of ideas (and perhaps a future friendship).

> **Consider This...**
> Our views are shaped, limited, and often biased by our particular cultural perspective. By remaining open to multiple perspectives and diverse viewpoints we create opportunities to develop personal viewpoints that are more balanced, comprehensive, and accurate.

Reflection 5.2 On what topics do you hold strong opinions? Do you think any of those opinions would be more acceptable to people from some cultural backgrounds than others?

Human Relations Skills (a.k.a., "People Skills")

In addition to *interpersonal communication* skills—the ability to listen and speak well in the company of others—another key component of social intelligence are *human relations* skills—the ability to relate to others in a sensitive and humane manner. Sensitivity to others' feelings and emotions, also known as empathy, has been found to be more important for personal and professional success than intellectual ability (IQ) (Goleman, 1995; 2006). To improve this broader set of human relations or "people skills," the following practices are recommended.

Make a genuine effort to learn and remember the names of people you meet. Remembering people's names communicates to others that you know them as individuals. It gives them the feeling that they're not just anonymous faces in a crowd, but unique human beings with a distinctive identity. When you know and remember someone's name, you're noticing and acknowledging their individuality. (You do just the opposite when you forget a person's name, or never bother to learn it in the first place.)

Learning and remembering names isn't an inherited trait; it's a skill that can be developed through personal effort and intentional use of effective learning and memory strategies, such as those discussed below.

> *" We should be aware of the magic contained in a name. The name sets that individual apart; it makes him or her unique among all others. Remember that a person's name is to that person the sweetest and most important sound in any language. "*
> —Dale Carnegie, author of *How to Win Friends and Influence People*, 1936

Strategies for Remembering Names

▶ When you first meet someone, consciously pay close attention to the person's name when you first hear it. Although this may seem to be an obvious suggestion, it's often overlooked because when we first meet people, we tend to focus less on their name and more on what impression we're making on them, what impression they're making on us, or what we're going to say next.

- One way to improve your attention and strengthen your memory of a new name is to use the person's name soon after you first hear it. For instance, if your friend Jack has just introduced you to Jill, you might say something like: "Jill, how long have you known Jack?" This allows you to quickly rehearse the new name soon after we've heard it. This is an effective strategy for promoting name memory because most forgetting of new information occurs immediately after we're first exposed to that information (Underwood, 1983).
- Associate the person's name with other things you've already learned or know about the person. For instance, associate the person's name with: (a) your first impression of the individual's personality, (b) a physical characteristic of the person, (c) the topic of conversation you had with the person, (d) the place where you met the person, or (e) a familiar word that rhymes with the person's name. By making a mental connection between the person's name and some other piece of information, you enable your brain to make an actual physical (neurological) connection between the two, which is the biological basis of human memory.
- As soon as you have the opportunity, make an actual note of the person's name in writing. When we want to remember anything, we write it down (e.g., grocery shopping list or party invitation list). We can use the same foolproof strategy for learning names by keeping a *name journal* that includes the names of new people we meet, along with some information about them (e.g., what they do and what their interests are). You can make it a goal to meet one new person from a diverse group each day or week, and make a point of remembering that person's name by recording it in a name journal.

Refer to people by name when you greet and interact with them. Once you've learned a person's name, always refer to that person by name. For instance, saying, "Hi, Julio" will mean a lot more to Julio than simply saying "Hi" or, worse yet, saying "Hi, there"—which sounds like you're just acknowledging something "out there" that could be either a human being or an inanimate object. Continuing to use people's names after you've learned them serves to reinforce your memory of their names, and it continues to send them the message that you haven't forgotten who they are.

Although it may seem that learning and remembering names is not worth all this time and effort, it is. Not only is it probably the best way to open up channels of intercultural communication and develop friendships, it also promotes personal and professional success. In business, remembering names helps recruit and retain customers; in politics it wins votes; in education it promotes teacher-student rapport; and when interacting with individuals from diverse groups, it rolls out the welcome mat for interaction, collaboration, and friendship formation.

> "When I joined the bank, I started keeping a record of the people I met and put them on little cards, and I would indicate on the cards when I met them, and under what circumstances, and sometimes [make] a little notation which would help me remember a conversation."
>
> —David Rockefeller, prominent American banker, philanthropist, and former CEO of the Chase Manhattan Bank

Consider This . . .

Developing the habit of learning and remembering names isn't merely a matter of social etiquette, it is a powerful way to make others feel welcomed and validated, particularly if they are members of a minority group.

Show interest in people by remembering information about them. Going beyond knowing the names of people to knowing something about them lays the foundation for further interaction and the development of a deeper relationship. You can strengthen relationships with members of diverse groups by paying particular attention to interests that you may have *in common*; shared interests can serve as a springboard to shared conversations, and perhaps, to the formation of long-term friendships. This is particularly true for interactions with people from different cultures because our different backgrounds and prior experiences can often overshadow our commonalities, causing us to overlook them.

> "All that is necessary is to take an interest in other persons, to recognize that other people as a rule are much like one's self, and thankfully to admit that diversity is a glorious feature of life."
> —Frank Swinnerton, British novelist and literary critic

Noticing things we have in common with members of groups who are different than us is an excellent way to stimulate conversation and future friendships.

"OHHH, YOU LOVE KITTIES, TOO!"

> "If we obey this law, [it] will bring us countless friends. The law is this: Always make the person feel important."
>
> —Dale Carnegie, author of *How to Win Friends and Influence People*

> "You can make more friends in two months by becoming interested in others than you can in two years by trying to get other people interested in you."
>
> —Dale Carnegie, author of *How to Win Friends and Influence People*

Ask questions about others' personal interests, plans, and experiences. Pay particular attention to what's most important to them, what they care about, and what holds their attention (e.g., politics, sports, relationships). Introduce these topics when you have conversations with them. When you see them again, ask them about something they brought up in your last conversation. Try to get beyond the standard, generic questions that are routinely asked after people say "hello" (e.g., "What's goin' on?"). Instead, ask about something *specific* that you discussed during your previous conversation (e.g., "How was that math test you were worried about last week?"). This sends a message to others that you not only know *who* they are, but also know *what* they care about and matters to them.

When you remember specific information about people, particularly about people from groups that may see themselves as very different from you, it sends them the message that they're important to you. Because we're more likely to remember what matters to us, when we remember people's names and something about them, it sends them the message that *they* matter to us.

Furthermore, when you show genuine interest in others, you're likely to find that others start showing more interest in you. You will also find others referring to you as a good listener and a good friend.

Reflection 5.3 What would you say are universal human interests—topics of conversation that are of interest and importance to people from any cultural background?

Be a caring and sharing person. How often have you witnessed this rapid, ritualistic interchange between two people?

Person A: "Hi, how's it goin'?"
Person B: "Fine, how ya' doin'?"

No real personal information is shared by either person, and chances are that neither one expects nor wants to hear about how the other person is truly feeling (Goffman, 1967). Such social rituals are understandable and acceptable when people first interact with each other. However, if we want to continue interacting with that person and move the relationship beyond a superficial level, we need to move beyond these ritualistic routines and toward mutual sharing of more personal, meaningful information.

This can be done by showing authentic concern for other people's feelings. For example, instead of asking the routine question, "How's it goin'?" ask the person, "How are you feeling?" Studies show that when people disclose or share their feelings with others, it helps them feel understood and feel better about themselves (Reis & Shaver, 1988). Showing concern for others not only helps them feel more comfortable about sharing information with you, it also helps to create more opportunities for you to learn from and about the people you meet.

Developing friendships with peers from diverse groups in an excellent way to learn from human differences and develop self-confidence in relating to people with different cultural backgrounds.

As you become more comfortable interacting with others from diverse groups, engage in some self-disclosure—disclose (share) a little more of yourself. Naturally, you want to do this gradually and in small doses, rather than suddenly with "hot blasts" of intimate details about your personal life that are likely to blow others away. Selectively and gradually sharing information about yourself serves to show others that you trust them well enough to share a part of yourself. In turn, they will be more likely to trust you and share a part of themselves.

You can begin this interpersonal sharing process by noticing things that others have shared with you and by sharing something about yourself that relates to what they shared with you. Relating a similar experience of your own demonstrates empathy—your ability to understand the feelings of others—which is particularly important when interacting with others whose background experiences are different from your own. It lets them know you have something in common with them, which encourages them to share more of themselves with you (Adler & Towne, 2001). Friendships gradually build up through this progressive give-and-take process of sharing personal information—human relations experts refer to this process as the *intimacy spiral* (Cusinato & L'Abate, 1994).

Keep a diversity *journal* and record your personal reflections on diversity. Learning deeply from diversity requires both action and *reflection*. Studies show that college students learn most effectively from diversity experiences when they take time to reflect on these experiences and record their reflections by writing (Lopez, Gurin, & Nagda, 1998; Nagda, Gurin, & Lopez, 2003). Personal reflection naturally complements and follows active involvement. Both processes are needed for learning to be complete and "go deep." Active involvement is necessary to initially capture and engage *attention*—which enables you to "get into" the learning experience and get information through your attention filter and into your brain. However, reflection enables you to slow down, step back, and look back at the learning experience. This process of reflective review ensures the learning experience gets "locked" deeply into your long-term memory (Broadbent, 1970; Bligh, 2000).

Writing is an effective strategy for promoting reflection on diversity experiences (or any learning experiences) because it "forces" you to carefully and systematically think through the experience, and provides you with a visible product of your thought process that you can review later to stimulate further reflection (Applebee, 1984; Langer & Applebee, 1987).

Take a Leadership Role with Respect to Diversity

Your experiences with diversity may present an opportunity for you to develop leadership skills. Research shows that the most effective leaders are those that enable diverse individuals to see themselves as members of the same community and, by advancing the community's interest, they advance their own interests (Bass & Riggio, 2005).

By embracing diversity and creating a welcoming, inclusive community, you demonstrate leadership. Research shows that both white students and students of color feel a greater sense of belonging when they perceive themselves as members of a community that is open and welcoming to students from different ethnic and racial groups (Locks et al., 2008).

You can demonstrate diversity leadership by (a) modeling responsible social behavior, (b) making others feel welcome (particularly members of minority groups), (c) drawing out people who may be shy and including them in conversations and activities, and (d) being an empathic listener who provides an emotional sounding board for others.

Effective leadership involves effective communication and human relations skills. For example, effective leaders know their constituents names and interests (Hogan, Curphy, & Hogan, 1994), and they are good listeners (Johnson & Bechler, 1998). Successful leaders don't dominate dialogue and discussion; when they do speak, they use effective oral communication strategies to enable them to express their ideas efficiently and persuasively. They also communicate with social sensitivity, which enables them to effectively mediate and resolve interpersonal disagreements before they develop into conflicts. Although being a dynamic and eloquent speaker can be helpful in certain leadership roles, leaders are often effective not because of their spectacular oratory skills, but because of their outstanding interpersonal and human relations skills. Thus, the effective interpersonal communication and human relations skills discussed earlier in this chapter should not only improve your intercultural relationships, they should also develop your potential for intercultural leadership, enabling you to relate to others from diverse backgrounds and to promote harmony among diverse groups of people.

In addition to interpersonal communication and human relations skills, the following practices will enable you to demonstrate diversity leadership as a teacher and citizen.

Seek out views and opinions of classmates from diverse backgrounds. For example, during or after class discussions, ask students who are members of different ethnic and racial groups if their personal experiences support or contradict points made or positions during class discussions. Research indicates that free discussions among student groups, in which diverse viewpoints are openly sought and included, is one of the most effective ways to develop critical thinking skills (Kurfiss, 1988).

> **Consider This . . .**
>
> The goal of discussions with classmates is not to force conformity or convergence on a single "correct" answer or position. One key role of a leader during group discussions is to encourage others to express their positions—even if they may differ from the majority. By so doing, the leader promotes multiple perspective-taking and balanced thinking—which are two key characteristics of critical thinkers.

> " The nation's future depends upon leaders trained through wide exposure to that robust exchange of ideas which discovers truth out of a multitude of tongues. "
>
> —William J. Brennan, former Supreme Court Justice

Reflection 5.4 How would you define teamwork? What do you think are the key characteristics of successful learning teams (e.g., study groups or group projects)?

Form discussion groups with students from diverse backgrounds. You can demonstrate leadership and gain greater exposure to diverse perspectives by joining or forming diverse groups of students who differ in terms of such characteristics as gender, age, race, or ethnicity. You might begin by forming discussion groups composed of students from different cultural backgrounds, but who share common interests. For instance, you could form learning groups of students who have the same educational interests or career goals, but who differ with respect to race, ethnicity, or age. This practice gives diverse members of your group some common ground for discussion and can raise group awareness that although we may be members of different groups, we can, at the same time, have common interests and goals.

> **Consider This . . .**
>
> Including diversity in your discussion groups not only provides social variety, it also promotes the quality of the group's thinking by allowing its members to gain access to and learn from diverse perspectives and life experiences of people from different backgrounds.

Form learning teams with students from diverse backgrounds. A learning *team* is much more than a discussion group; it moves beyond discussion to *collaboration*—its members "co-labor" (work together) to reach the same learning goal. Research from kindergarten through college indicates that when students collaborate in teams, their academic performance and interpersonal skills improve significantly (Cuseo, 1996). Studies also show that merely having contact with others from different cultural backgrounds is often insufficient to promote intercultural appreciation and competence (Putnam, 2007). However, when interpersonal contact between individuals from different ethnic and racial groups involves collaboration and pursuit of a common goal, racial prejudice is reduced and interracial friendships are more likely to be formed (Allport, 1954; Amir, 1976). Scholars believe that these positive results are explained by the fact that when individuals from diverse groups work collaboratively on the same team toward the same goal, they all become members of the same "in-group" (us); nobody is a member of an "out-group" (them) (Pratto et al., 2000; Sidanius et al., 2000). For a summary of the characteristics of effective learning teams, see **Box 5.2**.

Box 5.2 Tips for Teamwork: Creating Successful Learning Teams

1. **Intentionally form diverse learning teams comprised of individuals with different cultural backgrounds and life experiences.**
   If you team up only with friends or classmates whose lifestyles and experiences are similar to your own, it can actually impair your team's performance. Your similar experiences can cause your learning to get off track and onto topics that have nothing to do with the learning task (e.g., what you did last weekend or what you are planning to do next weekend).

2. **Your team should identify and pursue a common goal.**
   Your team should create the same final product that represents their unified effort and accomplishment (e.g., a completed sheet of answers to questions, a list or chart of specific ideas). A collectively created end product helps individual members function as "we" rather than "me," and helps the team stay on task and moving in the same direction—toward their common goal.

3. **Each teammate should have equal opportunity and assume personal responsibility for contributing to the team's final product.**
   For example, all team members should be equally responsible for making a specific contribution to the team's final product—such as contributing a different piece of information to the team's overall topic or project final product (e.g., a specific chapter from the textbook or a particular section of class notes)—as if each teammate is bringing a different piece or part that's needed to complete the whole puzzle.

4. **All teammates should work interdependently—that is, they should depend on or rely upon each other to achieve their common goal.** Similar to a sports team, each member of a learning team should have a specific role to play. For instance, each teammate could assume one of the following roles:
   - manager—whose role is to assure that the team stays on track and moving toward their goal
   - moderator—whose role is to ensure that all members have equal opportunity to contribute
   - summarizer—whose role is to monitor the team's progress, identify what has been accomplished and what still needs to be done
   - recorder—whose role is to keep a written record of the team's ideas

Teammates may also assume roles that involve contributing a particular type of thinking to the learning task (e.g., analysis, synthesis, or application) or bringing a specific perspective to the final product (e.g., cultural, national, or international).

> "We are born for cooperation, as are the feet, the hands, the eyelids, and the upper and lower jaws."
> —Marcus Aurelius, Roman Emperor, 161–180 AD

5. **Before delving into the work task, teammates should take some social "warm up" time to interact informally with each other.**
Getting the opportunity to learn each other's names, backgrounds, and interests will enable group members to become comfortable with one another and develop a sense of team solidarity or identity, particularly if they come from diverse (and unfamiliar) cultural backgrounds. Once they get to know each other as individuals, they should become more comfortable about sharing their personal thoughts and viewpoints during teamwork.

6. **Teamwork should take place in a friendly, informal setting.**
The context or atmosphere in which group work takes place can influence the nature and quality of interaction among team members. People are more likely to work openly and collaboratively when they are in an environment that is conducive to relationship building. For example, a living room or a lounge area would provide a warmer and friendlier team-learning atmosphere than a sterile classroom.

7. **Learning teams should occasionally divide into smaller subgroups (e.g., as pairs or trios) so that teammates get an opportunity to work with each other on a more personal level, particularly if they are from different ethnic or racial groups.**
The smaller the group size, the greater the level of participation, involvement, and depth of interaction between group members. For example, it's much easier not to participate in a group of six than a group of two. If opportunities are created for different team members to work together, everyone gets at least one opportunity to work closely with every other member of the team. This can promote diversity appreciation by allowing each team member to experience working at a personal level with an individual from a minority group that's not represented in large numbers at your school.

When contact among people from diverse groups takes place under the above conditions, it has the greatest potential for having positive impact on learning and diversity appreciation. A win-win scenario is created: Learning is strengthened, and at the same time, prejudice is weakened.

Sources: Allport (1979); Amir (1969); Aronson, Wilson, & Akert (2005); Cook (1984); Sherif et al. (1961); and Wilder (1984)

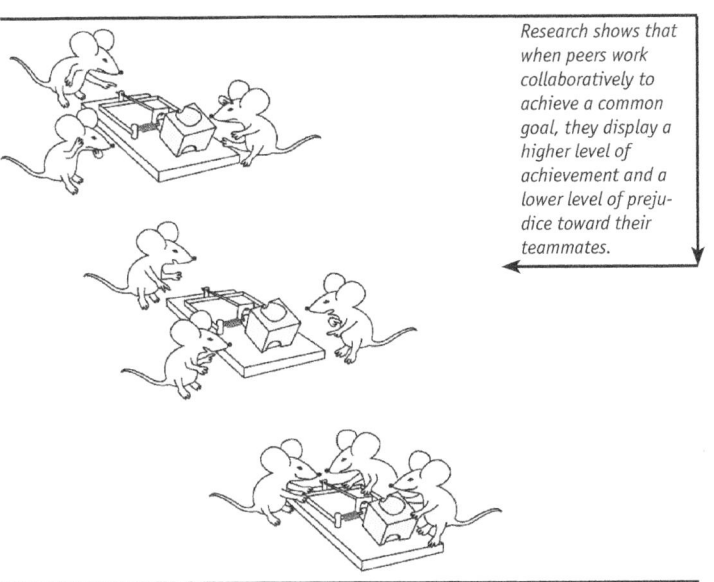

Research shows that when peers work collaboratively to achieve a common goal, they display a higher level of achievement and a lower level of prejudice toward their teammates.

> "TEAM = Together Everyone Achieves More"
> —Author Unknown

After concluding small-group discussions, take time to pause and reflect on the group experience. Ask yourself questions that trigger personal reflection on the ideas that were shared by diverse members of your group and carefully consider the impact of those ideas on you. For instance, you could ask yourself (and your teammates) the following questions:

- What major similarities in viewpoints or background experiences did all group members share? (What were the themes?)
- What major differences of opinion were expressed by members of diverse groups during the discussion? (What were the variations on the theme?)
- Were there particular topics or issues raised during the discussion that provoked intense reactions or very emotional responses from members of the group?
- Did the discussion cause any members of the group to change their mind about an idea or position they previously held?

Serve as a community builder and discover the common themes that unite the ideas and experiences of students from varied backgrounds. Look for common denominators—themes of unity that underlie diversity. Individuals from diverse ethnic and racial groups still share many common characteristics, such as being citizens of the same country, persons of the same gender, or members of the same generation. No matter what particular racial or ethnic group(s) an individual belongs to, humans of all races and ethnicities live in neighborhoods, are members of communities, develop friendships and intimate relationships, have basic human needs, progress through the same stages of the human life cycle, and struggle with universal issues of personal identity and eventual mortality.

Consider This . . .

> By learning about diversity (our differences), we simultaneously learn more about our commonality (our shared humanity).

Take a stand against prejudice at school by constructively disagreeing with those who make stereotypical statements or prejudicial remarks. Studies show that when members of the same group observe another member of their group make a prejudicial remark, the group's prejudice tends to increase—due, in large part, to the pressure of group conformity (Stangor, Sechrist, & Jost, 2001). In contrast, if a person's prejudicial comment is challenged by another member of his own group, particularly a member who is liked and respected, that person's prejudice tends to decrease, as does similar prejudice held by other members of the group (Baron, Byrne, & Brauscombe, 2006). Thus, by taking a leadership role and challenging prejudicial remarks made by a member of your own group, you not only help reduce that member's prejudice, you're also likely to reduce prejudice among all other group members who witness your challenge.

Consider This . . .

> By being open to diversity and actively opposing prejudice, you demonstrate civic character. You become a role model whose actions visibly demonstrate to other student citizens in your school community that valuing diversity has both educational and ethical value. You show others that appreciating diversity is not only a *smart* thing to do; it's also the *right* thing to do.

Summary and Conclusion

The following suggestions and strategies for meeting, interacting, and communicating with diverse cultural groups comprise the crux of this chapter.

A deep appreciation of diversity requires interacting with and learning from people of diverse cultural backgrounds. Studies show that learning is maximized when students move beyond acquiring knowledge about diversity vicariously from lectures and readings—to learning *experiencing* diversity through direct, interpersonal contact with people from diverse groups.

Intentionally create opportunities for intercultural interaction and conversation by placing yourself in situations and locations where you will come in regular contact with people from diverse groups. Spend time at places in schools where diverse groups of people are likely to congregate. Research indicates meaningful interactions and friendships are more likely to develop among people who are in physical proximity to one another.

Join a school club or organization that is devoted to diversity awareness (e.g., multicultural or international student club). Spending time in such venues will enable you to make contact with members of groups other than your own, and it sends a clear message that you value contact with people from diverse cultural backgrounds because you've taken the initiative to go to "their turf."

Engage in volunteer experiences that allow you to work in diverse communities or neighborhoods. Volunteer experiences in the local community beyond the borders of your campus may allow you the opportunity to interact with diverse groups of people who may not be found in large numbers within your school community.

Develop your interpersonal communication and human relations skills. These skills are important when interacting with all people; they become even more important when interaction takes place among people from diverse cultural backgrounds because their lack of familiarity and prior shared experiences can more easily lead to misinterpretation.

Work hard at being a good listener. If we make a conscious effort to listen attentively, we send others the message that they're worthy of our complete and undivided attention. This message is particularly important to send others from diverse groups because they may need greater assurance that we accept them and are truly interested in developing relationships with them.

Be aware of nonverbal messages you send while listening. Sending positive nonverbal signals when listening and speaking to members of diverse groups serves to increase their confidence about sharing personal ideas and experiences. This not only benefits those who speak to us, it also benefits us as listeners because listening to speakers who are more self-confident, and open about sharing their ideas, makes the challenging task of listening less difficult and more stimulating.

Make a genuine effort to learn and remember the names of people you meet. Refer to people by name when you greet and interact with them. Learning and remembering others' names is probably the best way to begin opening up channels for intercultural communication and potential friendships.

Show interest in people by remembering information about them. Knowing a person's identity and what interests them builds the foundation for further interaction and a deeper relationship. Pay particular attention to interests that you may have *in common* because shared interests can serve to stimulate conversations and the development of long-term friendships. Finding common interests is particularly important when interacting with people from different cultures because our differences can overshadow commonalities, causing us to overlook them.

Take a leadership role with respect to diversity. Students' experiences with diversity may present an opportunity for them to develop their leadership skills. Research shows that the most effective leaders are those who enable diverse individuals to see themselves as members of the same community, and that by advancing their community's interests, they advance their own interests (Bass & Riggio, 2005).

 **Exercise**

Don't say that about me!

Have students:

Step 1. Have future teachers select other future teachers with whom they identify and form two- to four-member groups comprised of other students who identify themselves as a member of the same group.

Step 2. Each group lists things that they never want to hear said again about their group and one thing that they would like to hear said about their group.

Step 3. In round-robin fashion, each group shares one item from both lists and continues to do so until all groups have reported all items from both lists.

Teaching for Diversity
Culturally Inclusive and Responsive Instructional Strategies

The effectiveness of diversity education depends not only on the content of the curriculum, it also depends on the *process* through which the curriculum is delivered—that is, the instructional strategies used by teachers to deliver the content. Deep, meaningful learning cannot take place without the use of teaching methods that are both student-centered and engaging.

Student-centered teaching starts with and focuses on the learner. Rather than focusing on what the teacher is covering in class, student-centered pedagogy puts the student at the center of the learning process by focusing *on the learner* and *what the learner is doing*. The goals of student-centered teaching are to (a) connect the content being taught with the experiences of the *learner*, (b) foster active student involvement in the learning *process*, and (c) promote the achievement of important student-learning *outcomes* (American College Personnel Association, 1994; Angelo, 1997; Barr & Tagg, 1995). Thus, effective student-centered pedagogy integrates student experiences into the learning process while engaging students in the process of learning (Gorski, 2010). Student-centered pedagogy also embodies the principles of democratic education because students are empowered to take an active, participatory role in the classroom and assume greater personal responsibility for their own learning (Gutmann, 1999a).

One way teachers can focus on the individual learner is through differentiated instruction which allows teachers to meet the learning needs of every student. Differentiated instruction provides students with multiple learning options so that each student can find their own meaning from the content and allows each student to express what they have learned on an individual level (Anderson, 2007; Tomlinson, 2001; 2004). The differences between a traditional classroom, differentiated classroom, and the inclusion of cultural competence in a differentiated classroom are illustrated in the following chart.

Traditional Classroom	Differentiated Classroom	*Differentiated Classroom Incorporating Cultural Competence*
Assessment takes place at the end of a unit of study	Assessment is ongoing, diagnostic, and has an influence on instruction	Assessment, instruction, classroom climate, and curricula use the strengths, interests, cultural background, home life, and real-life experiences of students to validate their individual identities
Whole class instruction	Variety of instructional strategies	Recognizes the influence of culture and utilizes cultural resources to mediate instruction
Adapted textbooks serve as the primary instructional resource	Multiple types of materials are utilized as instructional resources	Utilizes instructional resources that provide the viewpoints of all cultural and ethnic groups
Teacher is the problem solver and knowledge holder who "deposits" their knowledge to students	Students engage in problem solving, inquiry, and critical thinking	Students have an active role in all aspects of teaching and learning
Assignments have a quantitative focus	Assignments have a qualitative focus	Assignments are meaningful and purposeful to students, families and teachers

Source: Huber, J. (2010). Culturally responsive differentiated instruction. AEMP 2010 Education Forum, Los Angeles, CA. Retrieved from http://www.equityallianceatasu.org/sites/default/files/9.pdf.

FIGURE 6.1

Concept Map for Differentiating Instruction.

Source: Huber, J. (2010). Culturally responsive differentiated instruction. AEMP 2010 Education Forum, Los Angeles, CA.

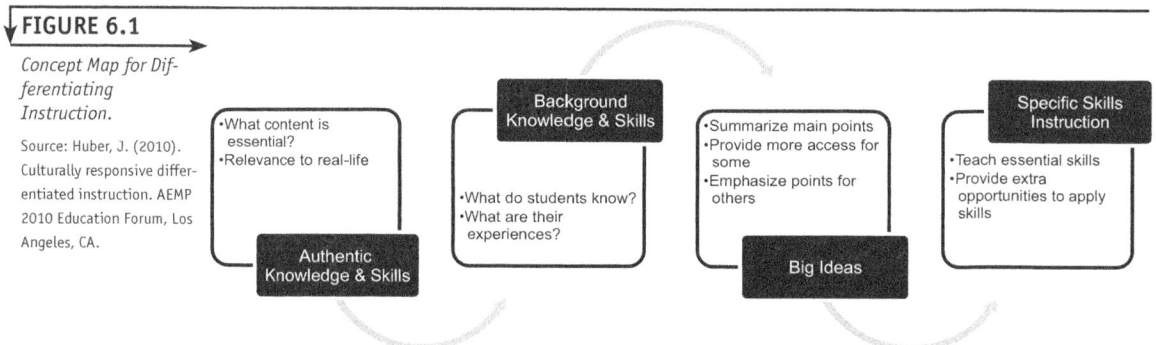

> "All aspects of teaching and learning in school must be refocused on, and rededicated to, the students themselves."
>
> —EdChange Multicultural Pavilion

Teachers have the ability to differentiate instruction based on content, process, and instructional product based on students' readiness, interests, and learning styles through a range of instructional strategies. These include: multiple intelligences, jigsaw, varied texts and supplementary materials, tiered lessons, independent study, learning contracts, varied questioning strategies, journal prompts, homework, and complex instruction (Tomlinson, 1999).

Research indicates that a key characteristic of *culturally competent* teachers is their use of student-centered teaching methods (Slavin & Madden, 2001; Tharp et al., 2000). For instance, studies show that the success of Hispanic students is compromised by instruction that does not engage them in the learning process (Haberman, 1991; Padrón & Waxman, 1993). Culturally competent teaching goes beyond exposing students to a culturally inclusive curriculum that incorporates achievements of people from diverse cultural backgrounds to also involving culturally inclusive pedagogy that enables students from diverse backgrounds to be equally engaged in the learning process.

One of the key intended outcomes of diversity education is to change students' attitudes toward cultural and group differences. Research repeatedly shows that trying to change people's attitudes or opinions by means of lectures (teacher presentations) is not effective (Bligh, 2000). After reviewing over 100 years of research on instructional strategies for producing attitude change, Bligh (2000) reached the following conclusion: "Lectures are relatively ineffective for teaching values associated with subject matter. Sermons rarely convince agnostics, but they give solidarity to the faithful. Similarly, lectures are ineffective in changing people's values, but they may reinforce those that are already accepted" (p. 12).

Furthermore, if teachers lecture to students about diversity instead of actively involving students in the learning process, they lose a golden opportunity to model the democratic process in the classroom; instead, they model an authoritarian or dictatorial approach to teaching diversity in which the lesson is dictated to students which may be viewed as suppressing students, rather than empowering them. The famous Brazilian educator, Paulo Freire, makes this point vividly in his classic book, *Pedagogy of the Oppressed (1970)*:

> *Narration (with the teacher as narrator) leads the students to memorize mechanically the narrated content. Worse yet, it turns them into "containers," into "receptacles" to be "filled" by the teacher. The more completely she fills the receptacles, the better a teacher she is. The more meekly the receptacles permit themselves to be filled, the better students they are. Education thus becomes an act of depositing, in which the students are to memorize mechanically the narrated content.*
>
> *This is the "banking" concept of education, in which the scope of action allowed to the students extends only as far as receiving, filing, and storing the deposits. In the banking concept of education, knowledge is a gift bestowed by those who consider themselves knowledgeable upon those whom they consider to know nothing. Projecting an absolute ignorance onto others, a characteristic of the ideology of oppression, negates education and knowledge as processes of inquiry. The banking concept maintains attitudes and practices, which mirror oppressive society as a whole: the teacher is the subject of the learning process, while the pupils are mere objects (pp. 71–73).*

After reviewing more than 50 research articles and reports, the Center for Strengthening the Teaching Profession (2009) identified several indicators of cultural competence and how they are demonstrated in the classroom environment.

Climate of Inclusion	➢ Students are given opportunity to provide feedback concerning expectations, standards, and evaluations ➢ Students are involved and comfortable ➢ Learning materials and classroom décor reflect the diversity of the students ➢ Cultural identity is expressed ➢ Students are grouped heterogeneously ➢ Multiple forms of assessment ➢ Environment that is safe, clean, encouraging, and welcoming ➢ Translators
Connections between Students' Prior Knowledge and Learning	➢ Journal writing ➢ Integration of home language ➢ Student engagement/participation
Rigor/High Expectations	➢ Rubrics ➢ Increasing level of classroom expectations that are communicated clearly ➢ Evidence of strong leadership in administrators and teachers ➢ Recognition of school alumni, emphasizing successes of former students ➢ Accessibility to differentiated instruction ➢ Positive behavioral supports
Classroom Practices That Are Hands-On, Cooperative, and Culturally Aligned	➢ Emphasis on human themes ➢ Democracy practiced ➢ Student choice and voice instruction ➢ Group work with roles ➢ Classroom arranged in a way that is conducive to community learning ➢ Balance of student-teacher talk ➢ Students are a part of the multicultural curriculum, combining individual learning styles while stretching their knowledge to learn other styles and contribute to the curriculum
Responsiveness Based on Cultural Knowledge of Student	➢ Multiple forms of assessment ➢ Teacher asks writing prompt questions ➢ Writing prompts are assigned in journal entries ➢ Encouragement of autobiographical writing ➢ Images displayed are positive ➢ Environment that is safe, clean, encouraging, and welcoming
Recognition of Varying Rates of Acculturation	➢ Demonstration of acceptance by teacher ➢ Absence of tokenism ➢ Use of student-driven cues ➢ Respect for privacy ➢ Encouragement of team building ➢ Use of ice-breakers ➢ Recognition of student progress and what is needed to get them where they need to be
Teacher Self-Awareness	➢ Awareness of self-identity and bias of instruction ➢ Honest ➢ Uses equitable practices ➢ Involved and engaged in children's learning ➢ Practices visual compassion and humility; not generalizing or dismissing items ➢ Encourages students to express their own cultural identity

Center for Strengthening the Teaching Profession (2009)

One way to convert the philosophy of democratic education and student-centered teaching into a practical action plan for teaching is to focus on creating three key, student-centered connections in the classroom:

1. The student-*teacher* connection: engaging student interaction with the instruction by building rapport with the class
2. The student-*subject* connection: engaging students with the subject matter through active-learning pedagogy
3. The student-*student* (peer-to-peer) connection: promoting student interaction with their peers by creating an inclusive classroom community

Consistent with the philosophy of student-centered teaching and democratic education, each of these connections begins with and centers on the student as the key agent in the learning process. These three student-connection points are used as a general framework for organizing the specific teaching strategies discussed in this chapter.

Making the Student-*Teacher* Connection:
Establishing Rapport with Your Class

Teacher-student rapport may be viewed as a precondition or prerequisite for student engagement in the learning process. If students feel comfortable relating to the teacher, they become more responsive to the teacher's attempts to engage them in the learning process. Teacher-student rapport creates a social and emotional classroom climate in which students feel comfortable and confident about interacting with their teacher and becoming actively involved with the subject matter being taught. Effective teaching goes beyond use of good teaching techniques and includes teacher characteristics and personal qualities that serve to humanize the classroom environment and promote student feelings of inclusiveness and self-worth (Jones, 1989).

On the *first day* of class, make an intentional effort to *learn students' names*. Taking some time to know students, and allowing students some time to get to know their teacher, should take place before beginning to cover curricular content. (In other words: "people before paper.") Before diving into the first lesson plan, the first item on the agenda should be to establish personal connections with students.

Learning the names of students as quickly as possible is probably the most effective way to establish early rapport with students and create a favorable first impression of the class. As an old saying goes, "You never get a second chance to make a first impression." Furthermore, learning students' names and using this knowledge to call on students by name is one way to effectively convey high expectations for students from all cultural backgrounds. As Forsyth and McMillan point out: "High expectations are communicated as teachers learn students' names and call on them by name" (1991, p. 58).

> Educators should be chosen not merely for their special qualifications, but more for their personality and their character, because we teach more by what we are than by what we teach.
>
> —Will Durant, American writer, winner of the Pulitzer Prize and Presidential Medal of Freedom, and former teacher and principal at a school designed to educate working class children

Carl Rogers, renowned humanistic psychologist, artfully expresses the value of knowing your students: "I think of it as prizing the learner. It is a caring for the learner. It is an acceptance of this other individual as a separate person, a respect for him as having worth in his own right." Said in another way, effective teachers provide students with personal validation (Rendón, 1994). When students are personally validated, they are valued as unique human beings, recognized as individuals, and feel significant—that they matter to their teacher (Schlossberg, 1989). Once they are personally validated, students are able to relate more easily and openly to the teacher, feel more comfortable about asking questions, and become more willing to seek out the teacher's advice or assistance.

Once students' names have been learned, *continually refer to students by name.* Although it is important to learn students' names as soon as possible, it is even more important to show you know who they are by using their names each time you address them.

> Is not knowing who you're talking to as bad as not knowing what you're talking about?
>
> —Dr. Benjamin DeMott, professor emeritus of English at Amherst College, literary critic, and social commentator

Personalize **the classroom experience by learning and remembering** *information about individual students.* In addition to learning each student's personal identity, teachers should learn something personal *about* each student in class. When teachers go beyond knowing who their students are to knowing something about them, it provides students with an additional dose of personal validation.

One effective way to learn more *about* students is by having them complete a *student information sheet,* whereby they respond to questions about themselves on a sheet of paper in class (Cuseo, 2004b). The student information sheet can be used on the first day of class to learn about each student's background, interests, goals, etc. It may also be used to initiate out-of-class conversations with students, which, in turn, is likely to increase their willingness to speak up in class. The student information sheet can also be a valuable tool for helping teachers identify forms of diversity that may not be clearly visible (e.g., students' family background, current living situation, and future aspirations). Teachers can also use this information to intentionally create heterogeneous learning groups of students with diverse experiences.

PERSONAL INSIGHT

One of my most successful teaching strategies is something I do on the first day of class. I ask my students to complete a "student information sheet" that includes their name and some information relating to their past experiences, future plans, personal interests, etc. I respond to the same questions that I ask my students by writing my answers on the board while they write theirs on a sheet of paper. (This allows my students to get to know me while I get to know them.) After I've collected all their information sheets, I call out the names of individual students, asking them to raise their hand when their name is called. This allows me the opportunity to associate their name and face. To help me remember their names, after I call each name I very rapidly jot down a quick word or abbreviated phrase next to the student's name for later review (e.g., something distinctive about the student's face or the specific area of the room in which the student is seated).

I save the students' information sheets and refer back to them throughout the term. For example, I record the student's name and strongest interest on a post-it note, and I stick it in my class notes near that topic.

When we get to that topic in class (which could be months later), I immediately see the student's names posted by it. When I begin to discuss the topic, I mention the name of the student who had expressed interest in it on the first day of class (e.g., "Gina, we're about to study your favorite topic."). Students really perk up when I mention their name in association with their topic of interest; plus, they're amazed by my apparent ability to remember their personal interests from the first day of class so much later in the term. Students rarely ask me about how I managed to remember their personal interests, so they're not aware of my post-it note strategy. Instead, they just think I've got extraordinary social memory and social sensitivity (which is just fine with me).

Joe Cuseo

Allow students an opportunity to *share their personal histories*. To appreciate diverse cultural experiences, we have to become aware of them. One way to do so is by asking students to write a short, autobiographical story about their personal journeys. To give students some direction and focus for this writing assignment, they could relate their personal stories to such topics as: (a) turning points in their life, (b) past experiences or decisions that they or their family has made that continue to affect their life (positively or negatively), and (c) role models or sources of inspiration in their life.

Students could share their personal histories in small, intentionally formed groups comprised of students with very different background experiences. Allowing students from a variety of backgrounds to share their personal stories may enable them to see that others have different personal journeys and experienced different challenges.

Have students bring an *artifact* to class that reflects their cultural background (e.g., food, clothing, music, art) and ask them to briefly describe its role or significance in their life. This practice represents a nonthreatening, nonverbal way to initiate discussion of students' personal stories and cultural experiences. It also creates a classroom community that reflects and respects cultural differences—which is a hallmark of effective multicultural education (National Council for the Social Studies [NCSS], 1991).

Interact with students in a *personable* and *empathic* manner. This recommendation may be implemented by the following practices:

▶ Greeting students when you enter class and when you see them on campus or in the school.
▶ Welcoming back students after a weekend or vacation break.
▶ Acknowledging the return of an absent student (e.g., "Glad to see you're back, we missed you last time.")
▶ Wishing students good luck on a forthcoming exam.
▶ Expressing concern to students who are not doing well or who've been excessively absent (e.g., "Everything okay?" "Anything I can do to help?").
▶ Acknowledging emotions expressed by students in class (e.g., "You seem excited about this topic." "I sense that you're growing tired or bored, so let's take a short break from this task.").

Provide *personalized* feedback to students. Students are more likely to attend to and respond nondefensively to feedback when it's delivered in a personalized, nonthreatening manner. Teachers may deliver personalized feedback to students by using the following strategies:

- Addressing students by name in written and spoken remarks.
- Comparing students' present performance with their previous work and noting areas of personal improvement.
- Signing their name at the end of written messages to students so that teacher feedback is delivered in a warm form that simulates a personal letter.

If it's too time-consuming for you to write a personal note to all students on every returned assignment or exam, personal notes may be written to a smaller subset of students in class (e.g., students with last names A–M); then on the following assignment, a different subgroup of students may be sent personal notes (last names M–Z).

For students struggling in class, a *personal note on returned assignments or exams* could be written that invites, requests, or requires them to see the teacher outside of class time. This written note could be reinforced by a private verbal comment before or after class. The importance of reaching out to struggling or low-achieving students is supported by research indicating these students are often the least likely to initiate or seek out extra help on their own (Knapp & Karabenick, 1988).

Consider *refraining* from using *red ink* to correct student errors on exams and assignments. No definitive line of research supports this suggestion; it is based entirely on the intuitive feeling that students may associate the color red with apprehension ("red flag" or "red alert") or humiliation ("red-faced"). Culturally competent teachers do not want their students to experience these feelings when processing teacher feedback because it's likely to cause students to react emotionally or defensively, rather than rationally and constructively. Delivering written feedback to students in a color other than red, which has such a long history of negativity, may help reduce the likelihood that students feel personally threatened by the feedback and lower the risk that it will adversely affect their self-esteem or self-efficacy.

Personally acknowledge or recognize students for their effort and participation. Be on the lookout for opportunities to compliment or reinforce students when they demonstrate motivation (e.g., thank them for their attention and involvement in class). Studies of K–12 teachers who generate the greatest gains in student achievement indicate that reinforcing effort is one of their common practices (Marzano, Pickering, & Pollock, 2001). Such recognition is an effective practice to use with all students, and it is an especially effective way to personally validate the efforts of minority students (Rendón & Garza, 1996).

Share personal examples and anecdotes that relate to class material. This practice shows students that the teacher is human—a real person with whom they can identify and emulate. Furthermore, by sharing personal experiences, teachers model honest self-disclosure, which increases the likelihood that students will do the same. It can also promote learning by encouraging students to connect class material to their personal lives.

Sharing personal anecdotes can deepen learning by providing students with real, "human" examples that concretely illustrate course concepts and bring them to life (literally). Peter Elbow (1986) eloquently articulates the advantages of teacher anecdotes:

> *We should reveal our own positions, particularly our doubts, ambivalences, and biases. We should show we are still learning, still willing to look at things in new ways, still sometimes uncertain or even stuck. We can increase the chances of our students being willing to undergo the necessary anxiety involved in change if they see we are willing to undergo it (p. 150).*

Use student *journals* as a vehicle for personalizing interaction with students and for building rapport with the class. A journal may be defined as a series of written reflections on, or reactions to, personal experiences *over an extended period of time*, which provides students with a *chronological record of their thoughts and feelings*. Journals may be assigned in the form of a: (a) *"free" journal,* whereby students have complete freedom to write about any personal issue they like; or (b) *"prompted" journal,* in which students write a response to a specific, teacher-posed prompt (e.g., "My first impression of this topic is . . ."). Students could also be given a prompt that asks them to review their previous journal entries to detect patterns of consistency or change that may have occurred over time.

If teachers respond regularly (or even periodically) to student journals, it enables them to engage in an ongoing dialogue or personal conversation with students—in writing—which strengthens teacher-student rapport. This ongoing student-teacher dialogue may take place on paper or online (e.g., an *electronic journal.*)

Maintain and express your *sense of humor*. Fear of being perceived as "unprofessional" or "losing control" of the class may inhibit some teachers from incorporating content-relevant and socially appropriate humor in the classroom. Being funny is not necessarily being frivolous. A humorous *personal anecdote* that relates to, or helps drive home, the educational point of the lesson should not be withheld from the class.

Using *cartoons* to illustrate concepts is also an effective way to use humor to engage students. A concept-relevant cartoon supplies students with a visual and an emotionally stimulating illustration that can capture their attention to what is being taught and their retention of it.

Cartoons may be easily delivered via PowerPoint slides or document cameras and projected before class begins (e.g., to capture students' attention as they enter the classroom), which can create a positive first impression of the class session and induce anticipatory interest. Cartoons may also be used to break up lengthy teacher presentations with content-relevant humor in order to sustain (or regain) student attention.

Teachers who adorn their classroom or office door with educationally relevant cartoons and witty sayings may also reduce student trepidation about interacting with them inside or outside the classroom.

Making Student-*Student* (Peer) Connections:
Promoting Peer Interaction and Creating a Sense of Community among Classmates

In addition to the student-teacher relationship, another key interpersonal connection in the classroom that can affect student learning is the relationship between students. The first few class sessions can shape students' first impression of their classmates, which, in turn, can shape their attitude toward the class. Thus, building a sense of class community among students should be among the first "topics" covered at the start of the term. Providing early opportunities for students to know their teacher and to know each other provides the social foundation on which an engaging classroom learning environment can be built.

> " Students are likely to learn more from classroom instruction when they feel accepted and valued by their teachers and peers. "
> —Cheryl Bernstein Cohen, author of *Teaching about Ethnic Diversity*

> " Tell me and I'll listen. Show me and I'll understand. Involve me and I'll learn. "
> —Teton Lakota Indian saying

Moreover, developing positive peer relations can foster the formation of interpersonal bonds and create a classroom climate within which open and honest discussion of diversity can take place. The power of diversity education lies in the *process* of enabling students to directly experience and appreciate human differences more so than it does on the content of teacher lectures about why students should appreciate human differences.

To establish an early sense of class *community*, use *icebreaker* activities to "warm up" students to each other. An effective icebreaker that may be used for this purpose is the "Classmate Scavenger Hunt." This procedure involves using information gathered from a student-information sheet (completed on the first day of class) to construct a list of statements associated with each student in class (Cuseo, 2004a). Students mill around the room and find each person in class who "matches" (belongs to) that personal statement. A key advantage of this exercise is that it enables *each student to meet and interact with every other student* in class, and it does so in a nonthreatening fashion.

"Diversity Bingo" is another popular icebreaker whose procedural steps and advantages are similar to those of the Classmate Scavenger Hunt. Each student is given a bingo game card that contains a grid of squares, with each square containing a statement or question that relates to an individual in class. Students take their bingo cards and mingle around the classroom to find the person that matches the statement.

Compared to other icebreaker activities, the key advantage of both the Classmate Scavenger Hunt and Diversity Bingo is that all students are equally and simultaneously involved—that is, at all times during the activity, all students are engaged, either asking a question of a classmate or responding a classmate's question.

Engaging Students in *Small Group* Work

Learning becomes less teacher-centered and more student-centered when the teacher steps off the stage and allows students to work in small groups. Brain imaging studies reveal that when learning takes place in the context of social interaction, greater activity takes place in thinking parts of the brain than when we learn alone (Carter, 1998). Thus, group work may be viewed as a natural, "brain compatible" form of learning (Jensen, 1998). The human brain may be biologically wired to learn socially because human interaction and collaboration have played a critical role in the survival of our species (e.g., our ancient ancestors hunted and gathered in groups).

Small group work (two to four students) allows multiple students to become equally involved in the learning process at the same time, including those who may not be assertive or aggressive enough to speak up in a larger group context. As a general rule, the level of student involvement in a group-learning situation is inversely related to the size of the group—that is, as the group's size increases, the level of individual involvement decreases. Thus, having students work in pairs (groups of two) is a particularly powerful way to involve all students in the learning process at the same time, either as a speaker or a listener. Because a group of two represents the smallest possible group size, it is the group size that provides students with the most face-to-face interaction and the opportunity for maximum involvement in the learning process. Pair work implements the effective teaching principle of "time on task," which means the more time students spend actively engaged in the learning process, the more learning takes place (McLeod, Fisher, & Hoover, 2003). As Spencer Kagan (1998) points out, when teachers make decisions about instructional practices, they should keep two key principles in mind:

- The *Equality* Principle: Will the practice allow all students to be *equally* involved?
- The *Simultaneity* Principle: Will the practice allow all students to be involved at the *same time*?

Traditional teacher-centered instructional methods for involving students, such as posing a question to the whole class, involve students *unequally* (only students who raise their hand) and *sequentially* (another student responds only after the previous student has responded). Research indicates that whole-class questioning typically involves only a small percentage of students in class—those who are willing to compete for and answer the questions posed; thus, a small minority of students tends to do the vast majority of talking (Karp & Yoels, 1976). Furthermore, the small proportion of the class that speaks up often represents those students who are the most confident, outgoing, and verbally assertive (Boyer, 1987) rather than the more reserved or reticent students who are fearful about speaking in large groups (Bowers, 1986), and underrepresented students who are less likely to be verbally active in traditional classroom settings (Astin et al., 1972; Levitz, 1992).

In contrast, pair work maximizes the involvement of all students, and it also has the practical advantage of allowing for quick and convenient group formation: students can quickly turn to the person on the right, left, front, or back without having to move their desks or move out of their desks.

When to Use Small Group Work

The positive impact of small group work may be maximized if it's strategically introduced at the following key times during a class period.

- At the *start* of class—to activate students' interest and prior knowledge. For example, a class session can begin by using a group activity known as "*active knowledge sharing.*" This practice involves providing students a *list of questions* relating to the subject matter to be covered (e.g., words to define, people to identify, or a pretest of prior knowledge). Students then pair up to answer the questions as best as they can, after which they dialogue with other pairs to compare and share answers that their original pair was unable to answer.

    Small group work may also be introduced *before* beginning a whole-class discussion. For example, students may formulate questions in small groups that are addressed in a whole class discussion following their small group work.

- *During* class—to intercept attention loss and interject active involvement at key points in a teacher's presentation. For example, after a critical point is reached during a teacher's presentation, students may work in pairs to compare notes or generate specific examples of concepts covered by the instructor.

    Small group work may also take place *after* a class discussion; for example, group members could be asked to (a) identify positions or issues that they think were overlooked during the discussion, and (b) discuss whether their viewpoints were changed or strengthened as a result of the discussion.

- At the *end* of class—to create a sense of "closure" (meaningful ending) to the class session and to consolidate student retention of key information covered in the lesson. For example, a class period may conclude with a small group task in which students work in pairs, checking each other's class notes for accuracy and completeness.

Strategies for Improving the Quality of Small Group Learning

The quality and impact of small group learning may be strengthened by use of the following strategies.

Allow students some time to gather their thoughts individually *before* they discuss them in small groups. For example, *think-pair-share* groups may be formed, whereby students are given a minute to think privately about a topic or concept before joining a partner to share their ideas. Providing students with personal reflection time prior to group discussion can enrich the quality and depth of ideas that are subsequently exchanged. Prediscussion thought time also increases the probability that shy or verbally apprehensive students will contribute their ideas, because research indicates that students who are apprehensive about communicating in classroom settings are more likely to participate in a discussion when they're given the time and opportunity to think about what they're going to say before saying it (Neer, 1987).

Have groups keep a *visible record* of the ideas they generate. If possible, provide each group with a flip chart or transparency sheet on which their ideas are to be recorded and potentially displayed. This practice serves to help keep group members "on task" by holding them accountable for creating a concrete, final product that they may be asked to share with the whole class.

Notify students that *any member* of the group may be called on to *report* their group's ideas. This serves as an incentive for all members to listen actively to the ideas shared by their teammates and conveys the message that the teacher has high expectations for all students to participate.

Have small groups come to the *front of class* to report their work (e.g., as a student panel). Asking students to present their group's work to the whole class holds them more accountable for the quality of their work because they know it will be displayed publicly. This practice may also reduce students' fear of public speaking by allowing them the opportunity to speak to a large group as a member of a small, supportive group—rather than by asking the student to deliver a stand-alone presentation in front of the whole class.

***Intentionally* form small discussion groups comprised of students from *diverse* backgrounds.** This practice implements two common recommendations cited by educational scholars for promoting critical thinking and attitude change: (a) students should be given opportunities to "collaborate and 'stretch' their understanding by encountering divergent views" (Kurfiss, 1988, p. 2), and (b) teachers should intentionally create an "atmosphere of disequilibrium [cognitive dissonance created by encountering the unfamiliar] so that students can change, rework, or reconstruct their thinking processes" (Meyers, 1986, p. 14).

One caveat should be heeded when forming small learning groups comprised of diverse students: If there are just a few students from a particular cultural group in class, students from that underrepresented group should not be spread across groups in a way that isolates them (Rosser, 1988). For instance, if there are four students of color in class, it may be tempting to place each one of them in a different learning group in order to spread their diversity across groups. However, it's more advisable to place these four students in only two groups, one pair per group, because having at least one other student of color in their group will help them feel more comfortable about expressing their minority experiences and viewpoints. In subsequent group discussions, new groups may be formed to ensure that white students who were not previously exposed to the perspective of students of color are grouped with them and experience their perspective.

Also, be sure that underrepresented students in all groups are given equal opportunity to participate. One effective procedure for doing so is by using a cooperative learning strategy called "Talking Chips" (Kagan, 1992). This procedure includes four short steps:

1. Each team member is given a symbolic "talking chip" (e.g., a checker, coin, or playing card).
2. Teammates are instructed to place the chip in the center of the team's workspace when they make an individual verbal contribution to the team's discussion.
3. Teammates can speak in any order, but they cannot speak again until all chips are in the center—an indication that every team member has spoken.
4. After all chips have been placed in the center, team members retrieve their respective chips for a second round of discussion—which follows the same rules of equal participation.

During small group discussions among students from diverse backgrounds, instruct the groups to be on the lookout for patterns of *commonality* and *unity* that accompany or transcend their differences. When students focus their attention on differences during discussions of diversity, it can divert their attention away from detecting what they all have in common. If students are not mindful of the unity that coexists with diversity, repeated discussions of diversity may inadvertently intensify or magnify group divisiveness and separatism. In fact, research indicates that when diversity education focuses on differences alone, disenfranchised groups are likely to experience feelings of further isolation and alienation (Smith, 1997).

To minimize this risk, students should be reminded that when they're discussing diversity, they're discussing variations on a common theme—their shared humanity. While students explore their diversity, they should also be encouraged to dig below the surface of their cultural differences to uncover their deeper commonalities—the universal experiences that unite them both as citizens of the same country and as members of the same species. To best promote this process of appreciating both their diversity and their shared humanity, it may be more effective to instruct students to begin their diversity discussions by identifying their commonalities—*before* they launch into discussion of their differences. For example, before beginning a discussion of cultural differences, students might first discuss the common elements of all cultures (e.g., language, family, artistic expression, rituals). Initially identifying their similarities can help defuse initial defensiveness and divisiveness by providing students with common ground on which to build an open and honest discussion of diversity.

Students can build a solid foundation of commonality by identifying universal human themes, such as common dimensions of human cultures (e.g., those

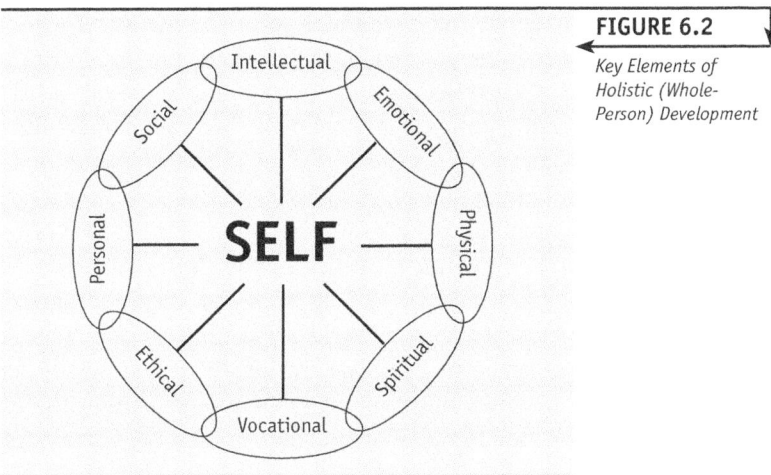

FIGURE 6.2

Key Elements of Holistic (Whole-Person) Development

identified on p. 8), or common dimensions of holistic (whole-person development)—such as those depicted in **Figure 6.2.**

The following instructional strategies may also be especially effective for realizing the twin objectives of helping students appreciate human differences (diversity) and embrace human commonalities (humanity).

- Form *homogeneous* groups of students who share similar demographic characteristics (e.g., same-gender groups or same-race/ethnicity groups) and have them share their personal views or experiences with respect to a diversity-related issue (e.g., prejudice or discrimination). Ask each group to record its main ideas in writing and form a panel to report their group's ideas and field questions from other students in class. During the panel report and discussion, the teacher can serve as panel moderator whose role is to highlight the common themes and variations on those themes that emerge across different the separate groups.
- Create *heterogeneous* discussion groups of students with different demographic characteristics. At the conclusion of these discussions, build in reflection time for students to think about examples of both diversity and unity that emerged during the group process. Reflection following discussion gives the brain time to "process" ideas that it was exposed to during the discussion and promotes storage of those ideas in students' long-term memory (Rosenshine, 1997). This practice implements the following standard for effective multicultural education identified by the National Council for the Social Studies (1991): "Does the curriculum help students participate in cross-ethnic and cross-cultural experiences and reflect upon them?" (p. 39).

To ensure reflection after participating in diversity-related discussions, students could be asked to write a one-minute paper that asks them to take a minute to write about the similarities and differences in the ideas or experiences reported by diverse members of their discussion group. For example, students could write reflections to such questions as: (a) What major *differences* in perspectives did you detect among group members during your discussion? (b) What major *similarities* in viewpoints or background experiences did all group members share? (c) What particular topics or issues raised during your discussion seemed most important to *all* members of your group?

▸ Form *heterogeneous* groups of students who differ with respect to a demographic characteristic and are *homogeneous* with respect to another characteristic (e.g., students of the same gender who differ with respect to their race, ethnicity, or socioeconomic status). This practice increases student awareness that members of different ethnic or racial groups can, at the same time, be members of the same group—who share common experiences, needs, and concerns.

Occasionally structure small group work so that it moves beyond discussion to *collaboration*. The critical feature that distinguishes discussion groups from collaborative learning groups is that the latter do not simply generate ideas; instead, they go a step farther and try to reach *consensus* or a *unified group decision* about the ideas they generate. The key to converting a discussion group into a collaborative group is to choose an action verb for the group task that signals to students that they are to make a *group decision* about the ideas they generate. For example, rather than simply asking students to "list" their ideas, a collaborative group may be asked to *categorize* or *prioritize* their ideas—which asks group members to come together and reach a united and unitary group decision.

Transform group work into true *teamwork* by implementing the key procedural features of *cooperative learning*. Cooperative learning may be defined as a structured form of collaborative learning that converts group work into teamwork by having group members work toward the same, common goal (encouraging collective responsibility) while assuming specific roles that are complementary (ensuring *interdependence*) and identifiable (ensuring individual accountability); the role of the teacher during the cooperative learning is to serve as a roving *facilitator, coach,* or *consultant* to the learning groups (Cuseo, 1992; Johnson, Johnson, & Smith, 1991; Slavin, 1990).

More specifically, cooperative learning methods are designed to foster teamwork by implementing and incorporating the following seven procedural features into the group experience.

1. *Positive interdependence* among team members (social responsibility)—for example, students assume complementary roles and submit a single, jointly created work product.
2. *Individual accountability* (personal responsibility)—for example, as the group conducts its work, each group member has a clearly defined role and contribution to make to the team's final product.

3. *Intentional team formation*—for example, students from diverse backgrounds are placed on the same team.
4. *Intentional team building*—for example, students engage in an icebreaker activity and develop a team identity that helps them build an esprit de corps prior to engaging in the work task.
5. Students are prepared for teamwork by receiving explicit instruction on how to make effective teams work (e.g., students are instructed on what it means to work collaboratively, disagree constructively, and achieve consensus).
6. The teacher assumes an active role during the group learning process, functioning as a *coach and consultant* during the learning process—for example, roaming the room, troubleshooting problems, encouraging effort, and recognizing/reinforcing instances of effective teamwork.
7. Students "*process*" (reflect on) the quality of their teamwork after the learning task is completed—for example, each member assesses how well the group worked as a team and the quality of their personal contributions to the team.

When the seven procedural features are incorporated into small group work, research indicates that students experience significantly greater gains in cognitive, social, and emotional development (Johnson & Johnson, 1989; Slavin, 1990). For instance, one practice employed by effective K–12 teachers who've been found to promote the largest gains in student achievement is the use of cooperative learning procedures that supply students with a defined purpose or role to play in the group-learning process (Marzano, Pickering, & Pollock, 2001). There is also evidence that cooperative learning methods are especially effective for elevating the academic achievement of Hispanic and African American students (Aronson & Gonzalez, 1988; Posner & Markstein, 1994).

Moreover, when teachers use cooperative learning to create diverse learning teams, they access and harness the educational power of diversity by enabling students to experience different perspectives within the supportive context of a small, collaborative group of peers working together toward a common goal. Thus, cooperative learning capitalizes on student diversity found in the classroom and utilizes it as a social resource for diversity education (Gorski, 2010).

> *"The multicultural curriculum should help students develop the skills necessary for effective interpersonal, interethnic, and intercultural group interactions."*
> —National Council for the Social Sciences

Making the Student-*Course* (Subject) Connection:
Engaging Students with the Subject Matter

Project REACH (Respecting Ethnic and Cultural Heritage) is a successful multicultural education program which currently includes more than 60,000 students and hundreds of teachers in 12 states in the subject matter of middle school social studies. The project is based on four phases:

1. **Human Relation Skills.** Students participate in activities focused on self-awareness, self-esteem, interpersonal communication, and understanding group dynamics.
2. **Cultural Self-Awareness.** Students research their family history, community, and personal culture.
3. **Multicultural Awareness.** Students utilize American history textbooks that incorporate a multicultural viewpoint.
4. **Cross-Cultural Experience.** Textbook material is personalized through discussion among students and adults from differing ethnic groups.

Research indicates that when students are exposed to engaging teaching methods in the classroom, they experience significant gains in academic achievement; this is particularly true for ethnic minority students (Wiggan, 2008). Unfortunately, research also indicates that students are reporting higher levels of *academic disengagement* in school—they frequently report feeling bored in class, missing class, and spending little time on their studies outside of class (Sax et al., 1997; Sax et al., 2005). One characteristic of instructors who are perceived to be "outstanding teachers" is that they "strive to make courses interesting" (Davis, Wood, & Wilson, 1983). These findings underscore the importance of teaching methods that motivate students to learn.

The following research-based practices are recommended as teaching strategies for combating academic disengagement and stimulating students' intrinsic interest in learning.

Frequently interject thought-provoking questions during class presentations to promote student involvement in the learning process. Research indicates that frequent use of questions is a characteristic of teachers whose students make the greatest gains in academic achievement (Rosenshine, 1971; Rosenshine & Stevens, 1986). Questions create temporary states of doubt or puzzlement in students' minds that can motivate them to resolve the doubt and seek answers. Also, when teachers ask thought-provoking questions, they model intellectual curiosity and reflective inquiry that their students can emulate.

Careful forethought should be given to the type of questions posed to students because not all questions are equally effective in triggering student involvement. How a question is framed or phrased often determines whether it will successfully stimulate student involvement. As one instructional development specialist suggests: "You must highlight them [questions] in your outline. You should know *exactly* what questions, word for word, you are going to ask" (Welty, 1989, p. 42).

The types of questions that are most likely to trigger student involvement are summarized in **Box 6.1.**

Box 6.1 Questions That Most Effectively Elicit Student Involvement

- *Open-ended* questions that have more than one correct or acceptable answer. Such questions invite multiple responses, welcome a diversity of perspectives, and encourage *divergent* thinking—expansive thinking that does not force students to "converge" on one (and only one) correct answer (Cuseo, 2005).
- *Conditionally phrased* questions (e.g., "What *might* be . . . " "What *could* be . . . ?" "What *may* be . . . ?"), with tentative phrasing, send students a clear verbal signal that a diversity of answers is possible and acceptable. This encourages students to think creatively and reduces their fear or embarrassment about giving "the" correct answer or the specific answer the teacher (authority figure) is "looking for." When students are asked a factual question for which there is one and only one correct answer, it means that there's a limitless number of incorrect answers that can be given to it. Consequently, students are less likely to volunteer an answer to such questions because the odds of being right are clearly not in their favor.
- *Higher-order thinking* questions that ask students to think at a level higher than rote recall of factual information. For example, questions that call for:
  a. critical thinking (e.g., What do you think are the strengths and weakness of this idea?), or
  b. creative thinking (e.g., What may be another way to look or interpret this issue?)
- *Focused* questions that are clearly tied to (focus on) a specific concept or issue. "Does anybody have any questions or comments this time?" is an unfocused question because it isn't anchored or tied to any particular point or idea. In contrast, "What might be possible causes of prejudice?" is a focused question that's more likely to elicit student responses.
- *Personalized* questions that situate students in a relevant, real-life situation and ask them how they would respond in this situation. For instance, if the topic under discussion is test-taking skills, students could be asked the following question: "Suppose you were about to take a test and you experience memory block for something you know you studied. What might you try doing to overcome the block and trigger your memory?" Questions like this implement the principle of "situated learning"—the principle that learning is more likely to take place when students are placed or situated in a real-life context (Bransford, Brown, & Cocking, 1999) which encourages them to *apply* the concept being learned to their personal lives.
- Questions that invite responses from a *student group*, particularly a group whose ideas have yet to be heard. For example, "I haven't heard the perspective of females on this issue. May I ask some of the ladies in class to share their ideas?"
- Questions that call for *all* students to respond *nonverbally*.
  For example, students can respond with a simple show of hands to a question such as: "How many of you agree with the following statement . . . ?" or "How many of you had an experience similar to . . . ?" Other ways in which students can respond nonverbally include:
  a. Have students *vote with their feet* on an issue by moving to one of four *corners* of the room, with each corner representing one of four options: "strongly agree," "agree," "disagree," or "strongly disagree";
  b. Ask students to *move to either side of the room* depending on where they stand (literally) with respect to a debatable point or issue. (The center aisle may be used as "middle ground" where students may stand if they're unsure or think they need more information before deciding.) For example, ask students where they stand on the issue of whether or not schools should have a dress code.
  c. Supply students with "clickers" (classroom response systems) that allow them to anonymously choose an answer to a multiple choice question and use computer technology to calculate and project the percentages of students choosing each option.

When students are asked to respond nonverbally, all students are able to get involved at the same time—not just the most verbally assertive students who answer faster (or louder) than their classmates. Nonverbal exercises can also serve as a stimulus to trigger subsequent discussion. For instance, students could be asked *why* they ended up occupying a particular place or space in the first place. After students have discussed the reason behind their position, the class may be given an opportunity to change their positions if ideas expressed during the class discussion caused them to change their mind; students could then be asked why they changed their mind (position). Once students have responded nonverbally to a question, it gets their thinking going and can generate mental and motivational momentum that moves them to respond verbally as well.

When making an instructional presentation (teacher talk), intersperse student-involvement activities at three key junctures: *before*, *during*, **and** *after* **the presentation.** It may be useful to conceive of teacher presentations in terms of three distinct segments or stages: *beginning, middle,* and *end*. An effective *learning sequence* can then be created by intentionally planning to engage students at each of these three key times:

1. at the *start* of the presentation—to "warm up" and *activate* students' preexisting ideas about the topic;
2. *during* the presentation—to "break up" or *punctuate* teacher-delivered information with activities that involve students; and
3. *after* the presentation—to "wrap up" and *consolidate* the information that was presented by having students reflect on it and connect with it (i.e., relate it to their personal life).

Listed next are specific strategies for involving students at each of these three stages in the learning sequence.

Pre-Presentation Strategies: involve students *before* the presentation by activating their preexisting feelings, attitudes, or knowledge (and misconceptions) about the to-be-presented information. Any of the following practices may be used for this purpose. For example, before a presentation on diversity, ask students to jot down the ideas that come to their mind when they hear the world "diversity."

- *Pre-Tests:* give students a short, nongraded assessment of their knowledge or skills with respect to the upcoming topic (e.g., a short series of true-false questions).
- *Background Knowledge Probes:* asking students to jot down what they already know (or think they know) about an upcoming topic and how they got to know it (i.e., the source of their knowledge) (Angelo & Cross, 1993).
- *Background Interest Probes:* students are asked what they would like to know about the upcoming topic or what questions they would like answered about it (Cross & Angelo, 1989).
- *Verbal "Whips":* in rapid succession, students take turns verbalizing the first thought that comes to mind in response to the topic that's about to be covered in class.
- *Shared Presentation:* students first share what they think they know about the day's topic and record their ideas on the board. After students have shared all their ideas, the teacher acknowledges the good ideas that students have already mentioned (e.g., by underlining them on the board), then adds his or her own ideas to create a jointly produced composite, or "master," list that represents the collaborative effort of both the students and their teacher.

These pre-presentation practices draw students into the learning process by drawing out their prior knowledge and misconceptions about the topic to be covered. They also implement a teaching practice that has been found to promote significant gains in student achievement: activating students' prior knowledge and experiences before beginning a lesson, and using this information during the lesson (Marzano, Pickering, & Pollock, 2001).

Within-Presentation Strategies: during a presentation, pause for students to engage in an active-learning exercise with respect to the information that's been presented thus far. This practice serves to interrupt or intercept the attention loss that normally occurs when students listen to teacher-delivered information for a stretch of time (Bligh, 2000). Research on effective teachers reveals that one practice they use is to teach new material in small steps to break it into small pieces or parts, and immediately after each part is taught, students are given the opportunity to respond to it or practice it (Rosenshine & Stevens, 1986). It's been found that if teachers pause periodically during a presentation to allow students a minute or two to reflect and discuss the concept being taught, they are more likely to recall that concept when tested on it at a later point in time (Ruhl, Hughes, & Schloss, 1987).

Any of the following strategies may be used to punctuate teacher presentations with activities that engage students in the learning process.

- *Pauses for Reflection:* students write a short, reflective response to a focused question designed to promote higher-level thinking about the material presented.
- *"Writing-to-Discuss" Exercises:* students engage in a short, thought-provoking writing exercise and then they use their written responses as a springboard for class discussion. This is not only an effective way to break up teacher talk time, it also enhances the quality of class discussions because students had time to think through their thoughts (and capture them in writing) before expressing them orally. Writing before discussing may be an especially effective practice for promoting the involvement of students whose cultural backgrounds encourage them not to speak out spontaneously in the presence of adult authority figures, such as teachers.
- *Problem-Solving Presentations:* students listen to a series of short presentations (e.g., 5 to 10 minutes) that includes a succession of focused problems, each of which is followed by student discussion of possible solutions to the problem (Bonwell & Eison, 1991). This strategy can be used throughout an entire class period by alternating between teacher "mini-presentations" on thought-provoking problems followed by a student discussion on how best to solve or resolve the problem.

Infusing pauses for student involvement periodically throughout a class period also implements a teaching practice that has been found to promote high gains in student achievement: *providing all students with frequent opportunities for active practice* (Rosenshine, 1971; Rosenshine & Stevens, 1986). Effective teachers provide opportunities for all students to respond and check their understanding before moving on to the next concept (Rosenshine, 1997). In contrast, less effective teachers tend to ask the class a question about what was covered, call on a student who raises his or her hand and answers it (often correctly because it's likely to be a student who "got it"), and then moves on to teach the next segment of the lesson.

Post-Presentation Strategies: following a teacher presentation, students engage in activities that require *retrospection* (reflective review) and *consolidation* (registration) of ideas they acquired during the presentation.

The *one-minute paper* is an effective tool for promoting student reflection following teacher presentations. A one-minute paper may be defined as a short, informal writing exercise (taking one minute or less to complete) that's designed to prompt each student to reflect on the day's lesson. Any of the following questions may serve as the stimulus or prompt for one-minute papers:

- What do you think was the major *purpose or objective* of today's class?
- What do you think was the most *important* point discussed today?
- Without looking at your notes, what *stands out in your mind* (or what do you *recall most vividly*) about today's class?
- Looking back at your notes, what would you say was the *most interesting* idea or *most useful* strategy discussed in today's class?
- Could you relate *personally* to anything discussed in today's class?
- Did you see any *connections* between what was discussed in class today and what's been covered in any of our *other classes*?
- What was the most *surprising* or *unexpected* idea you encountered in today's class?
- What do you think was the most *puzzling, confusing, or disturbing* idea covered in class today?
- What *helped* (or *hindered*) your understanding of today's presentation?
- During today's class, what idea(s) struck you as things that you could use *immediately*?
- Do you see any way in which the material discussed in today's class *relates to your current or future life*?

Use *Writing-To-Learn* Exercises to Engage Students with the Subject Matter

Students can become actively involved with the subject matter by writing about it. Writing in school doesn't always have to involve formal assignments, such as essays and reports, it can also take the form of a variety of "writing-to-learn" activities that differ from formal writing assignments in three major ways: (a) they're shorter, requiring less amount of student time to complete; (b) they're written primarily for the benefit of the writer—as an aid to thinking and learning; and (c) they don't require extensive teacher commentary, correction, or grading (Tchudi,

1986). These characteristics of writing-to-learn exercises allow them to be used flexibly as in-class activities.

Writing-to-learn activities are particularly well-suited for younger students and English-as-a-second-language (ESL) students because they require less writing experience and skill refinement than do formal writing assignments.

> **Consider This . . .**
>
> Students still benefit cognitively when they write to learn, even if they're still learning to write.

One-minute papers qualify as a writing-to-learn exercise that can be conveniently used to engage students in the classroom. Another efficient writing-to-learn exercise is *freewriting*, whereby students quickly record their thoughts, feelings, or free associations on a topic without worrying about their writing mechanics such as punctuation or spelling.

A writing-to-learn strategy that can be over an extended period of time are *learning logs*, in which students keep an ongoing record of their learning experiences. For instance, students can write regular entries in their learning log about (a) what they're learning that's most significant or useful, (b) how they're going about learning it (their learning habits or strategies), and (c) how they feel about it (e.g., their level of interest or boredom with respect to a particular topic).

Involve students in role playing exercises. Role plays may be defined as *dramatic enactments* of scenarios involving characters with whom students can identify. Drama can serve as a powerful stimulus for engaging students as both actors in a skit and as reactors to a skit. Students can play the role of themselves, or they can take on the role of different people to gain different perspectives (e.g., a majority student plays the role of a minority student). Student actors can also be asked to reverse roles during the skit to gain a more balanced perspective.

> *" Role playing of various ethnic and cultural experiences should be interspersed throughout the curriculum to encourage understanding of what it means to belong to various ethnic groups. "*
> —National Council on the Social Studies (1991)

Role plays are more effective than teacher presentations for promoting empathy and attitude change, particularly with respect to diversity-related issues. Having someone assume the role of a blind person by wearing a blindfold for an extended period of time is much more likely to promote empathy for the visually handicapped than a teacher's lecture on the subject.

One way to get the entire class involved in a role play is to have all students assume the same role. For example, the class could serve as members of an advisory committee or a group of experts, while the teacher adopts the role of learner (Erickson & Strommer, 1991). For example, the teacher assumes the role of a new international student who has just immigrated to this country and the class serves as an advisory committee of American citizens whose role is to help the recent immigrant prepare for a citizenship test by learning the essentials of American history and its governmental system.

Scripts. Similar to role plays, scripts actively involve students in dramatic scenarios; the only difference is that the characters *read* their parts. Students take on different characters in a script, or they may be asked to improvise and complete an unfinished script as if they were one of the characters.

Simulations. These are reality-based exercises that actively engage or immerse students in an environment that simulates (approximates) a real-life experience. For instance, *BaFa'-BaFa'* is a popular intercultural simulation that has students assume membership in either the Alpha or Beta culture, each with its own set of cultural values, expectations, customs, and language. Members of each "culture" visit, observe, and interact with members of the other ("foreign") culture, thereby simulating the experience of what it's like to try to fit in and function effectively in a culture that differs radically from one's own. The intended learning outcomes of this simulation is reduction of ethnocentrism and promotion of empathy for those who must adapt to, and become assimilated into, an unfamiliar culture (e.g., an immigrant).

Case Studies. Cases or case studies are actual events or fictional scenarios that closely approximate real-life events that require students to reach a decision about how to handle a problem, or resolve an issue or dilemma, for which there is no single "correct" answer or solution (Christensen & Hansen, 1987). Cases are typically presented in written form, and students read them individually before joining teams to discuss what the best option is for solving the problem presented in the case.

Cases demonstrate to students that attempting to solve real-life problems is often a "messy" or ambiguous process that involves multiple alternatives and potential solution strategies. Cases also stimulate student motivation because they engage students in the learning process because they require them to take action and make a decision.

"Good case studies promote empathy with the central characters; students can see themselves in the situation or story" (Erickson & Strommer, 2005, p. 252).

Listed here are examples of cases relevant to diversity education.

> By providing students with opportunities to use decision-making abilities and social action skills in the resolution of problems affecting ethnic, racial and cultural groups, schools can contribute to more effective education for democratic citizenship.
> —National Council on the Social Studies (1991)

- News items relating to human rights issues drawn from national media (TV, movies, or newspaper articles)
- Instances of intergroup conflict that have taken place on campus, in the school or in the local community
- Educational documentaries that poignantly capture the experiences of people who have encountered prejudice or discrimination
- Actual events that the teacher has experienced or observed—both personally and professionally
- Experiences solicited from students in class—for example, prejudice experienced or witnessed themselves, their friends, or their family members have encountered or witnessed.

Student discussions of cases can be given more structure or focus by posing open-ended questions that ask students to think about:

- the likely cause(s) of the incident,
- if and how it could have been prevented,
- whether students can identify with any characters involved in it, or
- whether students have had personal experiences similar to those being depicted in the case.

Meyers and Jones (1993) suggest that the following types of questions—based on approaches taken by prominent case-study educators—can be used to promote higher-level thinking in response to cases and other problem-based tasks.

- *Implication* questions (e.g., "If events like this continue, what might be the consequences?")
- *Analytical/Evaluative* questions (e.g., "What particular action is at the root of this problem? Which action played the most pivotal role?")
- *Predictive/Hypothetical* questions (e.g., "If the roles of the main characters were switched, what would have happened?")

Providing students with opportunities to predict and test hypotheses about causes and effects is an effective teaching practice that is associated with significant gains in student achievement (Marzano, Pickering, & Pollock, 2001).

Whenever possible, allow students the opportunity to make *personal choices* about what they will learn. When students from any cultural background are allowed to make their own educational choices, it improves their sense of control of the learning process and their intrinsic interest in learning (Ginsberg & Wlodkowski, 2009). Thus, whenever possible, allow students to choose what they will learn and how they will learn it. For example, students may be given a *topic "menu"* of topics from which they may choose to read or write about the topic that most interests them. Members of diverse student groups who opt for the same topic could be grouped together to complete a team project on their topic of common interest.

At the start of class sessions, present a *prompt* that grabs student attention and stimulates anticipatory interest in the day's topic. An evocative visual stimulus can be an especially effective way to "set the stage" and initially capture student attention at the very *start* of class or a new unit of instruction. This can create a sense *of positive anticipation* or a positive "anticipatory set" (a state of heightened curiosity or favorable expectation) about the upcoming learning experience (Hunter, 1994). The following prompts may be used for this purpose:

- a thought-provoking *quote* (e.g., a "classic quote" chosen from a famous or influential person)
- a provocative *passage* (e.g., poignant paragraph or short poem)
- a powerful *picture* or *image* (e.g., of a hate crime)
- an engaging *video vignette* (e.g., from a popular movie)

▶ an intriguing *artifact* (e.g., relevant historical or cultural object)
▶ a topic-relevant *cartoon* (e.g., one that visually depicts or drives home a point about the topic being covered)

Concepts are better remembered if their verbal presentation is accompanied by a visual image (Paivio, 1990). Research on K–12 teachers who generate the greatest gains in student achievement reveals that one of their common practices is using "nonlinguistic representations," which are visual representations of concepts that they teach in class (Marzano, Pickering, & Pollock, 2001).

The power of visual memory may be traced to the critical role that the sense of vision played in the early survival of the human species—for example, visually recalling where food and shelter were located. Humans relied on vision to process information long before they could speak or write; thus, the human brain may be innately wired for better visual than verbal memory (Milner & Goodale, 1995). This may be one reason why we remember faces better than names.

Induce *surprise or incredulity* among students by confronting them with paradoxes, incongruities, counterintuitive findings, or controversial ideas. Class may be started with a statement that contradicts logic or common belief; for example: "Memorizing information is not the best way to learn it" or "People don't work better under pressure!" Erickson and Strommer (1991) point out that interesting teacher presentations "open with a problem, question, quandary, or dilemma. Or they start with something students take for granted and confront them with information or observations indicating things are not so obvious or certain as they initially appear. Or they present a list of incongruous facts or statistics and ask, 'How can this be?'" (p. 98).

End **class with an** ***unanswered*** **question or** ***unresolved issue, a dilemma that builds positive anticipation for the next class session.*** This strategy serves to stimulate student interest in the same way that a TV sequel concludes an episode with an uncertain ending, which motivates viewers to view the next episode.

Use popular *games* to stimulate student interest and involvement in learning factual information. Games can be an engaging method for delivering factual material to students in a way that's more engaging than stand-and-deliver teacher presentations. Game formats can be used that are similar to those seen in TV game shows, such as "Jeopardy" or "Family Feud." Learning teams can be created to generate further excitement by fostering friendly competition between teams and collaboration within teams.

The "Who Wants to Be a Millionaire?" game format is ideal for involving all students in class. Students may volunteer to be contestants, or they may compete to be contestants by being the first to give a correct answer to a "toss up" question. The student participating as a contestant can use the game's "lifeline" supports to involve other members of the class, such as "poll the audience" (show of hands) or "phone a friend" (ask another student in class).

Incentives for becoming a contestant can be created by awarding participating students prizes that vary in value—depending on the number or complexity of the questions they answer correctly (e.g., gift certificates of varying value). The teacher can assume the role of game show moderator and make periodic instructional contributions by adding a few informative or explanatory comments after a contestant provides a correct or incorrect answer, thereby enabling collateral learning to take place as the game proceeds.

Understand that individual students may have different learning styles, the way in which they prefer to perceive and process information. Some students may prefer to take in information by reading about it, listening to it, seeing an image or diagram of it, or physically touching and manipulating it. Students may also vary in terms of whether they like to receive information in a form that is very structured and orderly, or in an unstructured form that allows them the freedom to explore, play with, and restructure it in their own way. Once information has been received, students may also differ in terms of how they prefer to process or deal with it. Some might like to think about it on their own, whereas others may prefer to talk about it with someone else, make an outline of it, or draw a picture of it.

Expose students to a variety of instructional methods and classroom learning experiences. Instructor delivery of factual information may be made more engaging by varying:

a. instructional *formats* (e.g., short teacher presentations, whole-class discussions, small group discussions, paired peer interactions, self-reflection exercises, cases, role plays, simulations, panels, guest speakers), or
b. instructional *modalities or media* (e.g., accompanying verbal information with projections of visual images—such as pictures and photos—or visual movement—films, DVDs, or YouTube videos).

Changes in learning formats and modalities produce changes in routine that sustain student attention by providing students with different sources of sensory and psychomotor stimulation. Such variations in sensory and postural stimulation induce changes in students' internal state of arousal, which serve to combat the attention loss that typically takes place when humans are repeatedly exposed to the same stimulus conditions (McGuinness & Pribram, 1980).

Diversifying instructional methods also helps teachers accommodate differences in students' learning styles. It's unrealistic to expect a teacher to accommodate the individual learning styles of all students at all times. However, if a teacher periodically varies instructional formats and learning modalities, it allows every student in class to periodically experience an instructional format that most closely matches their preferred learning style (Erickson & Strommer, 2005).

Some research suggests that different learning styles tend to be associated with different cultural backgrounds. Thus, by varying instructional formats and modalities of instruction to accommodate different learning styles among students from different cultural, ethnic, and gender groups, teachers are implementing "equity pedagogy" (Banks & Banks, 1995)—that is, culturally responsive or culturally inclusive pedagogy.

Highlight the *relevance* and *usefulness* of the material that students are being asked to learn. Students demonstrate higher levels of academic achievement when they perceive the material they're learning to be personally useful (Jones & Watson, 1990). Students are also more likely to engage in higher-level thinking about academic material they perceive as relevant (Roueche & Comstock, 1981).

The following practices are suggested for enhancing the personal and practical relevance of material being taught, thereby increasing students' level of engagement with the material.

- When introducing a topic, share with students *why* the topic is relevant to their lives. Identifying student learning goals or outcomes at the beginning of an instructional unit is a teaching practice that has been found to result in greater gains in student achievement (Marzano, Pickering, & Pollock, 2001). Setting learning goals at the outset of a lesson sets the stage for students to see the relevance of the lesson's topic to their current or future life, which in turn, will increase their motivation to learn it (Ginsberg & Wlodkowski, 2009).
- Use ideas, comments, and questions that *students bring up in class,* or that they choose to *write about* in papers and journals, to help guide selection of teaching examples and illustrations. Teachers should consider keeping a "teaching journal" and review it to identify trends or patterns in course topics that trigger the most student interest. If certain topics seem to hold student attention and generate numerous questions, make note of them and incorporate them into your future class presentations, or use them as focus points for future class discussions.
- Ask students to draw from their own experiences to *provide examples* of concepts being taught in class.
- Facilitate learning of abstract concepts by asking students to *apply* them to a situation or context relevant to their current life (e.g., "How might you apply this idea to what you're currently experiencing at home or in your local community?").
- After finishing a class topic or instructional unit, seek student *feedback* on its usefulness or relevance (e.g., after the unit is completed, ask them to provide feedback in the form of a one-minute paper).

Accompany each class exercise and assignment with a clear *rationale* that articulates *why* they're being asked to complete it. Taking just a little time to justify assignments by clearly pointing out its current or future value to students will help them become more enthused about completing it and less prone to perceive the work as "busy work" or "pointless homework."

Highlight the social relevance of concepts by relating them to *current events*. The following practices are strategies for implementing this recommendation.

- Illustrate concepts and principles by using examples from *popular media* (TV, movies, etc.). Students could be asked to identify their favorite programs or movies, or what they like to read (either online or in print). This information can provide the teacher with insight into students' special interests and provide additional ideas for illustrating course concepts in ways that connect with students' current life experiences. Students may also be encouraged to write letters of protest to popular media outlets that promote racial or cultural stereotypes, thereby raising students' consciousness and social activism with respect to these issues.
- Be alert to newsworthy events occurring *at school* and in the *local community* (e.g., events reported in the local school newspaper). Using late-breaking, news-making information in class highlights the contemporary relevance of what is being taught in the classroom, and it also models for students the value of keeping up with current events and relating classroom learning to "real life." A document camera may be used to conveniently project headlines and stories from the daily newspaper that relate to the day's lesson.

Engage Students in *Future Life-Planning* Assignments

Students can be engaged in thinking about their future by connecting their current learning experience with their future goals and life plans. Research on minority college students indicates that they are more likely to persist to graduation if they're given frequent opportunities to connect their current academic experience with their future career goals (Richardson, 1989). Students may be asked to develop a long-range, personal growth or life success plan that goes beyond educational and vocational goals to include *personal development* goals (e.g., goals relating to social, emotional, physical, and/or spiritual dimensions of self-development).

Such assignments encourage students to adopt a future-oriented perspective and to make meaningful connections between where they are now in life and where they want to go in life. This encourages goal setting and goal-directed behavior, which has been found to increase personal motivation and commitment (Boekaerts, Pintrich, & Zeidner, 2000; Locke & Latham, 1990).

Summary and Conclusion

Student-centered pedagogy is the essence of good teaching. It puts the student at the center of the learning process by focusing *on the learner* and *what the learner is doing*. The goals of student-centered teaching are to (a) connect the content being taught with the experiences of the *learner,* (b) foster active student involvement in the learning *process,* and (c) promote the achievement of important student-learning *outcomes*. Classroom engagement is important for the teacher and student and provides the foundation for lifelong learning.

NAME _____ DATE _____

Exercise

Self-Assessment of Cultural Competence

This exercise is designed for you to self-assess and then develop an action plan to assist you as a teacher. Please be honest in your answers. As a member of the teaching profession, the knowledge you have of yourself and others is important and reflected in the ways you communicate and interact. This individual assessment instrument was developed to assist you in reflecting upon and examining your journey toward cultural competence.

The following statements are about you and your cultural beliefs and values as they relate to the organization. Please check the ONE answer that BEST DESCRIBES your response to each of the statements.

Individual Assessment	Almost Always	Often	Some-times	Almost Never
1. I reflect on and examine my own cultural background, biases, and prejudices related to race, culture, and sexual orientation that may influence my behaviors.	☐	☐	☐	☐
2. I continue to learn about the cultures of the consumers and families served in the program, in particular attitudes toward disability; cultural beliefs and values; and health, spiritual, and religious practices.	☐	☐	☐	☐
3. I recognize and accept that the consumer and family members make the ultimate decisions even though they may be different compared to my personal and professional values and beliefs.	☐	☐	☐	☐
4. I intervene, in an appropriate manner, when I observe other staff engaging in behaviors that appear culturally insensitive or reflect prejudice.	☐	☐	☐	☐
5. I attempt to learn and use key words and colloquialisms of the languages used by the consumers and families served.	☐	☐	☐	☐
6. I utilize interpreters for the assessment of consumers and their families whose spoken language is one for which I am not fluent.	☐	☐	☐	☐
7. I have developed skills to utilize an interpreter effectively.	☐	☐	☐	☐
8. I utilize methods of communication, including written, verbal, pictures, and diagrams, that will be most helpful to the consumers, families, and other program participants.	☐	☐	☐	☐
9. I write reports or any form of written communication, in a style, and at a level which consumers, families, and other program participants will understand.	☐	☐	☐	☐
10. I am flexible, adaptive, and will initiate changes, which will better serve consumers, families, and other program participants from diverse cultures.	☐	☐	☐	☐
11. I am mindful of cultural factors that may be influencing the behaviors of consumers, families, and other program participants.	☐	☐	☐	☐

Developed by the AUCD Multicultural Council
Adapted in part from Goode, T.D. (2009). *Promoting Cultural Diversity and Cultural Competency Self Assessment Checklist for Personnel Providing Services and Support to Children with Special Health Needs and Their Families.* Washington, DC: Georgetown University Child Development Center.

Effective Culturally Inclusive Assessment of Student Learning and Academic Performance

The goal of this chapter is to equip prospective teachers with skills for improving the quality, validity, and equity of assessing student learning. The following principles and strategies also improve the quality of teaching and promote the academic achievement of students from diverse cultural backgrounds.

Comprehensive assessment of student learning should be holistic—it should evaluate the development of the student as a whole person. Effective assessment goes beyond standardized test scores to include important aspects of personal development, such as:

> *" An obvious question to pose when developing assessment instruments is, 'To what extent does this assessment promote quality and diversity simultaneously'?"*
> —Ginsberg & Wlodkowski, *Diversity & Motivation*

a. Development of *Lifelong Learning and Thinking Skills* (e.g., learning how to learn, how to think deeply, and how to acquire and communicate knowledge)
b. *Emotional* Development (e.g., understanding, controlling, and effectively expressing emotions)
c. *Social* Development (e.g., human relations skills, intercultural communication skills, leadership development, and civic engagement)
d. *Ethical* Development (e.g., clarifying one's values and developing personal character)

 **PERSONAL INSIGHT** On a regular basis, you will hear terminology like formative and summative assessment. In addition, you will hear that the accreditors (i.e., NCATE or your regional accreditor) will want to make sure that you are explicit in stating and assessing student learning outcomes and using a continuous assessment model to make it happen. The many years that I have been in higher education and working closely with P–12, I haven't seen a more successful strategy than those who use a model that stresses that all can learn and all will learn. To do this you will need to do regular (formative) assessment as to ensure that you can address the specific learning needs of the student are addressed. This process is generally effective for all students and specifically beneficial for students of greatest need.

Aaron Thompson

e. *Physical* Development (e.g., acquiring and applying knowledge about the human body to prevent disease, maintain wellness, and promote peak performance), and
f. *Identity* Development (e.g., formulating a positive self-concept and sense of personal direction)

Effective assessment should include evaluating changes that take place in students' attitudes, behaviors, and cognition (thinking). Student learning may take place in three key forms or dimensions, sometimes referred to as the "ABCs" of student assessment:

A = *Affective*—learning represented by change in students' *attitudes*, *perspectives* or viewpoints (e.g., changes in their attitude toward school or their views of different cultural groups).
B = *Behavioral*—learning demonstrated by a change in students' *habits* (e.g., student improvement in study and work habits), or in students' *actions* (e.g., becoming more engaged in class).
C = *Cognitive*—learning demonstrated by gains in *knowledge* and *thinking* processes (e.g., acquisition of curricular knowledge, self-knowledge, or critical thinking skills).

Effective assessment utilizes *multiple* and *varied* methods of student performance evaluation. A cardinal principle of effective assessment is employing multiple methods, rather than relying exclusively on a single method or source of evaluation. Use of multiple methods allows for cross-validation and minimizes the risk that students' performance results reflect the particular method used to assess their learning rather than the full scope of what they actually learned.

Culturally inclusive assessment is also maximized by use of different assessment methods because they are more likely to be sensitive to the diverse cultural backgrounds and learning styles of students in class. Thus, use of multiple and varied evaluation methods to assess student achievement provides a more balanced system of assessment that increases (a) assessment *validity*—because the limitations of one evaluation method are more likely to be counterbalanced by the strengths of the others, and (b) assessment *equity*—because different evaluation formats more effectively accommodate the variety of learning styles and skill sets that diverse students bring to the learning process.

Research indicates that students vary appreciably in terms of what evaluation procedures they're most comfortable with (Lowman, 1984; McKeachie, 1986); for example, students whose writing skills are not yet well developed may feel less comfortable with (and may be unduly penalized by) exams that are comprised solely of essay questions. By utilizing diverse evaluation methods, all students will have at least occasional opportunities to demonstrate their knowledge and skills in a way that is most compatible with their preferred style of learning (Sedlacek, 1993; Suskie, 2000). "Students generally need a range of opportunities and ap-

> "Principals and teachers who want to be leaders of student learning should consider using multiple forms of assessment."
>
> —Leadership for Student Success: A Partnership of the Laboratory for Student Success and the Institute of Leadership Development, Washington, DC

proaches to demonstrate what they know" (Ginsberg & Wlodkowski, 2009, p. 272).

Effective assessment includes a balanced blend of *quantitative* and *qualitative* data on student performance. Evidence of student learning can be gathered in *quantitative* form (numerical data that can be summarized statistically such as student scores on tests and other performance measures), or *qualitative* form (nonnumerical or "human" data in the form of spoken and written words that can be analyzed for themes or patterns such as students' written comments on exams and assignments, or spoken comments made during oral presentations or class discussions).

These two basic forms of data should be viewed as *complementary* sources of evidence for student learning with offsetting advantages and disadvantages. For instance, *quantitative* assessment data is more efficiently scored (number crunching by machine rather than a person or multiple persons) and easier to collect in large amounts. However, it often captures the outcome or product of learning without providing much information about the process of learning (or failure to learn). In contrast, collecting and analyzing *qualitative* assessment data is more time-consuming and labor intensive, but it can often provide information about the thought processes that lead students to student learning (or failure to learn). For instance, students' written reflections on what they are at each step of solving a math or science problem can provide valuable information on the underlying thought processes that lead successful students to arrive at the correct solution and common reasons why students make mistakes.

The following practices are recommended for providing students with *multiple and varied* evaluations of their knowledge and skills.

Use assessment methods that evaluate student performance for work done *in class* (e.g., quizzes or exams) and *out of class* (e.g., take-home tests, assignments, or projects). Timed classroom-based tests may be one student's meat, but another's poison. Evaluating student achievement by methods other than tests provides more opportunity and greater equity for students who are not strong test takers.

One strategy that teachers could use to intentionally diversify assessment is to conceptualize student evaluation methods in terms of the following categories and to be sure that they're using at least one assessment method per category:

a. *product* assessments: written essays, stories, research reports, projects, etc.
b. *performance* assessments: tests, oral presentations, debates, science demonstrations, artistic expression (e.g., visual arts, drama, music, etc.), and
c. *process-focused* assessments: oral questioning, interviews, journaling, portfolio development, etc. (Ginsberg & Wlodkowski, 2009).

Assess students' ability to demonstrate their knowledge through *different communication modes or modalities* (e.g., written reports, oral reports, multimedia presentations). Just as students have different learning styles for acquiring knowledge, they may have different styles for expressing or demonstrating their knowledge. An English teacher, identified as "outstanding" by students and faculty colleagues, provides a good example of how teachers can encourage use of diverse forms of knowledge expression: She requires every student in class to write two essays on topics that she assigns; on the third assignment, however, students are given five or six methods for evaluation from which to choose. Among the options offered to students is a third written essay, a creative writing piece, a dramatic act to be performed in front of class (alone or as part of a team project), or an original video presented in class that students develop either individually or in teams. Students are also allowed to create and submit additional options for teacher approval (Wilson, 1987).

Draw test questions from a *variety of informational sources* (class presentations, discussions, assigned readings, etc.). Culturally inclusive evaluation recognizes that knowledge is acquired from and applied to multiple settings and cultural contexts.

On exams, include both "*subjective*" and "*objective*" test questions (e.g., essay and multiple choice questions). Students are encouraged to use and develop different cognitive abilities when exposed to questions that ask them to supply their own answers, versus selecting an answer from alternatives supplied for them. Essay questions require students to *recall* knowledge by producing it on their own, which promotes the development of writing and synthesis skills. In contrast, multiple choice questions require students to *recognize* important distinctions by choosing from possible alternatives, which promotes the development of reading and analytical reasoning skills.

Neither of these types of questions is superior to or more "authentic" than the other. During their educational career and beyond, students will be required to synthesize information in writing and make discriminating choices based on information they read. Both of these mental activities have the potential to promote critical thinking or other forms of higher-level reasoning. As one educational measurement scholar puts it: "Producing an answer is not necessarily a more complex or difficult task, or one more indicative of achievement than choosing the best of available alternatives" (Ebel, 1972, pp. 124–125). Anyone who has reviewed or taken standardized tests for admission to college, graduate school or professional school can attest to how multiple choice questions are capable of assessing higher-level cognitive skills. If multiple choice questions test only factual knowledge or rote memory, it is, as Clegg and Cashin point out, "the result of poor test craftsmanship and not an inherent limitation of the item type; a well-designed multiple-choice item can test higher levels of student learning" (1986, p. 1). Conversely, as Erickson and Strommer observe, "Many essay questions masquerade as tests of complex thinking skills when, in fact, they can be answered on the basis of memorization" (1991, p. 137).

Thus, teachers should not automatically exclude any particular testing format when constructing exams. Instead, they should be ready to incorporate a balanced blend of essay (writing), multiple choice, and true-false questions. It may also be possible to integrate different test question formats into a single test question. For example, writing can be incorporated into multiple choice or true-false questions by giving students the option of clarifying their choices in writing, or by requiring them to write a justification for their answer to certain multiple choice or true-false questions. Also, students may only be allowed to earn maximum credit on designated multiple choice questions if they both choose the correct alternative *and* explain (in writing) why it's the correct choice (Zinsser, 1988). Allowing students the opportunity to explain or express their interpretation of what the "correct" answer is also serves to validate the way in which students perceive "reality" or the "truth" and helps them move away from dualistic (right or wrong) thinking and thinking that the person in authority is always "right" (knows the truth) (Butler, 1993).

> *Assessment experiences that reward students who best conform to the instructor's norms and values serve as additional evidence of cultural bias.*
> —Ginsberg & Wlodkowski, *Diversity & Motivation*

Exams are more likely to be inclusive and equitable if they engage students in a variety of test-preparation and test-taking skills. This variety also encourages students to exercise and develop the full repertoire of test-taking skills that they'll be expected to use at higher levels of education and on certification exams required for entry into certain occupations (e.g., nursing, teaching, and law).

Include assignments that require students to work both *independently* (individually) and *interdependently* (in groups or teams). Developing independence and interdependence are important dimensions of personal development (Chickering, 1969; Chickering & Reisser, 1993). Assessing student performance in both of these contexts creates a more diversified and comprehensive system of student performance evaluation.

For *group projects*, assess group members on both their *independent (individual)* work and their *interdependent (collective)* work. Survey research indicates that high-achieving students report high levels of great dissatisfaction with group projects in which all members of their group receive the same, undifferentiated grade (Fiechtner & Davis, 1992). High-achieving students complain that their individual effort and contribution to the group's final product often exceeds the efforts of their less motivated teammates, yet these "free riders" or "social loafers" are inequitably awarded the same grade. For this reason, resist the temptation to conveniently assign a single "group grade" to all members of the group. Instead, build assessment of *individual accountability* or *personal responsibility* into the evaluation of students' group work. One way to ensure that the individual responsibility of each group member can be readily identified and evaluated is by having each member assume responsibility for contributing a distinct or unique component to the group's final product (e.g., a particular piece or unit of information, or a different cultural perspective). To ensure that each member also demonstrates some degree of *collective responsibility* to the group, individual members could be assessed on how well they connect or integrate their personal contributions with the contributions made by other group members.

Student Learning Is Promoted by *Frequent Assessment*

Each assessment of student performance represents only an *estimate* of what that student has learned or achieved. Some assessments will overestimate student learning whereas others will underestimate it. These errors of measurement tend to be distributed randomly across different assessments given at different times, so the best way to reduce the magnitude of measurement errors is to base the student's final grade on multiple assessment measures; this will allow random errors of measurement to balance out or cancel each other out (Gage & Berliner, 1984; Gronlund, 1985). Measuring student achievement on the basis of only a few high stakes assessment tasks can lead to inaccurate judgments, "especially with learners whose experiences, behaviors, beliefs, and values challenge an instructor's ways of understanding" (Ginsberg & Wlodkowski, 2009, p. 273).

In addition to improving test validity by providing a larger sample of student performances on which to base grades, frequent assessment has the following advantages.

- Frequent assessment encourages students to "stay on top of things" and work more *consistently*. Assessment frequently requires students to distribute their study time more evenly throughout the term.
- Frequent assessment requires students to learn and retain a more limited amount of material at one time, giving them the opportunity to learn the material more deeply. It's probably safe to say that students will learn smaller amounts of material more deeply and larger amounts of material more superficially. Tests that assess large amounts of information tend to encourage "surface learning" and memorization of facts, while diminishing students' depth of thinking and motivation to think (Ginsberg & Wlodkowski, 2009; Wieman, 2007).
- More frequent assessment is likely to result in students being assessed earlier in the term; thus, they receive *earlier feedback* in the learning process that can be used to make early adjustments to improve future performance. Furthermore, when students receive earlier feedback, they are more *motivated* to attend to it and use it for performance-improvement purposes because they know they'll have time to rectify early errors and achieve a good final grade. Furthermore, early and frequent assessment allows teachers to better understand "the different abilities and backgrounds that are present among students and may suggest strategies for dealing with this diversity" (Education Commission of the States, 1995).

Frequent assessment can be incorporated into students' work on larger, long-range projects by having them submit early graded "installments" of work segments at interim points throughout the term. For instance, if the project involves a research report, students could submit early installments of their work in the following sequence: (a) topic identification and tentative bibliography after the first month, (b) outline by the end of the second month, (c) first draft by the third month, and (d) final draft during the last week of class. These submitted installments are also an effective way for teachers to combat plagiarism and "ghost writing."

Furthermore, requiring shorter-term installments of work reduces the likelihood that students will *procrastinate* and assures them that they're "on the right track" as their work proceeds. An additional reason why this short-term installment strategy may be effective for writing assignments is suggested by research indicating that "writer's block" is less likely to be experienced when writing is done in small steps with specific deadlines for completing each step (Hull, 1981; Rennie & Brewer, 1987).

Hold High Expectations for All Students

It can often be difficult to explain verbally or capture in words what constitutes "excellence" or "A" work—as reflected in the common expression: "I can't tell you what it is, but I know it when I see it." Excellence may be more effectively communicated to students by allowing them to see examples of excellent work.

The following strategies may be used to help students to literally "see" what constitutes high-quality work.

Provide students with *models* of excellent (grade "A") work. High-quality work submitted by students in previous classes may be saved and shown to current students. These illustrations of excellence could be one student's total work product, or pieces of different students' work that illustrate excellence with respect to a particular performance criterion (e.g., separate illustrations of a student's work that demonstrates excellent overall organization, clarity of written expression, or critical thinking). Providing students with such concrete illustrations should also reduce the likelihood that they will voice the same complaint as the following college freshman: "I'm not really sure how my essay answers can be improved to give her what she wants" (Erickson & Strommer, 1991, p. 49).

> *Evidence that other students—students just like them—have done excellent work is a strong motivator.*
> —Robert E. Scott & Dorothy Echols Tobe, *Communicating High Expectations*

Teachers could develop a file of former students' outstanding work to share with current students as models to aspire to, or emulate.

Distribute anonymous copies of students' written work from previous classes that range in quality, and ask the class to rank the students' work and identify their reasons (criteria) for their ranking. Research shows that students' writing improves if they first identify instances of good/bad writing and participate in the process of developing criteria for evaluating the quality of their own writing (White, 1985).

Provide students with a *checklist of criteria* that will be used to evaluate the quality of their work. The criteria that a teacher uses to determine high-quality work should not remain a mystery to students; they should be shared with students so that they are positioned to self-assess their performance before being formally assessed by the teacher. For writing assignments, the following criteria and illustrative descriptions might be shared with students to clarify what a well-written paper looks like and motivate them to meet these criteria in their own work.

- *Organization*. The paper should include:
  a. an introduction,
  b. a conclusion,
  c. clear transitions between paragraphs, and
  d. well-defined section headings.
- *Documentation*. The paper should include:
  a. a variety of sources that are used in a balanced fashion—as opposed to over-reliance on one or two references,
  b. use of some primary sources—as opposed to exclusive reliance on secondary references (e.g., textbooks), and
  c. a blend of historical sources and current publications.
- *Presentation*. The paper should be presented in a manner consistent with stated guidelines about formatting features, such as:
  a. page margins,
  b. line spacing,
  c. paper length,
  d. references cited in the body of the paper, and
  e. references cited in the reference section at the end of the paper.

Students' family members may also be apprised of these criteria so that they can support the student's efforts at developing competence and achieving excellence.

Before administering an exam to students, provide them with as much relevant information as possible about its *content* and *format*. For instance, prior to exams, students could be informed about:

- the number and nature of questions (essays, multiple choice, etc.),
- relative point value of test questions,
- amount of time allowed to complete the exam,
- materials that students need to bring to the exam, and
- permissible test-taking aids (e.g., calculators, dictionaries).

The less uncertainty students experience prior to an exam, the less test anxiety they will experience during the exam.

Prior to the *first* exam of the term, share a previously used exam to allow students to familiarize themselves with your testing style. It may be worth taking a portion of class time to discuss the layout and expectations of an old exam before students encounter their first test of the term.

To prepare students for major exams, provide them with *study guides* that *identify specific learning objectives (intended learning outcomes)*—that is, what information students are expected to know and how they'll be expected

to show they know it. Providing students with specific study objectives prior to exams does not mean that the teacher is "giving away" test answers. Teachers can ensure that students focus their study time on learning what they should learn without being accused of narrowly "teaching to the test." Students can be directed to critical class concepts and instructed how they can learn these concepts deeply without being shown the exact test questions that will appear on the exam. For instance, a student guide may alert students to the fact that they will be expected to *evaluate* bias in the reporting of historical incidents or *apply* the concept of privilege to a current event without knowing what specific test questions will be used to assess their ability to evaluate and apply these particular concepts.

One way to specify the content and thinking skills that students are expected to demonstrate on a test or assignment is by creating a "table of specifications" (Tyler, 1950), also known as a "content-by-process matrix," which lists what content (concepts) are to be assessed and the thinking processes that students are expected to use in relation to that content. (See the table below.)

TABLE OF SPECIFICATIONS
Thinking Process:

Content Area:	Comprehension	Application	Evaluation
Bias			
Privilege			
Discrimination			

This content-by-process matrix can function as an organizational blueprint for devising exams and assignments that are balanced and comprehensive. By ensuring that evaluation items appear in each cell of the matrix, the teacher ensures that students will be evaluated on a balanced, representative sample of important concepts and thinking skills.

Research shows that students tend to study material that they expect will be on the test and will use cognitive processes while studying that they think they'll be expected to use on the test. When students are given study objectives that involve higher-level thinking skills, they are more likely to engage in higher-level thinking with respect to the concepts they're studying and also demonstrate greater retention of those concepts (Marton & Saljo, 1976). These findings strongly suggest that supplying study objectives that involve higher-level thinking skills (e.g., application, evaluation, synthesis) will increase the probability that these cognitive skills will be practiced during students' study time and utilized during test time.

Moreover, at-home study time provides students with the time they need to engage in higher-level thinking. Test time should be the time when students demonstrate those higher-level thinking skills they've practiced and honed during their study time. It is unrealistic to expect students to display higher-level thinking from scratch during the restricted time frame of an in-class exam because studies show that performing under time pressure inhibits and restricts higher-level thought processes, such as critical and creative thinking (Hart, 1983). Thus, students shouldn't be expected to study facts and then be able to integrate or synthesize those facts during a timed exam. However, if students are provided with specific study objectives that encourage them to engage in integration or synthesis during study time, requiring them to write an already mentally prepared synthesis during test time is a reasonable expectation and represents a valid demonstration of their higher-level thinking skills.

Providing students with specific learning objectives to prepare for exams has multiple advantages, which include the following.

- Specific learning objectives *increase students' motivation to study* because their performance expectations are made explicitly clear. Since students know where to focus their study efforts, they are more likely to study because they see a clearer connection between effort expended and grade achieved. Perhaps nothing can be more disheartening and demotivating for students than to study hard and then discover later (during the test) that they "studied the wrong things." When people do not see a connection between the efforts they expend and the outcomes they achieve, it decreases their sense of self-efficacy (Bandura, 1997) and increases their feeling of "learned helplessness" (Seligman, 1998).

- Learning objectives enable students to *self-monitor* their learning and identify specific concepts they're having difficulty understanding *before* they're tested on those concepts. Thus, specific study learning objectives empower students to engage in early self-diagnosis, helping them troubleshoot and pinpoint sources of confusion before they adversely affect their test score.

- Specific learning objectives can *reduce test anxiety* by reducing students' feeling of uncertainty and supplying them with a support structure for test preparation. Research indicates that when performance expectations match the reality of the performance task, less performance anxiety is experienced (Tracey & Sherry, 1984). Thus, equipping students with specific study objectives serves to reduce their test anxiety by reducing their uncertainty about how they will be expected to perform—that is, what they will be expected to know and be able to do on the test (which should also reduce teacher frustration with having to repeatedly answer the perennial student question: "Will this be on the test?").

It's less likely that students will ask questions like this if they're supplied with study guides containing specific learning objectives.

- Specific study objectives help teachers *identify and prioritize* the most essential concepts for students to learn. When teachers take the time to identify the most critical or most powerful ideas that students should grasp, it ensures that students will be assessed for learning concepts that are most important for them to learn—that is, they will spend their out-of-class study time on material that is central or crucial, not peripheral or trivial.

    Even if teachers don't "teach to the test," students will "study to the test" because they'll study what they expect to be on the test (Frederiksen, 1984; Gamson, 1993). By providing students specific study objectives, teachers direct students' test expectations and preparation toward the most crucial concepts. Not all course material is equally important; learning objectives increase the likelihood that amid the wealth of information presented to students in class and in readings, they will find and devote their study time to learning what is most important to learn.
- Providing students with study objectives before exams promotes *teacher rapport with the class*. When a teacher takes the time and effort to supply students with study guides it reduces the likelihood that they'll perceive their teacher as someone playing a game of "keep away"—withholding information about the test, then "ambushing" them later with "trick" test questions.

> *The only instructional sin greater than teaching obsolete or trivial information is to test and grade students about such knowledge.*
>
> —Stanford Ericksen, *The Essence of Good Teaching*

Multiple-choice questions require recognition memory similar to that used to identify the correct criminal from a line-up of possible suspects.

▶ Specific study objectives increase *test validity* by ensuring that test questions are derived exclusively from the same pool of learning objectives that students are studying. In assessment terminology, providing students with specific learning objectives increases "content validity" because it ensures that the content that students are expected to learn is consistent with the content that appears on the test (Gronlund, 1985).

Naturally, study guides comprised of specific learning objectives (outcomes) will take time to construct, but the short-term cost in time should be far outweighed by its long-term benefits for teaching and learning.

Instruct students how to *self-monitor* the quality of their academic performance and level of achievement at all points during the term. When students are uncertain about "where they stand" in class, it can produce grade anxiety. Research indicates that one distinguishing characteristic of successful students is that they engage in *self-monitoring*—that is, they are aware of how well they are learning and where they stand in class (Pintrich, 1995; Weinstein, 1994). One way to empower students to self-monitor their academic progress is by encouraging them to save and track their grades for completed tests and assignments. After each assignment or exam, have students add its points to their cumulative total so they can determine their overall class grade at all times throughout the term.

Use students' performance patterns on tests and assignments as feedback to assess *the quality of your exams* **and the** *effectiveness of your teaching*. One way that teachers can acquire this feedback is to have students complete a brief, post-exam evaluation form that includes questions such as the following:

- Was there anything on the exam that you didn't expect to see?
- Was the grade you received on this test the grade you thought you were going to receive?
- How much time did you spend preparing for this test?
- Do you think your test grade was what you deserved for the amount time and effort you put into studying for the test?
- Which questions or parts of the exam did you find to be most challenging? Least challenging?
- Now that you have experienced the test, would you have studied for it differently? In what way(s)?
- Did you learn anything while taking the exam (e.g., acquired any new knowledge or thinking skill)? (McMullen-Pastrick & Gleason, 1986)

These questions can be used as a springboard for launching students into an honest discussion of quality of their test preparation and the quality of the test itself. The information gleaned from this discussion can be used by teachers to improve the clarity and validity of their exams. One characteristic of effective teaching in general and teaching of diverse students in particular is the ability to access and respond to student feedback (Ginsberg & Wlodkowski, 2009).

Another effective way in which teachers can assess and improve the quality of their validity of tests is by performing an *item analysis* on student answers to test questions. Item analysis involves computing the percentage of students that answer different multiple choice or true-false questions correctly, and students' average score on different essay questions. Teachers can use this information to identify specific test items on which a *majority* of students performed poorly, which may suggest that the test item was ambiguously written, or that students received inadequate instruction on the concept tested by these items. Teachers can use this feedback to immediately adjust students' test score and grade so that they are not unfairly penalized for missing such items. This information may also be used to improve the clarity of these test questions and the quality of teaching provided on the concepts assessed by these questions.

Item analysis also has another powerful purpose: it helps teachers construct *moderately challenging* exams—that is, exams comprised of test items that are neither overly simple nor overly difficult. A large body of research suggests that moderately challenging tasks generate higher levels of intrinsic motivation than tasks that are extremely difficult or extremely easy (Csikszentimihalyi, 1990, Schiefele & Csikszentimihalyi, 1995). Reviewing students' average scores on individual test questions can provide information on whether the question was moderately challenging by assessing its level of difficulty. Test items that proved to be too easy or too difficult could be eliminated, rewritten, and reevaluated on a future test. By engaging in an ongoing process of reviewing and modifying test items in this fashion, teachers can eventually end up with a comprehensive set of moderately challenging questions that can be included on their exams.

Adopt a *learning-for-mastery* model of assessment whereby students are given the opportunity to *retake exams or resubmit assignments* in order to *improve* the quality of their work and their class grade. Students should have the opportunity to learn from their initial evaluation and use it as feedback to improve their performance. When students are able to repeat and improve their performance on a test or assignment, research indicates that they make significant gains in learning and academic achievement (Bloom, 1984; Fitzgerald, 1987). This finding suggests that giving students an opportunity to review their exams and correct their mistakes would be a highly effective educational practice.

Providing students opportunities to repeat and improve their work is consistent with the "mastery learning" model of education. This model takes the position that initial differences in student performance on a test or other measure of learning do not reflect differences in their learning ability or potential. Instead, this original variation in performance levels reflects differences in the amount of time, practice, and feedback that individual students need to master the material—which are due, in part, to differences in their prior learning experiences and cultural backgrounds. If initially low-performing students are given more time and chances to learn the material, they will eventually achieve a level of mastery comparable to those students who performed well on the original test.

The mastery learning model acknowledges that there are individual differences among students in their natural learning abilities or talents. However, these represent differences in the *speed* at which students can learn a particular concept or skill, rather than differences in their ability or potential to learn it (Bloom, 1968; 1978; Carroll, 1963).

Naturally, if students are given the opportunity to relearn the material and be reevaluated for performance improvement as suggested by the mastery learning model, it is likely to result in an upward shift in the distribution of course grades. For teachers who are concerned that giving students these extra opportunities to improve their performance will result in "grade inflation," that fear can be mitigated by *averaging* students' first and second scores rather than replacing their first score with their improved, second score. If the ultimate purpose of education is to maximize the academic achievement of all students, instructional practices that promote better learning should produce a welcomed upward shift of grade distribution. If students are willing to put in the extra time and effort to correct their mistakes and elevate their performance, teachers should not feel guilty or be chastised for "lowering academic standards."

Grades should reflect what students actually learn and should be *criterion*-referenced—that is, based on absolute standards or criteria (e.g., percentage of questions answered correctly)—rather than norm-referenced (i.e., based on the percentage of peers they score higher than or beat out). Teachers should not let

> "We need to distinguish between bad inflation resulting from unjustifiably high grades and good grade inflation [resulting] from more effective pedagogy and consequently improved achievement."
>
> —Craig Nelson, professor emeritus of Biology, Indiana University; president, International Society for the Scholarship of Teaching and Learning

unchallenged expectations that they should have a "normal" distribution of grades (bell-shaped curve) distract them from using student evaluation methods that most effectively promote student learning for all students.

Competitive "curve grading" is not only inconsistent with mastery learning and having high expectations for all students, it may also detract from interethnic and interracial harmony because research in social psychology reveals that when people engage in *competitive* interaction with members of racial or ethnic groups who are unfamiliar or initially disliked, negative attitudes toward these people are intensified (Burgess & Sales, 1977; Swap, 1977). In contrast, grading according to absolute standards is also more likely to result in greater student collaboration with respect to school work and less invidious social comparisons (Boyer, 1987).

Grading according to absolute standards is also more likely to promote improvement in the quality of teacher's teaching and test construction. As Erickson and Strommer (1991) point out:

> *Grading according to [absolute] standards is more likely to point out problems and lead to improvements in teaching and test-taking practices. If several students do poorly on an exam, the low grades usually prompt some serious soul searching. Was instruction adequate? Was the exam poorly constructed? Or did students simply not study enough? We can correct such problems, but only if we detect them. Grading on a curve too often hides ineffective teaching, poor testing, and inadequate learning. So long as we give a reasonable number of A's and B's and not too many D's or F's, no one makes a fuss (pp. 154–155).*

Assessment designed to promote student learning should take precedence over assessment designed to distribute class grades. Rather than perpetuating testing practices that focus less on assessing student learning and more on spreading out and sorting out students into grade categories, good teachers use assessment as a vehicle for improving their teaching and helping students from all cultural backgrounds attain clearly defined learning outcomes and high levels of academic achievement. Effective, culturally inclusive assessment begins with the educational philosophy that the teacher's role is to nurture and cultivate the growth of all students, rather than excavate and weed out "weak" students.

> *"Grading on a curve does not allow all students to see how close they are coming to high standards of performance. If all students reach the standard, it is okay for all to reach the highest grade."*
> —Ginsberg & Wlodkowski, *Diversity & Motivation*

Student Learning Is Promoted by the Delivery of Performance-Improving *Feedback*

According to the aforementioned "mastery learning model," all students are capable of achieving a high level if they are given the practice time to do so. The mastery model also stipulates that if students make effective use of performance feedback, it will expedite their ability to learn from their mistakes and master the

> "People can't learn without feedback. It's not teaching that causes learning. Attempts by the learner to perform cause learning, dependent upon the quality of feedback and opportunity to use it."
> —Grant Wiggins, *Feedback: How Learning Occurs*

material. When students receive informative feedback that they can use to improve their performance (as opposed to just a grade, test score, or where they rank in class), they are more likely to make an effort to improve their performance and take personal responsibility for mastering the material or gaining competence in the skills they are being asked to learn (Zimmerman & Kitsantas, 2005).

Feedback enhances and accelerates student learning when it is: (1) prompt, (2) proactive, (3) precise, (4) practical, (5) persuasive, (6) personalized, and (7) positive. These characteristics of effective feedback are defined in **Box 7.1**.

Box 7.1 Effective Teacher *Feedback:* Seven Central Features

1. ***Prompt:*** delivered *soon after* performance is completed.

2. ***Proactive:*** delivered *early* in the learning process, thus allowing for quick diagnosis and correction.

3. ***Precise:*** focuses specifically on and clearly identifies what the student needs to do to *correct* mistakes and improve performance.

4. ***Practical:*** provides students with an *incentive* to actually use the feedback provided and immediately apply it to improve their performance and grade.

5. ***Persuasive:*** provides good reasons *why* improvement should be made by relating it to the achievement of students' personal goals, thus increasing student motivation to *take action* on the feedback provided.

6. ***Personalized:*** delivered in an *individualized* and *nonthreatening* manner that targets personal *actions* or *behaviors* needing improvement, rather than the student's general character or group membership.

7. ***Positive:*** includes recognition of student *strengths* and conveys *optimism* that productive change can be made in areas that need improvement.

What follows is a more extensive description of these "seven Ps" of effective feedback and teachers may implement them in the classroom.

1. *Prompt* Feedback

    Research supports the value of immediate feedback for promoting students' motivation to learn (Malone, 1981) and their retention of course concepts (Kulik, Jaksa, & Kulik, 1978). Although teachers may not be able to provide students with immediate feedback following a test, they can still provide students with prompt feedback by having an answer key ready or solutions posted for review as soon as students complete their work. An instructor identified as "outstanding" (by students, faculty, and administrators) points out that there is another advantage of prompt feedback: "[It] indicates to the students the importance of what they are doing and my interest and concern for their learning the material" (Davis, Wood, & Wilson, 1983, p. 235).

2. *Proactive* Feedback

Feedback is more useful when it's delivered early in the learning process, thereby allowing students ample opportunity to remedy shortcomings before they eventuate in poor grades and damaged self-esteem. Teachers can give short, ungraded exams or assignments early in the term so that students receive early feedback and use it to improve their subsequent graded performance.

Research on student motivation suggests that the majority of students approach academic challenges with "performance goals" in mind—they view learning situations as tests of their competence and strive to be judged as competent rather than incompetent. These students tend to attribute failure to low ability (rather than to low effort), feel ashamed or dejected when they do not perform well, and do not persist on tasks if they are not initially successful. In contrast, a minority of students approach academic challenges with "mastery" goals—they view learning situations as opportunities to improve their ability and do not define initial mistakes as failures; instead, they persist if they're not initially successful and experience pride or pleasure as they overcome mistakes in the process of mastering academic tasks (Dweck & Leggett, 1988).

Because this research indicates that most students have performance goals rather than mastery goals, teachers should give strong consideration to designing assignments that enable students to explore some early success in class. These early success experiences should help them develop "mastery" goals, increase their initial self-confidence, and strengthen their ability to persist on more difficult tasks encountered later in the term.

3. *Precise* Feedback

In addition to knowing where they stand in class, students need to know *how* to go about rectifying their mistakes so they can avoid making those same mistakes again. Effective feedback should inform and demonstrate to learners what particular aspects of their performance need improvement.

It's difficult for students to improve their performance when the only feedback they receive is a generic grade (Brophy, 2004). Even providing students with general written comments like, "Your paper needs more organization" lacks the specific feedback of comments such as: "Your paper needs an introduction, a thesis statement, and a conclusion that summarizes the paper's major points." Research conducted at Harvard University indicates that improvement in student writing is related to the *specificity* of action strategies that were included in the feedback they received from their instructors (Light, 1992).

4. *Practical* Feedback

Feedback becomes "constructive" when students build on it to improve their performance and experience practical benefits for doing so. One straightforward strategy for getting students to use feedback constructively is by requiring students to correct their mistakes. In two independent studies of this practice, when instructors returned exams to students, they listed brief references to the textbook pages and/or class notes after every test question. On test questions that were answered incorrectly, students were required to write a short paragraph that identified the correct answer and explain why it was correct. When compared to students in other sections of the same course who didn't receive this feedback and were not asked to correct their mistakes, students who received feedback and corrected their error: (a) scored higher on the same final exam, (b) liked the course more, and (c) felt more confident of their abilities in the course subject (Clark, Guskey, & Benninga, 1983; Guskey, Benninga, & Clark, 1984).

An alternative to *requiring* students to correct their mistakes is simply to provide them with a strong *incentive* to do so. For instance, students could be allowed to redeem some (or most) of their lost points and improve their grade if they correct and resubmit their answers.

5. *Persuasive* Feedback

    Effective feedback also motivates students to improve their performance by articulating *why* improvement is important for achieving their current goals and future plans. Teachers cannot assume that students see the purpose of academic learning and its value in "real life." When students are given feedback on *how* to improve their performance, they should also be reminded about *why* making the effort to use that feedback will lead to self-improvement and attainment of personal goals.

6. *Personalized* Feedback

    Students are more likely to attend to feedback and respond in a nondefensive manner if it's delivered in a personalized manner. This may be accomplished through such practices as (a) addressing the student by name when providing written feedback, (b) noticing something about the student (e.g., mentioning that you've noticed the student's increased level of involvement and participation in class), (c) signing your name at the end of your comments so that your written feedback simulates a personal letter, or (d) asking about something you know is currently going on in the student's life in a postscript to your feedback (e.g., athletic endeavors or family matters).

7. *Positive* Feedback

    Feedback becomes more balanced and less likely to damage students' self-esteem if it includes positive information, such as complimentary comments about specific aspects of the student's work. During the rush to correct and return tests or assignments as promptly as possible and justify to students why they have lost points and received a grade less than A, it's easy to forget to take a moment to offer students' praise and encouragement. To guard against this "criticism trap," the following practices are recommended as strategies for delivering positive feedback:

    - In addition to pinpointing the sources of students' mistakes, make a conscious effort to identify aspects of their work that were done correctly or effectively (e.g., "You got most of this problem right; it's just this one part that we need to work on.")

> *Positive feedback places emphasis on improvement and progress rather than on deficiencies and mistakes.*
>
> —Ginsberg & Wlodkowski, *Diversity & Motivation*

- Acknowledge students' *strengths*, even if those strengths don't relate directly to the specific criteria used to grade their work (e.g., the creativity of the answers provided, or the care they took to answer all parts of all questions).
- Even if further improvement is needed, point out aspects of students' work that have *improved* during the course of the term, (e.g., "You still have a little way to go but you've come a long way since the beginning of the term.")

Use a "forgiving" grading system that allows students to make up exams on which they performed poorly, or allow them to drop their lowest test score. These practices demonstrate teacher sensitivity to students who may be taking a test or completing an assignment while ill, stressed, or distracted by non-academic issues. Allowing students to drop their lowest performance score also has the advantage of reducing the need for teachers to construct and proctor make-up tests for students who missed the exam because the teacher can use the missed test as the student's lowest score and not count it toward the student's overall course grade. This practice is most appropriate for smaller tests (e.g., quizzes), rather than major exams that all students should be expected to complete. Used in this manner, the practice of dropping the lowest score will not unduly dilute the course's academic rigor or lower your grading standards.

Whatever particular way a teacher decides to implement a forgiving grading system, it will still send a strong signal to students that they have a caring teacher who is sensitive to the life circumstances and personal adjustments of students from diverse backgrounds.

Student Learning Is Enhanced by Exercises or Assignments That Promote *Self-Assessment* and *Self-Awareness*

Self-assessment is a learning process that enables students to look inward and gain insight into themselves as learners, thinkers, and individuals in a diverse world (Brookfield & Preskill, 2005). Teachers can promote this learning-for-self-awareness process by having students complete self-assessment inventories that require them to examine their (a) learning styles and learning habits, (b) educational and occupational interests, and (c) personal values, personality, and wellness habits. Students may also be asked to keep time diaries or learning logs to promote self-awareness of where their time and energy goes. These types of assignments encourage students to *engage* students in two important lifelong learning habits: *personal reflection* and *self-examination*.

The educational impact of self-assessment and self-awareness assignments can be strengthened by the following practices.

Provide students with a *comparative reference point* so that they can interpret their results in relation to others. Self-assessment becomes more meaningful when students are able to view their individual results in relation to national norms (if available), class averages, or the averages of student subgroups in class (e.g., males and females, minority and majority students). Comparative self-assessment is an effective way to expose students to diverse perspectives and gain a frame of reference that can sharpen their self-awareness and self-insight.

To make the comparative-assessment process more involving and interactive, *score lines* may be created whereby students line up in the order of their scores on a self-assessment instrument or inventory. Teachers could complete the same self-assessment inventories along with their students and join the score line. Completing an exercise with students often increases their interest and motivation to partake in it. When students see their teacher doing what they're being asked to do, their participation is validated and they receive the message that the task is important enough for their illustrious teacher to complete as well. (Furthermore, students are often extremely curious to see their teacher's results and how it compares with their own.)

As a *final, cumulative self-assessment assignment*, have students write a personal essay or autobiography that asks them to integrate and reflect on the results of separate self-assessments they completed throughout the term. To lend some definition and structure to this assignment, teachers could include focus questions that ask students to review their self-assessments for patterns that may reveal (a) personal *strengths and weakness*, (b) *consistencies* and *discrepancies* between their stated or espoused values and their enacted values, (c) their intentions and goals, (d) assets and resources available to them for realizing their goals, and (e) potential *blocks* or *barriers* that must be overcome to achieve their goals.

Intentionally stimulate students' *intrinsic interest* in and *motivation* for completing tests and assignments The following practices may be used to promote student enthusiasm for and effort in class *exams*.

Include test questions that relate to *current events* or that ask students to apply course concepts to contemporary, real-life situations (e.g., situations involving family relations, peer influence, or future educational choices and occupational choices). This practice serves to increase the probability that students will perceive the test as a relevant learning experience (rather than a grade determination ritual). Assessment becomes "authentic" when it's connected to students' life circumstances and frames of reference (Wlodkowski, 2008).

Have students *construct and submit test questions* for possible inclusion on exams. This practice should increase students' intrinsic interest in the test and is likely to decrease test anxiety by increasing their sense of perceived control over the test situation (Thompson, 1981), and sends students the message that their teacher respects their ideas.

The following practices may be used to promote student enthusiasm and effort on class *assignments*.

> " Assessment that is culturally responsive illuminates the connection between knowledge as others have defined it and meaning that is relevant to individual experiences and belief systems. "
> —Ginsberg & Wlodkowski, *Diversity & Motivation*

Accompany assignments with a clear *rationale* indicating *why* you're asking students to complete them. By taking just a little time to justify assignments and articulate their value, students will be less likely to perceive them as mere "busy work." Relevant to this recommendation is research indicating that "writer's block" is more likely to occur on assignments that writers perceive to be trivial or insignificant (Rennie & Brewer, 1987).

Have students *reflect on the intended learning outcomes* for class assignments. This practice may be effectively implemented by including a final step for each course assignment that asks students to write a short, one-minute reflection on the intended learning outcome of the assignment and whether or not it was met.

When assigning projects or papers, try to provide students with a *topic menu* from which they may choose a topic that most interests or excites them. Providing students with choices about what they will learn increases their intrinsic motivation to learn by increasing their sense of self-determination (i.e., students perceive the source of their motivation as internal, within themselves), rather than external (i.e., being controlled or coerced to learn by outside forces such as the demands of teachers or parents) (Deci & Ryan, 1991). Students who opt for the same topic could be grouped together to complete a team project on their topic of common interest.

Devise assignments that ask students to *apply* course concepts to relevant events occurring *on campus* or in *the local community* (e.g., by having students peruse the campus and city newspapers). Student assignments could be constructed that ask students to locate current events in the popular media and relate them to course issues (e.g., creating a collage or scrapbook comprised of course-relevant newspaper articles, pictures, and cartoons). Students could also peruse the classified section of the local newspaper to find an ad for a position that interests them, and write a persuasive letter to prospective employers in which they articulate why they would be an ideal candidate for the position. Employers from the local community may be invited to class to discuss what they look for in a well-written letter of application.

> "The closer assessment procedures come to allowing learners to demonstrate what they have learned in the areas where they will eventually use that learning, the greater will be their motivation to do well."
> —Ginsberg & Wlodkowski, *Diversity & Motivation*

Create assignments that encourage students to *make connections across different topics or instructional units*. For example, students could be asked to relate ideas currently being discussed in a unit on diversity to material previously covered in a unit on American history. Encouraging students to make connections across topics is a teaching practice that is consistent with the principles of implementing "brain-based" or "brain-compatible" learning, because the human brain is wired to seek patterns and make connections (Caine & Caine, 1991). In fact, learning itself is stored in the brain in the form of neurological connection between brain cells (neurons) (Cuseo, Fecas, & Thompson, 2010).

Periodically during the term, give students an assignment that asks them to *summarize or integrate* the most important concepts covered in the class up to that point. Synthesis represents one of the higher forms of thinking (Anderson & Krathwohl, 2001), and asking students to periodically reflect and connect ideas is an effective way to engage them in this higher-level thinking process. If done toward the end of the term, synthesis allows to gain a meaningful sense of "closure" that comes from "tying things altogether" and seeing the "bigger picture."

Summary and Conclusion

The word assessment has taken on a negative connotation among educators over the last several decades. We argue that assessment can be an important tool in improving instruction and offering feedback to students to improve the learning process if properly employed. Good assessment is essential for improving the quality, validity, and equity of student learning. A continuous philosophy of formative and summative assessment will improve the quality of teaching and promote the academic achievement of students from diverse cultural backgrounds.

# Exercise

Writing a Culturally Competent Lesson Plan

The learning outcome: At the end of this class, the student will have a comprehensive understanding of how science is truly a multicultural discipline.

Some questions to consider:
1. How will you ensure your class of 25 eighth graders that come from different cultural backgrounds, different learning styles, different races, different abilities, and different motivations will get the best learning experience?
2. How long will this process take?
3. What outside resources do you need?
4. What makes you the most uncomfortable about this assignment?

Glossary

Ableism: prejudice or discrimination toward people who are disabled (i.e., who are physically, mentally, or emotionally handicapped).

Achievement gap: difference in academic performance between ethnic groups.

Ageism: prejudice or discrimination toward a certain age group, particularly the elderly.

Anti-Semitism: prejudice or discrimination toward Jews or people who practice Judaism.

Apartheid: a strict system of racial segregation and discrimination against nonwhite people, which was once national policy in South Africa.

Bias: predispositions toward viewing something positively or negatively before the facts are known.

Classism: prejudice or discrimination based on social class, particularly toward people of lower socioeconomic status.

Cross-cultural: occurring between or across different cultures.

Cultural acceptance: valuing the differences and similarities that all humans share while viewing differences as a positive.

Cultural acknowledgment: the act of acknowledging the differences that exist between individuals, races, and entire cultures. In addition, it is viewing those existing differences as somewhat more positive than negative.

Cultural action: the process of recognizing differences and responding to them in a positive manner. This encapsulates the process of applying a method to accomplish your goal of becoming culturally competent.

Cultural awareness: an awareness of one's own biases and the effects they may have on yourself and others.

Cultural competence: the ability to appreciate cultural differences and to interact effectively with people from different cultural backgrounds.

Cultural sensitivity: an understanding that your internal biases have affected those around you (both those you know personally and those you do not).

Culturally inclusive assessment: the utilization of multiple forms of assessment to accommodate multiple cultures and learning styles.

Culture: a distinctive pattern of beliefs and values that are learned by a group of people who share the same social heritage, traditions, and style of living (e.g., language, fashion, food, art, music, values, beliefs).

Curriculum (mainstream): a traditional, Eurocentric, male-centered curriculum that largely ignores the contributions and perspective of nondominant groups.

Differentiated instruction: provides students with multiple options for learning to allow them to seek out their own meaning from content and express what they have learned on an individual level.

Discrimination: unequal and unfair treatment of a person or group of people; discrimination is prejudice put into action.

Diversity: the variety of differences that exist among people who comprise humanity (the human species).

Egocentric: to view the world as if one is at the *center* of it, showing little interest in or empathy for others.

Egoistic: to be *selfish* and unwilling to share with others or help others.

Egotistic: conceited and lacking humility.

Empathy: sensitivity to the emotions and feelings of others.

Ethnic group (ethnicity): a group of people sharing the same cultural characteristics, which have been learned or acquired through shared social experiences.

Ethnocentrism: considering one's own culture or ethnic group to be "central" or "normal," and viewing cultures that are different as "deficient" or "inferior."

Genocide: mass murdering of a certain group of people that is motivated by prejudice.

Groupthink: the tendency for tight, like-minded groups of people to think so much alike that they overlook flaws in their own thinking, which can lead to poor group decisions.

Hate crime: an extreme, aggressive act of discrimination that is motivated solely by prejudice (e.g., vandalism, assault, or genocide).

Hate group: an organization whose primary purpose is to stimulate prejudice, discrimination, and hostility toward members of minority groups (e.g., Ku Klux Klan, Neo-Nazis, White Supremacists).

Heterosexism: belief that heterosexuality is the only acceptable sexual orientation.

Homophobia: extreme fear and/or hatred of homosexuals.

Human relations skills: the ability to relate to others in a socially sensitive and humane manner.

Humanity: the universal aspects of the human experience that are shared by all people, regardless of what their particular cultural background happens to be.

Individuality: differences among individuals within the same group.

Institutional racism: a subtle form of racism that is rooted in organizational policies and practices that disadvantage certain racial or ethnic groups (e.g., race-based discrimination in mortgage lending, housing, and bank loans).

Intercultural communication: communication that takes place between members of different cultures.

Interdependence: a style of collaborative teamwork in which group members rely on each other to achieve a common goal.

International diversity: cultural differences that exist between different nations.

Interpersonal communication skills: the ability to listen and speak well when interacting with others.

Interpersonal intelligence (social intelligence): the ability to understand, empathize, and relate to other people.

"Jim Crow" laws: formal and informal laws created by whites after the abolition of slavery to continue their control over black labor.

Learning styles: individual differences in preferred ways of learning (i.e., personal preference for the way in which information is taking in or received, and the way in which information is processed once it has been received).

Looking-glass self: how people act and react to an individual (positively or negatively) reflects back on the individual and affects the person's self-concept or self-esteem (positively or negatively).

Majority group: a group whose membership accounts for more than one-half of the population.

Minority group: a group whose membership accounts for less than one-half of the population.

Multicultural: cultural differences that exist within the same society.

Multicultural curriculum: incorporates diverse perspectives into mainstream curriculum.

Multiple intelligences: different talents or abilities that individuals display, which can vary from person to person.

Multiple perspective-taking: viewing an issue from multiple angles and vantage points, including the perspectives of time (e.g., past, present, or future), place (e.g., national, international, or global), and person (e.g., social, emotional, or physical dimension of self).

Overrepresented group: a group whose percentage (proportion) of a specific population is higher than its percentage of the general population. For example, the majority of Americans who live below the poverty line are people of color, yet people of color represent a minority of the overall (general) population in America.

Prejudice: a negative prejudgment of a person or group of people.

Privilege: an advantage given to, or enjoyed by, a person or group of people.

Qualitative: nonnumerical data obtained through multiple ways, including assessment.

Quantitative: numerical data obtained through multiple ways, including assessment.

Race: a group of people who have been socially categorized on the basis of some distinctive physical traits, such as skin color or facial characteristics.

Racism: prejudice or discrimination based on skin color.

Regionalism: prejudice or discrimination based on the geographical region in which an individual has been born and raised.

Religious bigotry: denying the fundamental human right of other people to hold religious beliefs, or to hold religious beliefs that differ from one's own.

Segregation: the decision of a group to separate itself, either socially or physically, from another group.

Selective listening: selecting or "tuning into" conversational topics that relate only to the listener's personal interests or that support the listener's personal viewpoints, and "tuning out" everything else.

Selective memory: tendency to remember information that is consistent with one's beliefs, while forgetting information that is inconsistent with it or contradicts it.

Selective perception: tendency to see what is consistent with one's belief, while failing to see information that contradicts it.

Self-assessment: a learning process that enables students to look inward and gain insight into themselves as learners.

Self-awareness: a process that enables students to take inventory of their learning styles and habits, educational and career interests, and personal values and interests.

Sexism: prejudice or discrimination based on sex or gender.

Social identity: the group(s) an individual identifies with, which can shape or influence one's personal identity.

Socialization: characteristics that have been learned through social experiences.

Society: a group of people organized under the same social system (e.g., same system of government, justice, and education).

Socioeconomic status: stratification of groups of people into social classes based primarily on their *income* level and level of *education*.

Stereotyping: viewing members of the same group in the same way, such that all individuals in the same group (e.g., same race or gender) are viewed as having the same personal characteristics.

Underrepresented group: a group whose percentage (proportion) of a specific population represents less than its percentage of the general population. For example, the percentage of women in the specific field of engineering is far less than their percentage in the general population.

Xenophobia: extreme fear or hatred of foreigners, outsiders, or strangers.

References
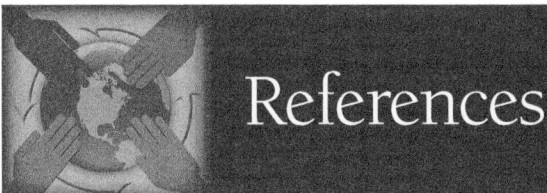

Aaronson, D., Barrow, L., & Sander, W. (2007). Teachers and student achievement in the Chicago public high schools. *Journal of Labor Economics, 25*(1), 95–136.

Abdul-Adil, J.K., & Farmer, A.D. (2006). Inner-city African American parental involvement in elementary schools: Getting beyond urban legends of apathy. *School Psychology Quarterly, 21*, 1–12.

Acredolo, C., & O'Connor, J. (1991). On the difficulty of detecting cognitive uncertainty. *Human Development, 34*, 204–223.

ACT. (2006). *Ready for college and ready for work: Same or different?* Iowa City, IA: Author.

Adelman, C. (2004). *Principal indicators of student academic histories in postsecondary education, 1972–2000.* Washington, DC: U.S. Department of Education.

Adler, R.B., & Towne, M. (2001). *Looking out, looking in: Interpersonal communication* (10th ed.). Orlando, FL: Harcourt Brace.

Aikenhead, G.S. (1997). Toward a First Nations cross-cultural science and technology curriculum. *Science Education, 81*, 217–238.

Aikenhead, G.S. (2001). Integrating Western and Aboriginal sciences: Cross-cultural science teaching. *Research in Science Education, 31*, 337–335.

Alliance for Excellent Education. (2009). Teaching for a new world: Preparing high school educators to deliver college and career ready instruction. Retrieved January 10, 2012, from http://www.all4ed.org/files/TeachingForANewWorld.pdf.

Allport, G.W. (1954). *The nature of prejudice.* Cambridge, MA: Addison-Wesley.

Allport, G.W. (1979). *The nature of prejudice* (3rd ed.). Reading, MA: Addison-Wesley.

American College Personnel Association (1994). *The student learning imperative: Implications for student affairs.* Washington, DC: Author.

American Council on Education (2008). Making the case for affirmative action. Retrieved October 25, 2008, from http://www.acenet.edu/bookstore/descriptions/making_the_case/works/research.cfm.

American Heart Association. (2006). Fish, levels of mercury and omega-3 fatty acids. Retrieved January 13, 2007, from http://americanheart.org/presenter.jthml?identifier=3013797.

American School Counselor Association. (2010). 2008–2009 Student to counselor ratios. Retrieved January 10, 2012, from http://www.schoolcounselor.org/content.asp?contentid=460.

Amir, Y. (1969). Contact hypothesis in ethnic relations. *Psychological Bulletin, 71*, 319–342.

Amir, Y. (1976). The role of intergroup contact in change of prejudice and ethnic relations. In P. A. Katz (Ed.), *Towards the elimination of racism* (pp. 245–308). New York: Pergamon Press.

Anderson, K.M. (2007). Differentiating instruction to include all students. *Preventing School Failure, 51*(3), 49–54.

Anderson, L.W., & Krathwohl, D.R. (Eds.) (2001). *A taxonomy for learning, teaching, and assessing: A revision of Bloom's taxonomy of educational objectives.* New York: Longman.

Anderson, M., & Fienberg, S.E. (2000). Race and ethnicity and the controversy over the U.S. census. *Current Sociology, 48*(3), 87–110.

Angelo, T.A. (1997). The campus as learning community: Seven promising shifts and seven powerful levers. AAHE Bulletin, *4*(9), 3–6.

Angelo, T.A., & Cross, P. (1993). *Classroom assessment techniques: A handbook for college teachers* (2nd ed.). San Francisco: Jossey-Bass.

Applebee, A.N. (1984). Writing and reasoning. *Review of Educational Research, 54*(4), 577–596.

Archer-Banks, D.M. (2008). African American parental involvement in their children's middle school experience. *Journal of Negro Education, 77,* 143–156.

Aronson, E. (1978). *The jigsaw classroom.* Beverly Hills, CA: Sage.

Aronson, E., & Gonzalez, A. (1988). Desegregation, jigsaw and the Mexican-American experience. In P. Katz & D. Taylor (Eds.), *Eliminating racism.* New York: Plenum.

Aronson, E., Wilson, T.D., & Akert, R.M. (2005). *Social psychology* (5th ed.). Upper Saddle River, NJ: Pearson/Prentice Hall.

Aronson, E., Wilson, T.D., & Akert, R.M. (2007). *Social psychology* (6th ed.). Upper Saddle River, NJ: Pearson/Prentice Hall.

Arum, R., & Roska, J. (2011). *Academically adrift: Limited learning on college campuses.* Chicago, IL: University of Chicago Press.

Assessment & Teaching of 21st Century Skills. (n.d.). What are 21st century skills? Retrieved January 10, 2012, from http://atc21s.org/index.php/about/what-are-21st-century-skills/.

Association for Effective Schools. (1996). Correlates of effective schools. Retrieved January 10, 2012. from http://www.mes.org/correlates.html.

Astin, A.W. (1993). *What matters in college?* San Francisco: Jossey-Bass.

Astin, A.W., Vogelgesang, L.J., Ikeda, E.K., & Yee, J.A. (2000). *How service learning affects students.* Los Angeles: Higher Education Research Institute, UCLA.

Astin, H.S., Astin, A.W., Bisconti, A.S., & Frankel, H.H. (1972). *Higher education and the disadvantaged student.* Washington, DC: Human Service Press.

Aud, S., Fox, M., & KewalRamani, A. (2010). Status and trends in the education of racial and ethnic groups (NCES 2010-015). Washington, DC: U.S. Government Printing Office, U.S. Department of Education, National Center for Education Statistics. Retrieved January 10, 2012, from http://nces.ed.gov/pubs2010/2010015.pdf.

Aud, S., Hussar, W., Kena, G., Bianco, K., Frohlich, L., Kemp, J., & Tahan, K. (2011). The condition of education 2011 (NCES 2011-033). Washington, DC: U.S. Government Printing Office, U.S. Department of Education, National Center for Education Statistics. Retrieved January 10, 2012, from http://nces.ed.gov/programs/coe/pdf/coe_trc.pdf.

Avolio, B.J. (2005). *Leadership development in balance: Made/born.* Mahwah, NJ: Lawrence Erlbaum Associates.

Balfanz, R., & Legters, N. (2004). *Locating the dropout crisis.* Baltimore: Johns Hopkins University Center for Social Organization of Schools.

Bandura, A. (1997). *Self-efficacy: The exercise of control.* New York: Freeman.

Banks, J.A. (2006). *Cultural diversity and education: Foundations, curriculum, and teaching* (5th ed.). Boston: Allyn & Bacon.

Banks, J.A. (1995). Multicultural education and curriculum transformation. *The Journal of Negro Education, 64*(4), 390–400.

Banks, J. (1993). Approaches to multicultural curriculum reform. In J. Banks & C. Banks (Eds.), *Multicultural education: Issues and perspectives.* Boston: Allyn & Bacon.

Banks, J.A., & Banks, C.A.M. (Eds.) (1995). *Handbook of research on multicultural education.* New York: Macmillan.

Banks, J.A., Cookson, P., Gay, G., Hawley, W., Irvine, J.J, Nieto, S., Schofield, J.W., & Stephan, W. (2001). Diversity within unity: Essential principles for teaching and learning in a multicultural society. *Phi Delta Kappan, 83*(3), 196–203.

Banks, C.A.M. (1997). Parents and teachers: Partners in school reform. In J.A. Banks & C.A.M. Banks (Eds.), *Multicultural Education: Issues and Perspectives* (3rd ed., pp. 408–426). Boston: Allyn and Bacon.

Bar, M., Neta, M., & Linz, H. (2006). Very first impressions. *Emotion, 6,* 269–278.

Baron, R.A., Byrne, D., & Branscombe, N.R. (2006). *Mastering social psychology*. Boston: Pearson/Allyn and Bacon.

Barr, R.B., & Tagg, J. (1995). From teaching to learning—A new paradigm for undergraduate education. *Change*, Nov/Dec, 13–25.

Bass, B.M., & Riggio, R.E. (2005). *Transformational leadership* (2nd ed.). Mahwah, NJ: Lawrence Erlbaum Associates.

Blake, R., & Mouton, J. (1979). Intergroup problem solving in organizations: From theory to practice. In W. Austin & S. Worchel (Eds.), *The social psychology of intergroup relations*. Monterey, CA: Brooks/Cole.

Bennis, D., & Graves, I. (n.d.). Introduction to The Directory of Democratic Education. Retrieved from http://montana2010.wordpress.com/about/quote-from-aero-website/.

Bernstein, C. (1986). Teaching about ethnic diversity. Retrieved January 10, 2012, from http://www.ericdigests.org/pre-924/ethnic.htm.

Bligh, D.A. (2000). *What's the use of lectures*. San Francisco: Jossey-Bass.

Bloom, B. (1968). Learning for mastery. *Evaluation Comment, 1*(2), 1–5.

Bloom, B.S. (1978). New views of the learner: Implications for instruction and curriculum. *Educational Leadership, 35*(7), 563–576.

Bloom, B.S. (1984). *Taxonomy of educational objectives. Cognitive domain*. New York: Longman.

Bodian, S. (2006). *Meditation for dummies*. Hoboken, NJ: Wiley Publishing.

Boekaerts, M., Pintrich, P.R., & Zeidner, M. (Eds.). (2000). *Handbook of self-regulation*. San Diego: Academic Press.

Bok, D. (2006). *Our underachieving colleges*. Princeton, NJ: Princeton University Press.

Bonwell, C.C., & Eison, J.A. (1991). Active Learning: Creating Excitement in the Classroom. ASHE-ERIC Higher Education Report No. 1. Washington, DC: The George Washington University, School of Education and Human Development.

Bowman, B.T. (1995). Cultural diversity and academic achievement. Retrieved January 10, 2012, from http://www.ncrel.org/sdrs/areas/issues/educatrs/leadrshp/le0bow.htm#author.

Bowers, J.W. (1986). Classroom communication apprehension: A survey. *Communication Education, 35*(4), 372–378.

Boyer, E.L. (1987). *College: The undergraduate experience in America*. New York: Harper & Row.

Brandt, R. (1994). On educating for diversity: A conversation with James Banks. *Educational Leadership, 52*(9), 31–35.

Bransford, J., Brown, A., & Cocking, R. (1999). *How people learn: Brain, mind, experience, and school*. Washington, DC: The National Academies Press.

Bridgeman, B. (2003). *Psychology and evolution: The origins of mind*. Thousand Oaks, CA: Sage.

Broadbent, D.E. (1970). Review lecture. *Proceedings of the Royal Society of London B*, 333–350.

Brookfield, S.D. (1987). *Developing critical thinkers*. San Francisco: Jossey-Bass.

Brookfield, S., & Preskill, S. (2005). *Discussion as a way of teaching: Tools and techniques for democratic classrooms* (2nd ed.). San Francisco: Jossey-Bass.

Brookings Institution, The. (2008). Demographic keys to the 2008 election. Washington, DC: Brookings Institute. Retrieved January 10, 2012, from www.brookings.edu/~/media/Files/events/2008/1020_demographics/ 20081020_demographics.pdf.

Brophy, J. (2004). *Motivating students to learn* (2nd ed.). Mahwah, NJ: Erlbaum.

Brown, T.D., Dane, F.C., & Durham, M.D. (1998). Perception of race and ethnicity. *Journal of Social Behavior & Personality, 13*(2), 295–306.

Bruffee, K.A. (1993). *Collaborative learning: Higher education, interdependence, and the authority of knowledge*. Baltimore: Johns Hopkins University Press.

Burgess, J.M., & Sales, S. (1977). Attitudinal effects of "mere exposure": A reevaluation. *Journal of Experimental Social Psychology, 7*, 461–472.

Butler, J. (1993). *Bodies that matter*. Routledge: New York.

Caine, R.N., & Caine, G. (1991). *Making connections: Teaching and the human brain*. Alexandria, VA: Association for Supervision and Curriculum Development.

California Newsreel. (2003). Race: The power of an illusion. Retrieved January 10, 2012, from http://newsreel.org/video/RACE-THE-POWER-OF-AN-ILLUSION.

Carroll, J. (1963). A model for school learning. *Teacher College Record, 64*, 723–733.

Carter, C.S. (1998). Neuroendocrine perspectives on social attachment and love. *Psychneuroendocrine, 23*, 779–818.

Cartledge, G., Singh, A., & Gibson, L. (2008). Practical behavior management techniques to close the accessibility gap for students who are culturally and linguistically diverse. *Preventing School Failure, 52*(3), 29–38.

Cawelti, G. (1999). *Handbook of research on improving student achievement*. Arlington, VA: Educational Research Service.

Center for Strengthening the Teaching Profession. (2009). Culturally responsive classroom descriptors. Retrieved January 10, 2012, from http://cstp-wa.org/sites/default/files/classroom_descriptors_web_0.pdf.

Chang, L., Chang, C.M., Stewart, S.M., & Au, E. (2003). Life satisfaction, self-concept, and family relations in Chinese adolescents and children. *International Journal of Behavioral Development, 33*, 421–429.

Chapman, C., Laird, J., & KewalRamani, A. (2010). Trends in high school dropout and completion rates in the United States: 1972–2008 (NCES 2011-012). Washington, DC: National Center for Education Statistics, Institute of Education Sciences, U.S. Department of Education. Retrieved January 10, 2012, from http://nces.ed.gov/pubs2011/2011012.pdf.

Chatman, S. (2008). Does diversity matter in the education process? an exploration of student interactions by wealth, religion, politics, race, ethnicity and immigrant status at the University of California. Research & Occasional Paper Series: CSHE.5.08. Center for Studies in Higher Education; University of California, Berkeley. Retrieved from http://cshe.berkeley.edu/publications/docs/ROPS.Chatman.Exploring.3.5.08.pdf.

Chickering, A.W. (1969). *Education and identity*. San Francisco: Jossey-Bass.

Chickering, A.W., & Reisser, L. (1993). *Education and identity* (2nd ed.). San Francisco: Jossey-Bass.

Chisholm, I.M. (1994). Preparing teachers for multicultural classrooms. *Journal of Educational Issues of Language Minority Students, 14*, 43–68.

Christensen, C.R., & Hansen, A. (1987). *Teaching and the case method*. Boston: Harvard Business School.

Cianciotto, J. (2005). *Hispanic and Latino same-sex couple households in the United States: A report from the 2000 Census*. New York: The National Gay and Lesbian Task Force Policy Institute and the National Latino/a Coalition for Justice.

Clark, C.R., Guskey, T.R., & Benninga, J.S. (1983). The effectiveness of mastery learning strategies in undergraduate education courses. *Journal of Educational Research, 74*, 210–214.

Clegg, V.L., & Cashin, W.E. (1986) Improving multiple-choice tests. IDEA Paper No. 16. Retrieved January 10, 2012, from http://www.theideacenter.org/sites/default/files/Idea_Paper_16.pdf.

Clewell, B., Anderson, B., & Thorpe, M. (1992). *Breaking the barriers: Helping female and minority students succeed in mathematics and science*. San Francisco: Jossey-Bass.

Colombo, G., Cullen, R., & Lisle, B. (1995). *Rereading America: Cultural contexts for critical thinking and writing*. Boston: Bedford Books of St. Martin's Press.

Conley, D. (2005). *The pecking order: A bold new look and how family and society determine who we become*. New York, Random House.

Cook, S.W. (1984). Cooperative interaction in multiethnic contexts. In N. Miller & M.B. Brewer (Eds.), *Groups in contact: The psychology of desegregation*. New York: Academic Press.

Cooley, C.H. (1922). *Human nature and the social order.* New York: Scribner's.

Coopersmith, J. (2009). Characteristics of public, private, and bureau of Indian education elementary and secondary school teachers in the United States: Results from the 2007–08 schools and staffing survey (NCES 2009-324). Washington, DC: National Center for Education Statistics, Institute of Education Sciences, U.S. Department of Education. Retrieved January 10, 2012, from http://nces.ed.gov/pubs2009/2009324.pdf.

Cross, P.K. (1982). Thirty years have passed: Trends in general education. In B.L. Johnson (Ed.), *General education in two-year colleges* (pp. 11-20). New Directions for Community Colleges, No. 40. San Francisco: Jossey-Bass.

Cross, K.P., & Angelo, T.A. (1989). Faculty members as classroom researcher. *American Association of Community and Junior College Journal, April/May*, 23–25.

Curran, M. (2007). Putting anti-oppressive language teacher education in practice. In K.K. Kumashiro & B. Ngo (Eds.), *Six lenses for anti-oppressive education: Partial stories, improbable conversations* (pp. 177–192). New York: Peter Lang.

Cuseo, J. (1992). Cooperative learning vs. small-group discussions and group projects: The critical differences. *Cooperative Learning and College Teaching*, 2(3).

Cuseo, J.B. (1996). *Cooperative learning: A pedagogy for addressing contemporary challenges and critical issues in higher education*. Stillwater, OK: New Forums Press.

Cuseo, J. (2002). Igniting student involvement, peer interaction, and teamwork: A taxonomy of specific cooperative leaning structures and collaborative learning strategies. Stillwater, OK: New Forums Press.

Cuseo, J. (2004a, February). Teaching the first-year seminar: How do we motivate students and maximize course impact? Presentation made at the Annual Conference on the First-Year Experience. Addison, TX.

Cuseo, J. (2004b). The empirical case against large class size: Adverse effects on the teaching, learning, and retention of first-year students. Posted manuscript, First-Year Assessment Listserv (FYA). Series. [On-line serial]. Policy Center for the First Year of College.

Cuseo, J. (2005). Questions that promote deeper thinking skills. On Course Newsletter, July. Retrieved January 10, 2012, from http://www.oncourseworkshop.com/Learning030.htm.

Cuseo, J.B., Fecas, V., & Thompson, A. (2010). Thriving in college and beyond: Research-based strategies for academic success and personal development (2nd ed.). Dubuque, IA: Kendall Hunt.

Cusinato, M., & L'Abate, L. (1994). A spiral model of intimacy. In S.M. Johnson & L. S. Greenberg (Eds.), *The heart of the matter: Emotion in marital therapy*. New York: Brunner/Mazel.

Csikszentimihalyi, M. (1990). Literacy and intrinsic motivation. *Daedalus, 119,* 115–140.

Darling-Hammond, L. (2000). Teacher quality and student achievement: A review of state policy evidence. *Educational Policy Analysis Archives*, 8(1). Retrieved January 10, 2012, from http://epaa.asu.edu/ojs/article/view/392/515.

Darling-Hammond, L., & Bransford, J. (2005). *Preparing teachers for a changing world: What teachers should learn and be able to do*. San Francisco: Jossey-Bass.

Davis, B.G., Wood, L., & Wilson, R.C. (1983). *ABCs of teaching with excellence*. Berkeley: University of California.

Deci, E.L., & Ryan, R.M. (1991). A motivational approach to self: Integration in personality. In R. Dienstbier (Ed.), *Nebraska symposium on motivation: Vol. 38, Perspectives on motivation* (pp. 237–288). Lincoln, NE: University of Nebraska Press.

Delpit, L. (1995). *Other people's children: Cultural conflict in the classroom*. New York: New York Press.

DeNavas-Walt, C., Proctor, B.D., & Smith, J.C. (2010). *Income, poverty, and health insurance coverage in the United States: 2009*. Current Population Reports, P60-238. Washington, DC: U.S. Government Printing Office, U.S. Census Bureau.

Diller, J.V., & Moule, J. (2004). Cultural competence: A primer for educators. Wadsworth Publishing.

Donahue, J., & Siegel, M.E. (2005). *Are you really listening: Keys to successful communication*. South Bend, IN: Ave Maria Press.

Dryden, G., & Vos, J. (1999). *The learning revolution: To change the way the world learns*. Torrance, CA: Learning Web.

Du Praw, M., & Axner, M. (1997). Toward a more perfect union in an age of diversity: Working on common cross-cultural communication challenges. Retrieved September 27, 2008, from http://www.pbs.org/ampu/crosscult.html.

Dweck, C.S., & Leggett E.L. (1988). A social-cognitive approach to motivation and personality. *Psychological Review, 95*, 256–273.

Ebel, R.L. (1972). *Essentials of educational measurement*. Prentice Hall.

Education Commission of the States. (1995). *Making quality count in undergraduate education*. Denver, CO: ECS Distribution Center.

The Education Trust. (2008). *Funding gaps 2008*. Washington, DC: Author.

Elbow, P. (1986). *Embracing contraries: Explorations in learning and teaching*. New York: Oxford University Press.

Encrenaz, T., Bibring, J.P., Blanc, M., Barucci, M.A., Roques, F., & Zarka, P. (2004). *The solar system*. Berlin: Springer.

Epstein, J.L. (1995). School/family/community partnerships: Caring for the children we share. *Phi Delta Kapplan, 76*, 701–712.

Erickson, B.L., & Strommer, D.W. (1991). *Teaching college freshmen*. San Francisco: Jossey-Bass.

Erickson, B.L., & Strommer, D.W. (2005). Inside the first-year classroom: Challenges and constraints. In J.L. Upcraft, J.N. Gardner, & B.O. Barefoot (Eds.), *Challenging and supporting the first-year student* (pp. 241–256). San Francisco: Jossey-Bass.

Etsy, K., Griffin, R., & Hirsch, M.S. (1995). *Workplace diversity*. Holbrook, MA: Adams Media Corporation.

Eyler, J., & Giles, D.E., Jr. (1999). *Where's the learning in service-learning?* San Francisco: Jossey-Bass.

Family Care Foundation. (2005). If the world were a village of 100 people. Retrieved December 19, 2006, from http://www.familycare.org.news/if_the_world.htm.

Feagin, J., & Feagin, C. (2003). *Racial and ethnic relations* (7th ed.). Upper Saddle River, NJ: Prentice Hall.

Feagin, J.R., & McKinney, K.D. (2003). *The many costs of racism*. Lanham, MD: Rowman & Littlefield.

Felstead, A., Gallie, D., & Green, F. (2002). Work skills in Britain 1986–2001. Retrieved December 22, 2006, from http://www.kent.ac.uk/economics/staff/gfg/WorkSkills1986–2001.pdf.

Feskens, K., & Kromhout E.J. (1994). Fish consumption and risk of stroke. The Zutphen Study. *Stroke, 25*, 328–332.

Fiechtner, S.B., & Davis, E.A. (1992). Why some groups fail: A survey of students' experiences with learning groups. In A.S. Goodsell, M.R. Maher & V. Tinto (Eds.), *Collaborative learning: A sourcebook for higher education*. Syracuse, NY: National Center on Postsecondary Teaching, Learning, & Assessment, Syracuse University.

Fields-Smith, C. (2003, April). "After it takes a village" African American parental involvement in the post desegregation era. Paper presented at the annual meeting of the American Educational Research Association, Chicago, IL.

Fitzgerald, J. (1987). Research on revision in writing. *Review of Educational Research, 57*(4), 481–506.

Fixman, C.S. (1990). The foreign language needs of U.S. based corporations. *Annals of the American Academy of Political and Social Science, 511,* 25–46.

Forsyth, D.R., & McMillan, J.H. (1991). Practical proposals for motivating students. In R.J. Menges & M.D. Svinicki (Eds.), *College teaching: From theory to practice.* New Directions in Teaching and Learning, no. 45. San Francisco: Jossey-Bass.

Frederiksen, N. (1984). The real test bias: Influences of testing on teaching and learning. *American Psychologist, 39,* 193–202.

Freire, P. (1970). *Pedagogy of the oppressed.* New York: Continuum.

Freire, P., & Macedo, D. (1987). *Literacy: Reading the word and the world.* South Hadley, MA: Bergin & Garvey.

Fritz, H. (1997). *George Washington and Slavery.* University of Missouri Press.

Gage, N.L., & Berliner, D.C. (1984). *Educational psychology* (3rd ed.). Boston: Houghton Mifflin.

Gamson, Z. (1993). Deep learning, surface learning. *AAHE Bulletin, 45*(8), 11–13.

Gardner, H. (1993). *Frames of mind: The theory of multiple intelligences* (2nd ed.). New York: Basic Books.

Gardner, H. (1999). *Intelligence reframed: Multiple intelligences for the 21st century.* New York: Basic Books.

Gemmil, G. (1989). The dynamics of scapegoating in small groups. *Small Group Behavior, 20,* 406–418.

Gerard, H., & Miller, N. (1975). *School desegregation.* New York: Plenum Press.

Gibb, J.R. (1961). Defensive communication. *The Journal of Communication, 11* (September), 3.

Ginsberg, M.B. (2005). Motivation, cultural diversity, and differentiation. *Theory into Practice, 44*(3), 218–225.

Ginsberg, M.B., & Wlodkowski, R.J. (2009). *Diversity and motivation: Culturally responsive teaching in college.* San Francisco: Jossey-Bass.

Gladwell, M. (2005). *Blink: The power of thinking without thinking.* New York: Little, Brown.

Goffman, E. (Ed.) (1967). *Interaction ritual: Essays in face-to-face behavior.* Chicago: Aldine.

Goleman, D. (1995). *Emotional intelligence: Why it can matter more than IQ.* New York: Random House.

Goleman, D. (2006). *Emotional intelligence: Why it can matter more than IQ.* New York: Bantom Books.

Goleman, D. (2007). *Social intelligence: The new science of human relationships.* Hutchinson.

Gonzalez, G., & Maez, L. (1995, Fall). Advances in research in bilingual education. *Directions in Language and Education, 1*(5), 694–701.

Gordon, R., Piana, L.D., & Keleher, T. (2000). *Facing the consequences: An examination of racial discrimination in U.S. public schools.* Oakland, CA: Applied Research Center.

Gorski, P. (1995). A course in race and ethnicity. Language of closet racism. Retrieved from http://curry.eduschool.virginia.edu/go/multicultural/langofracism2.html.

Gorski, P.C. (2010). EdChange, Multicultural Pavilion. Retrieved January 10, 2012, from http://www.edchange.org/multicultural/index.html.

Gorski, P.C. (2009). What we're teaching teachers: An analysis of multicultural teacher education coursework syllabi. *Teaching and Teacher Education, 25*(2), 309–318.

Green, M.G. (Ed.) (1989). *Minorities on campus: A handbook for enhancing diversity*. Washington, DC: American Council on Education.

Greene, J.P., & Winters, M. (2005). *Public high school graduation and college readiness: 1991–2002*. New York: Manhattan Institute for Policy Research.

Groen, M. (2008). The Whig party and the rise of common schools, 1837–1854," *American Educational History Journal, 35*(1/2), 251–260.

Gronlund, N.E. (1985). *Measurement and evaluation in teaching*. New York: MacMillan.

Gurin, P. (1999). Selections from The Compelling Need for Diversity in Higher Education, expert reports in defense of the University of Michigan: expert report of Patricia Gurin. *Equity and Excellence in Education, 32*(2), 37–62.

Guskey, T.R., Benninga, J.S., & Clark, C.R. (1984). Mastery learning and students' attributions at the college level. *Research in Higher Education, 20*, 491–498.

Gutmann, A. (1999a). Distributing higher education. In B.A. Pescosolido & R. Aminzade (Eds.), *The social worlds of higher education: Handbook for teaching in a new century* (pp. 370–383). Thousand Islands, CA: Pine Forge Press.

Gutmann, A. (1999b). *Democratic education*. Princeton, NJ: Princeton University Press.

Haberman, M. (1991). Pedagogy of poverty versus good teaching. *Phi Delta Kappan, 73*, 290–294.

Hall, R.M., & Sandler, B.R. (1982). *The classroom climate: A chilly one for women*. Association of American Colleges' Project on the Status of Women. Washington, DC: Association of American Colleges.

Hall, R.M., & Sandler, B.R. (1984). *Out of the classroom: A chilly campus climate for women*. Association of American Colleges' Project on the Status of Women. Washington, DC: Association of American Colleges.

Hamilton, D.L., & Sherman, S.J. (1989). Illusory correlations: Implications for stereotype theory and research. In D. Bar-Tal, C.F. Graumann, A.W. Kruglanski, & W. Stroebe (Eds.), *Stereotyping and prejudice: Changing conceptions* (pp. 59–82). New York: Springer-Verlag.

Hanushek, E. (2005). Some U.S. evidence on how the distribution of educational outcomes can be changed. Paper prepared for Schooling and Human Capital in the Global Economy: Revisiting the Equity-Efficiency Quandary, Munich, Germany.

Hart, L.A. (1983). *Human brain and human learning*. New York: Longman, Inc.

Hart Research Associates. (2009). Raising the bar: Employers' views on college learning in the wake of the economic downturn. Retrieved January 10, 2012, from http://www.aacu.org/leap/documents/2009_EmployerSurvey.pdf.

Haycock, K. (1998). *Good teaching matters . . . a lot*. Washington, DC: Education Trust.

Hill, P. J. (1991). Multiculturalism: The crucial philosophical and organizational issues. *Change, 23*(4), 38–47.

Hitchcock, C., Meyer, A., Rose, D., & Jackson, R. (2002). Technical brief: Access, participation, and progress in the general curriculum. Peabody, MA: National Center on Accessing the General Curriculum. Retrieved January 10, 2012, from http://www.cast.org/ncac/index.cfm?i=2830.

Hogan, R., Curphy, G.J., & Hogan, J. (1994). What we know about leadership: Effectiveness and personality. *American Psychologist, 49*, 493–504.

Holmes, M., & Wynne, E.A. (1989). *Making the school an effective community: Belief, practice, and theory in school administration*. Philadelphia, PA: Falmer Press.

Howard, T.C. (2002). Hearing footsteps in the dark: African American students; descriptions of effective teachers. *Journal of Education for Students Placed at Risk, 7*(4), 425–444.

Howes, C., Bryant, D., Burchinal, M., Clifford, R., Early, D., Pianta, R., Barbarin, O., & Ritchie, S. (2006). *National Center for Early Development and Learning (NCEDL) issued statement*. Chapel Hill, NC: NCEDL, FPG Child Development Institute.

Hugenberg, K., & Bodenhausen, G.V. (2003). Facing prejudice: Implicit prejudice and the perception of facial threat. *Psychological Science, 14*, 640–643.

Hull, G. (1981). Effects of self-management strategies on journal writing by college freshmen. *Research in the Teaching of English, 15*, 135–148.

Hunter, M. (1994). *Enhancing teaching*. New York: Macmillan College Publishing Company.

International Wellness Directory. (2009). The history of quackery. Retrieved January 10, 2012, from http://www.mnwelldir.org/docs/history/quackery.htm.

Ireson, J., & Hallam, S. (2005). Pupils' liking for school: Ability grouping, self-concept and perceptions of teaching. *British Journal of Educational Psychology, 75*, 297–311.

Jablonski, N.G., & Chaplin, G. (2002). Skin deep. *Scientific American* (October), 75–81.

Janis, I.L. (1982). *Groupthink: Psychological studies of policy decisions and fiascoes* (2nd ed.). Boston: Houghton Mifflin.

Jensen, E. (1998). *Teaching with the brain in mind*. Alexandria, VA: Association for Supervision and Curriculum Development.

Johnson, S.D., & Bechler, C. (1998). Examining the relationship between listening effectiveness and leadership emergence: Perceptions, behaviors, and recall. *Small Group Research, 29*(4), 452–471.

Johnson, D.W., & Johnson, R.T. (1989). *Leading the cooperative school*. Edina, MN: Interaction.

Johnson, D., Johnson, R., & Smith, K. (1998). Cooperative learning returns to college: What evidence is there that it works? *Change, 30*, 26–35.

Jones, D.J., & Watson, B.C. (1990). "High risk" students and higher education: Future trends. (ASHE-ERIC Higher Education Report No. 3). Washington, DC: The George Washington University, School of Education and Human Development.

Jones, M.G. (1989). Gender issues in teacher education. *Journal of Teacher Education, 40*, 33–38.

Jones, W.T. (1990). Perspectives on ethnicity. In L.V. Moore (Ed.), *Evolving theoretical perspectives on students* (pp. 59–72). San Francisco: Jossey-Bass.

Judd, C.M., Ryan, C.S., & Park, B. (1991). Accuracy in the judgment of in-group and out-group variability. *Journal of Personality and Social Psychology, 61*, 366–379.

Kagan, S. (1992). *Cooperative learning*. Laguna Niguel, CA: Resources for Teachers.

Kagan, S. (1998). New cooperative learning, multiple intelligences, and inclusion. In J. Putnam (Ed.), *Cooperative learning and strategies for inclusion* (2nd ed.). Baltimore, MD: Paul H. Brookes.

Karp, D.A., & Yoels, W.C. (1976). The college classroom: Some observations on the meaning of student participation. *Sociology and Social Research, 60*, 421–439.

Kelly, K. (1994). Out of control: The new biology of machines, social systems, and the economic world. Reading, MA: Addison-Wesley.

Khoshaba, D.M., & Maddi, S.R. (1999). Early experiences in hardiness development. *Consulting Psychology Journal, 51*, 106–116.

Kitayama, S., & Markus, H. (1994). Introduction to cultural psychology and emotion research. In S. Kitayama & H. Markus (Eds.), *Emotion and culture*. Washington, DC: American Psychological Association.

Kitchener, K., Wood, P., & Jensen, L. (2000, August). Curricular, co-curricular, and institutional influence on real-world problem-solving. Paper presented at the annual meeting of the American Psychological Association, Boston, MA.

Klein, L.G., & Knitzer, J. (2007). Promoting effective early learning: What every policymaker and educator should know. National Center for Children in Poverty. Retrieved from http://nccp.org/publications/pub_695.html

Knapp, J.R., & Karabenick, S.A. (1988). Incidence of formal and informal academic help-seeking in higher education. *Journal of College Student Development, 29*, 223–227.

Kober, N. (2001, April). *It takes more than testing: Closing the achievement gap. A report of the Center on Education Policy.* Washington, DC: Center on Education Policy.

Komives, Lucas, & McMahon, (2007). Exploring Leadership: For college students who want to make a difference. Jossey-Bass.

Kopkowski, C. (2006, November). Talk about it. *NEA Today Magazine.* Retrieved January 10, 2012, from http://www.nea.org/home/14439.htm.

Kozol, J. (1991). *Savage inequalities: Children in America's schools.* New York: Harper Collins.

Kulik, J.A., Jaksa, P., & Kulik, C.C. (1978). Research on component features of Keller's Personalized System of Instruction. *Journal of Personalized Instruction, 3*(1), 2–14.

Kurfiss, J. (1988). *Critical thinking: Theory, research, practice, and possibilities. ASHE-ERIC Higher Education Report No. 2.* Washington, DC: Association for the Study of Higher Education.

Ladson-Billings, G. (1995). Making mathematics meaningful in multicultural contexts. In W. Secada, E. Fennema, & L.B. Adajian (Eds.), *New directions for equity in mathematics education* (pp. 126–145). New York: Cambridge University Press.

Langer, J.A., & Applebee, A.N. (1987). *How writing shapes thinking. NCTE Research Report No. 22.* Urbana, IL: National Council of Teachers of English.

Laine, S. (2008). Afterword, in Lessons learned: New teachers talk about their jobs, challenges, and long-range plans. *Teaching in Changing Times, Issue No. 3.* Washington, DC: National Comprehensive Center for Teacher Quality/Public Agenda.

Lareau, A., & Horvat, E.N. (1999). Moments of social inclusion and exclusion: Race, class, and cultural capital in family-school relationships. *Sociology of Education, 72,* 37–53.

Latané, B., Liu, J.H., Nowak, A., Bonevento, N., & Zheng, L. (1995). Distance matters: Physical space and social impact. *Personality and Social Psychology Bulletin, 21,* 795–805.

LeBaron, M. (2003). *Bridging cultural conflicts: New approaches for a changing world.* San Francisco: Jossey-Bass.

Lee, V. E., & Burkam, D.T. (2002). *Inequality at the starting gate: Social background differences in achievement as children begin school.* Washington, DC: Economic Policy Institute.

Lee, O., & Buxton, C. (2008). Science curriculum and student diversity: Culture, language, and socioeconomic status. *The Elementary School Journal, 109*(2), 123–137.

Levine, D.U., & Levine, R.F. (1996). *Society and education,* Allyn and Bacon.

Levin, D.T. (2000). Race as a visual feature: Using visual search and perceptual discrimination tasks to understand face categories and the cross-race recognition deficit. *Journal of Experimental Psychology: General, 129*(4), 559–574.

Levitz, R. (1992). Minority student retention. *Recruitment & Retention in Higher Education, 6*(4), 4–5.

Light, R.J. (2001). *Making the most of college: Students speak their minds.* Cambridge, MA: Harvard University Press.

Light, R.J. (1992). The Harvard Assessment Seminars: Explorations with students and faculty about teaching, learning, and student life. Second report of the Harvard University Graduate School of Education and Kennedy School of Government.

Linville, P.W., Fischer, G.W., & Salovey, P. (1989). Perceived distributions of the characteristics of in-group and out-group members: Empirical evidence and a computer simulation. *Journal of Personality and Social Psychology, 57,* 165–188.

Locke, E.A., & Latham, G.P. (1990). *A theory of goal setting and task performance.* Englewood Cliffs, NJ: Prentice Hall.

Locks, A.M., Hurtado, S., Bowman, N.A., & Oseguera, L. (2008). Extending notions of campus climate and diversity to students' transition to college. *The Review of Higher Education, 31,* 257–285.

Lopez, G.E., Gurin, P., & Nagda, B.A. (1998). Education and understanding structural causes for group inequalities. *Journal of Political Psychology, 19*(2), 305–329.

Lowman, J. (1984). *Mastering the techniques of teaching*. Chapter 7, Planning course content to maximize interest. San Francisco: Jossey-Bass.

Malone, T. (1981). Toward a theory of intrinsically motivating instruction. *Cognitive Science, 4*, 333–369.

Marton, F., & Saljo, R. (1976). On qualitative differences in learning: Outcome and process. *British Journal of Educational Psychology, 46*(1), 4–11.

Marzano, R.J. (2003). *What works in schools*. Alexandria, VA: Association for Supervision and Curriculum Development.

Marzano, R.J., Pickering, D.J., & Pollock, J. (2001). *Classroom instruction that works: Research-based strategies for increasing student achievement*. Alexandria, VA: Association for Supervision and Curriculum Development.

Massey, D. (2003). Housing market rife with racial stereotyping. Retrieved from http://news.harvard.edu/gazette/2003/10.23/09-segregate.html.

Matlock, J. (1997). Student expectations and experiences: The Michigan study. *Diversity Digest*, 11. Washington, DC: Association of American Colleges and Universities.

McArthur, L.Z., & Friedman, S.A. (1980). Illusory correlation in impression formation: Variations in the shared distinctiveness effect as a function of the distinctive person's age, race, and sex. *Journal of Personality and Social Psychology, 39*, 615–624.

McGuinness, D., & Pribram, K. (1980). The neuropsychology of attention: Emotional and motivational controls. In M.C. Wittrock (Ed.), *The brain and psychology* (pp. 62–139). New York: Academic Press.

McIntosh, P. (2000). Interactive phases of personal and curricular re-vision with regard to race. In G. Shin & P. Gorski (Eds.), *Multicultural resource series: Professional development for educators*. Washington, D.C.: National Education Association.

McLeod, J., Fisher, J., & Hoover, G. (2003). *The key elements of classroom management: managing time and space, student behavior and instructional strategies*. Alexandria, VA: Association for Supervision and Curriculum Development.

McKeachie, W.J. (1986). *Teaching tips* (8th ed.). Lexington, MA: Heath.

McMullen-Pastrick, M., & Gleason, M. (1986). Examinations: Accentuating the positive. *College Teaching 34*(4), 135–139.

McKay School of Education. (2010). Diversity activities. Retrieved January 10, 2012, from http://education.byu.edu/diversity/activities.html.

Meadows, D.H. (2005). State of the village report updated in Family Care Foundation. Retrieved January 10, 2012, from http://www.familycare.org/special-interest/if-the-world-were-a-village-of-100-people/.

Meaney, K.S., Bohler, H.R., Kopf, K., Hernandez, L., & Scott, L.S. (2008). Service-learning and pre-service educators' cultural competence for teaching: An exploratory study. *Journal of Experiential Education, 31*(2), 189–208.

Mehrabian, A. (1972). *Nonverbal communication*. Chicago: Adline-Atherton.

Menken, K., & Holmes, P. (2000). *Ensuring English language learners' success: Balancing teacher quantity with quality*. Washington, DC: NCBE.

Meyers, C. (1986). *Teaching students to think critically*. San Francisco: Jossey-Bass.

Meyers, C., & Jones, T.B. (1993). *Promoting active learning: Strategies for the college classroom*. San Francisco: Jossey-Bass.

Milner, A.D., & Goodale, M.A. (1995). *The visual brain in action*. Oxford: Oxford Press.

Milville, M.L., Molla, B., & Sedlacek, W.E. (1992). Attitudes of tolerance for diversity among college students. *Journal of Freshman Year Experience, 4*, 95–110.

Mitrofanova, H. (2004). Building community-schools relations. Retrieved January 10, 2012, from http://lancaster.unl.edu/community/articles/communityschools.shtml.

Molnar, S. (1991). *Human variation: Race, type, and ethnic groups* (3rd ed.). Englewood Cliffs, NJ: Prentice Hall.

Morse, S.W. (1989). *Renewing civic capacity: Preparing college students for service and citizenship. ASHE-ERIC Higher Education Report No. 8.* Washington, DC: The George Washington University, School of Education and Human Development.

Moss, M., & Puma, M. (1995). *Prospects: The congressionally mandated study of educational growth and opportunity: First year report on language minority and limited English proficient students.* Washington, DC: U.S. Department of Education.

Myers, D. (1993). *Social psychology.* McGraw-Hill.

Nagda, B.R., Gurin, P., & Johnson, S.M. (2005). Living, doing and thinking diversity: How does pre-college diversity experience affect first-year students' engagement with college diversity? In R.S. Feldman (Ed.), *Improving the first year of college: Research and practice* (pp. 73–110). Mahwah, NJ: Lawrence Erlbaum.

Nagda, B.R., Gurin, P., & Lopez, G.E. (2003). Transformative pedagogy for democracy and social justice. *Race, Ethnicity, & Education, 6*(2), 165–191.

Nagda, B.A., Gurin, P., Sorensen, N., & Zúñiga, X. (2009). Evaluating intergroup dialogue: Engaging diversity for personal and social responsibility. *Diversity & Democracy, 12*(1), 4–6.

National Alliance to End Homelessness. (2007). Retrieved from http://www.endhomelessness.org/content/general/detail/1440.

National Association of Colleges & Employers. (2003). *Job Outlook 2003 survey.* Bethlehem, PA: Author.

National Center for Education Statistics. (2008). Table 41: Percentage distribution of enrollment in public elementary and secondary schools, by race/ethnicity and state or jurisdiction: Fall 1996 and fall 2006. Washington, DC: U.S. Department of Education.

National Clearinghouse for English Language Acquisition. (n.d.). The growing numbers of limited English proficient students, 1995/96 – 2005/06. Retrieved January 10, 2012, from http://www.ncela.gwu.edu/files/uploads/4/GrowingLEP_0506.pdf.

National Collaborative on Diversity in the Teaching Force. (2004). *Assessment of diversity in America's teaching force.* Washington, DC: Author.

National Council for the Social Studies. (1991). Curriculum guidelines for multicultural education. Retrieved January 10, 2012, from http://www.socialstudies.org/positions/multicultural.

National Council for the Social Studies. (1991). Social studies in the middle school: A report of the task force on social studies in the middle school. Retrieved January 10, 2012, from http://www.ncss.org/positions/middleschool.

National Education Association. (n.d.) Cultural competence for educators. Retrieved January 10, 2012, from http://www.nea.org/tools/30402.htm.

National Survey of Voters. (1998). Overview Report Conducted by DYG, Inc. Retrieved July 15, 2004, from http://www.diversityweb.org/research_and_trends/research_evaluation_impact/campus_community_connections/national_poll.cfm.

Neer, M.R. (1987). The development of an instrument to measure classroom apprehension. *Communication Education, 36,* 154–166.

Nicholas, R.W. (1991). Cultures in the curriculum. *Liberal Education, 77*(3), 16–21.

Nichols, M.P. (1995). *The lost art of listening.* New York: Guilford Press.

Nichols, R.G., & Stevens, L.A. (1957). *Are you listening?* New York: McGraw-Hill.

Norse, E.A. (1990). *Ancient forests of the Pacific Northwest.* Washington, DC: Island Press.

Office of Research. (1994). *What employers expect of college graduates: International knowledge and second language skills.* Washington, DC: Office of Educational Research and Improvement, U.S. Department of Education.

Ogbu, J. (1990). Overcoming racial barriers to equal access. In J. Goodlad & P. Keating (Eds.), *Access to knowledge: An agenda for our nation's schools* (pp. 59–89). New York: The College Board.

Oller, D.K. (1981). Infant vocalizations: Exploration and reflectivity. In R.E. Stark (Ed.), *Language behavior in infancy and early childhood* (pp. 85–104). New York: Elsevier/North-Holland.

Orfield, G. (1993). *The growth of segregation in American schools: Changing patterns of separation and poverty since 1968. A report of the Harvard Project on School Desegregation to the National School Boards Association.* Cambridge, MA: Harvard University Press.

Orfield, G., & Eaton, S.E. (1996). *Dismantling desegregation: The quiet reversal of Brown v. Board of Education.* New York: The New Press.

Orfield, G., & Lee, C. (2005). *Why segregation matters: Poverty and educational inequality.* Cambridge, MA: The Civil Rights Project at Harvard University.

Orfield, G., Losen, D., Wald, J., & Swanson, C. (2004). *Losing our future: How minority youth are being left behind by the graduation rate crisis.* Cambridge, MA: The Civil Rights Project at Harvard University. Contributors: Advocates for Children of New York, The Civil Society Institute.

Padrón, Y.N., & Waxman, H.C. (1993). Teaching and learning risks associated with limited cognitive mastery in science and mathematics for limited English proficient students. In Office of Bilingual Education and Minority Languages Affairs (Eds.), *Proceedings of the third national research symposium on limited English proficient students: Focus on middle and high school issues* (Vol. 2, pp. 511–547). Washington, DC: National Clearinghouse for Bilingual Education.

Paivio, A. (1990). *Mental representation: A dual coding approach.* New York: Oxford University Press.

Papalia, D.E., & Olds, S. (Eds.) (1990). *A child's world: Infancy through adolescence.* New York: McGraw-Hill.

Pascarella, E.T. (2001). Cognitive growth in college: Surprising and reassuring findings from the National Study of Student Learning. *Change,* November/December, 21–27.

Pascarella, E., & Terenzini, P. (2005). *How college affects students: A third decade of research* (Vol. 2). San Francisco: Jossey-Bass.

Pascarella, E., Palmer, B., Moye, M., & Pierson, C. (2001). Do diversity experiences influence the development of critical thinking? *Journal of College Student Development, 42,* 257–291.

Pascarella, E., Edison, M., Nora, A., Hagedorn, L.S., & Terenzini, P. (1996). Influences on students' openness to diversity and challenge in the first year of college. *Journal of Higher Education, 67,* 174–195.

Paul, R., & Elder, L. (2002). *Critical thinking: Tools for taking charge of your professional and personal life.* Upper Saddle River, NJ: Pearson Education.

Peoples, J., & Bailey, G. (2008). *Humanity: An introduction to cultural anthropology* (8th ed.). Belmont, CA: Wadsworth.

Pettigrew, T.F. (1998). Intergroup contact theory. *Annual Review of Psychology, 49,* 65–85.

Phinney, J.S., & Rotheram, J.J. (Eds.). (1987). *Children's ethnic socialization: Pluralism and development.* Newbury Park, CA: Sage.

Pierce, L. (1991). *Effective schools for national origin language minority students.* Washington, DC: The Mid-Atlantic Equity Center.

Pinker, S. (1994). *The language instinct.* New York: HarperCollins.

Pintrich, P.R. (1995). Understanding self-regulated learning. In P.R. Pintrich (Ed.), *Understanding self-regulated learning* (pp. 3–12). San Francisco: Jossey-Bass.

Posner, H.B., & Markstein, J.A. (1994). Cooperative learning in introductory cell and molecular biology. *Journal of College Science Teaching, 23,* 231–233.

Postsecondary Education Opportunity. (2005, June). Family income and higher education opportunity. *Opportunity, 156*(1).

Pratto, F., Liu, J.H., Levin, S., Sidanius, J., Shih, M., Bachrach, H., & Hegarty, P. (2000). Social dominance orientation and the legitimization of inequality across cultures. *Journal of Cross-Cultural Psychology, 31*, 369–409.

Putnam, R.D. (2007). E pluribus unum: Diversity and community in the twenty-first century. *Scandinavian Political Studies, 30*(2).

Ramsey, R.J., & Frank, J. (2007). Wrongful conviction: Perceptions of criminal justice professionals regarding the frequency of wrongful conviction and the extent of system errors. *Crime & Delinquency, 53*, 436–470.

Reis, H.T., & Shaver, P. (1988). Intimacy as an interpersonal process. In S.W. Durck (Ed.), *Handbook of personal relationships* (pp. 367–389). New York: Wiley.

Rendón, L. (1994). Validating culturally diverse students: Toward a new model of learning and student development. *Innovative Higher Education, (19)*1, 33–51.

Rendón, L.I., & Garza, H. (1996). Closing the gap between two- and four-year institutions. In L.I. Rendon & R.O. Hope (Eds.), *Education for a new majority: Transforming America's educational system for diversity* (pp. 289–308). San Francisco: Jossey-Bass.

Rennie, D., & Brewer, L. (1987). A grounded theory of thesis blocking. *Teaching of Psychology, 14*(1), 10–16.

Revilla, A.T., & Sweeney, Y.D.L.G. (1997). Low income does not cause low school achievement: Creating a sense of family and respect in the school environment. Retrieved January 10, 2012, from http://www.idra.org/IDRA_Newsletter/June_-_July_1997_High_-_Performing_High_Poverty_Schools/Low_Income_Does_Not_Cause_Low_School_Achievement/.

Reyes, P. (Ed.). (1990). *Teachers and their workplace: Commitment, performance and productivity.* San Francisco: Sage Publications.

Richardson, R.C., Jr. (1989). If minority students are to succeed in higher education, every rung of the educational ladder must be in place. *The Chronicle of Higher Education,* January 11, A48.

Riquelme, H. (2002). Can people creative in imagery interpret ambiguous figures faster than people less creative in imagery? *Journal of Creative Behavior, 36*(2), 105–116.

Rivera, B.D., & Rogers-Adkinson, D. (1997). Culturally sensitive interventions: Social skills training with children and parents from culturally and linguistically diverse backgrounds. *Intervention in School and Clinic, 33*, 75–80.

Rogers, C.R. (1975). Can learning encompass both ideas and feelings? *Education, 95*, 103–106.

Rogers, M., Hennigan, K., Bowman, C., & Miller, N. (1984). Intergroup acceptance in classroom and playground settings. In N. Miller & M.B. Brewer (Eds.), *Groups in contact: The psychology of desegregation* (pp. 187–212). Orlando, FL: Academic Press.

Rosenshine, B. (1971). *Teaching behaviors and student achievement.* London: National Foundation for Educational Research.

Rosenshine, B. (1997). Advances in research on instruction. In J.W. Lloyd, E.J. Kameanui, & D. Chard (Eds.), *Issues in educating students with disabilities* (pp. 197–221). Mahwah, NJ: Lawrence Erlbaum.

Rosenshine, B., & Stevens, R. (1986). Teaching functions. In M.C. Witrock (Ed.), *Handbook of research on teaching* (3rd ed., pp. 376–391). New York: Macmillan.

Rosser, S.V. (Ed.). (1988). *Feminism in the science and health care professions: Overcoming resistance.* New York: Pergamon Press.

Roueche, S.D., & Comstock, V.N. (1981). *A report on theory and method for the study of literacy development in community colleges.* Technical Report NIE-400-78-0600. Austin, TX: Program in Community College Education, The University of Texas at Austin.

Rudman, L.A., & Fairchild, K. (2004). Reactions to counter-stereotypic behavior: The role of backlash in cultural stereotype maintenance. *Journal of Personality and Social Psychology, 87*, 157–176.

Ruhl, K.L., Hughes, C.A., & Schloss, P.J. (1987). Using the pause procedure to enhance lecture recall. *Teacher Education and Special Education, 10*, 14–18.

Sadker, M., & Sadker, D. (1994). *Failing at fairness: How America's schools cheat girls.* New York: Charles Scribner's Sons.

Sanders, W.L., & Rivers, J.C. (1996). Cumulative and residual effects of teachers on future students' academic achievement. Knoxville, TN: University of Tennessee Value-Added Research and Assessment Center. Retrieved January 10, 2012, from http://heartland.org/policy-documents/cumulative-and-residual-effects-teachers-future-student-academic-achievement.

Sangrigoli, S., Pallier, C., Argenti, A.M., Ventureyra, V.A.G., & de Schonen, S. (2005). Reversibility of the other-race effect in face recognition during childhood. *Psychological Science, 16*, 440–444.

Sashkin, M., & Walberg, H.J. (Eds.). (1993). *Educational leadership and school culture.* Berkeley, CA: McCutchan.

Sax, L., Astin, A.W., Korn, W.S., & Mahoney, K.M. (1997). *The American freshman national norms for fall 1997.* Los Angeles, CA: Higher Education Research Institute, University of California, Los Angeles.

Sax, L.J., Hurtado, S., Lindholm, J.A., Astin, A.W., & Korn, W.S. (2005). *The American freshman: National norms for fall 2004.* Los Angeles, CA: Higher Education Institute, University of California.

Schiefele, U., & Csikszentimihalyi, M. (1995). Motivation and ability as factors in mathematics experience and achievement. *Journal for Research in Mathematics Education, 26*(2), 163–181.

Schlossberg, N.K. (1989). Marginality and mattering: Key issues in building community. In D.C. Roberts (Ed.), *Designing campus activities to foster a sense of community* (pp. 5–15). San Francisco: Jossey-Bass.

Schneider, E.C., Zaslavsky, A.M., & Epstein, A.M. (2002). Racial disparities in the quality of care for enrollees in Medicare managed care. *Journal of the American Medical Association, 287*(10), 1288–1294.

Seastrom, M.M., Gruber, K.J., Henke, R., McGrath, D.J., & Cohen, B.A. (2002). *Qualifications of the public school teacher workforce: Prevalence of out-of-field teaching, 1987–88 to 1999–2000* (NCES 2002-603). Washington, DC: U.S. Department of Education, National Center for Education Statistics.

Sedlacek, W. (1987). Black students on white campuses: 20 years of research. *Journal of College Student Personnel, 28*, 484–495.

Sedlacek, W.E. (1993). Employing noncognitive variables in admissions and retention in higher education. In *Achieving diversity: Issues in the recruitment and retention of underrepresented racial/ethnic students in higher education* (pp. 33–39). Alexandria, VA: National Association of College Admission Counselors.

Segall, M.H., Campbell, D.T., & Herskovits, M.J. (1966). *The influence of culture on visual perception.* Indianapolis, IN: Bobbs-Merrill.

Seligman, M.E.P. (1998). *Learned optimism.* New York: Pocket Books (Simon and Schuster).

Shah, A. (2008). Poverty facts and stats. Retrieved January 10, 2012, from http://www.globalissues.org/article/26/poverty-facts-and-stats.

Shapiro, S.R. (1993). *Human rights violations in the United States: A report on U.S. compliance.* New York: Human Rights Watch, American Civil Liberties Union.

Sherif, M., Harvey, D.J., White, B.J., Hood, W.R., & Sherif, C.W. (1961). *The robbers' cave experiment.* Norman, OK: Institute of Group Relations.

Shor, I. (1992). *Empowering education: Critical teaching for social change.* Chicago: University of Chicago Press.

Sidanius, J., Levin, S., Liu, H., & Pratto, F. (2000). Social dominance orientation, anti-egalitarianism, and the political psychology of gender: An extension and cross-cultural replication. *European Journal of Social Psychology, 30*, 41–67.

Slavin, R. (1980). Cooperative learning: What research says to the teacher. Baltimore, MD: Center for Social Organization of Schools.

Slavin, R.E. (1990). *Cooperative learning: Theory, research, and practice*. Englewood Cliffs, NJ: Prentice Hall.

Slavin, R.E., & Madden, N.A. (2001). *Reducing the gap: Success for All and the achievement of African-American and Latino students*. Washington, DC: Office of Educational Research and Improvement.

Smith, D. (1997). How diversity influences learning. *Liberal Education, 83*(2), 42–48.

Smith, R. (2005). Saving black boys: Unimaginable outcomes for the most vulnerable students require imaginable leadership. *School Administrator*, 1–7.

Smith, R.L. (1994). The world of business. In W.C. Hartel, S.W. Schwartz, S.D. Blume, & J.N. Gardner (Eds.), *Ready for the real world* (pp. 123–135). Belmont, CA: Wadsworth Publishing.

Snow, C. (2005). From literacy to learning. *Harvard Education Letter*, July/August.

Speidel, G. (1992). When children don't speak the language of instruction. *The Kamehameha Journal of Education, 3*(2), 93–107.

Stangor, C., Sechrist, G.B., & Jost, J.T. (2001). Changing racial beliefs by providing consensus information. *Personality and Social Psychology Bulletin, 27*, 484–494.

Stephan, W. (1986). The effects of school desegregation: An evaluation 30 years after Brown. In M.J. Sachs & L. Saxe (Eds.), *Advances in applied social psychology* (pp. 181–206). Hillsdale, NJ: Erlbaum.

Salinas, J.P. (2002). The effectiveness of minority teachers on minority student success. National Association of African American Studies & National Association of Hispanic and Latino Studies: 2000 Literature Monograph Series. Proceedings (Education Section) (Houston, TX, February 21–26, 2000).

Stephan, W. (1980). A brief historical overview of school desegregation. In W.G. Stephan & J.R. Feagin (Eds.), *School desegregation, past, present, and future* (pp. 3–22). New York: Plenum Press.

Stephan, W. (1978). School desegregation: An evaluation of predictions made in *Brown v. Board of Education*. *Psychological Bulletin, 85*, 217–238.

Suarez-Orozco, C., & Suarez-Orozco, M. (2002). *Children of immigration*. Cambridge, MA: Harvard University Press.

Suskie, L. (2000). Fair assessment practices: Giving students equitable opportunities to demonstrate learning. *AAHE Bulletin, 52*(9), 7–9.

Swap, W.C. (1977). Intergroup attraction and repeated exposure to rewards and punishers. *Personality and Social Psychology Bulletin, 3*, 248–251.

Tafjel, H. (1982). *Social identity and intergroup behavior*. Cambridge, England: Cambridge University Press.

Tatum, B.D. (2007). *Can we talk about race? And other conversations in an era of school resegregation*. Boston: Beacon Press.

Taylor, O. (1990). *Cross-cultural communication: An essential dimension of effective education*. Revised Edition.

Taylor, S.E., Peplau, L.A., & Sears, D.O. (2006). *Social psychology* (12th ed.). Upper Saddle River, NJ: Pearson/Prentice-Hall.

Tchudi, S.N. (1986). *Teaching writing in the content areas: College level*. New York: National Educational Association.

Tharp, R.G., Estrada, P., Dalton, S.S., & Yamauchi, L.A. (2000). *Teaching transformed: Achieving excellence, fairness, inclusion and harmony*. Boulder, CO: Westview.

Thompson, A., & Cuseo, J.B. (2009). *Diversity and the college experience*. Dubuque, IA: Kendall Hunt.

Thompson, A., & Luhman, R. (1997). Familial predictors of educational attainment: Regional and racial variations. In P. Hall (Ed.), *Race, ethnicity, and multiculturalism* (pp. 63–88). New York: Garland Publishing.

Thompson, G.L. (2003). Predicting African American parents and guardians satisfaction with teachers and public schools. *The Journal of Educational Research, 96*, 277–285.

Thompson, R.F. (1981). Peer grading: Some promising advantages for composition research and the classroom. *Research in the Teaching of English, 15(2)*, 172–174.

Tobias, S. (1978). *Overcoming math anxiety*. Boston: Houghton Mifflin.

Tomlinson, C.A. (1999). *How to differentiate instruction in mixed-ability classrooms*. Alexandria, VA: ASCD.

Tomlinson, C.A. (2001). *How to differentiate instruction in mixed ability classrooms* (2nd ed.). Alexandria, VA: Association for Supervision and Curriculum Development.

Tomlinson, C.A. (2004). The Mobius effect: Addressing learning variance in school. *Journal of Learning Disabilities, 37*. Alexandria, VA: Association for Supervision and Curriculum Development.

Tracey, T., & Sherry, P. (1984). College student distress as a function of person environment fit. *Journal of College Student Personnel, 25(5)*, 436–442.

Tyler, R.W. (1950). *Basic principles of curriculum and instruction*. Chicago: University of Chicago Press.

UNEP News Centre. (2010). UN opens biodiversity year with plea to save world's life-supporting ecosystems. Retrieved from http://www.unep.org/Documents.Multilingual/Default.asp?DocumentID=606&ArticleID=6439&l=en&t=long.

Underwood, B.J. (1983). *Attributes of memory*. Glenview, IL: Scott, Foresman, & Company.

U.S. Census Bureau. (2008a). An older and more diverse nation by midcentury. Retrieved August 20, 2008, from http://www.census.gov/Press-Release/www/releases/archives/population/012496.html.

U.S. Census Bureau. (2008b). Current population survey's annual social and economic supplement. Retrieved January 10, 2012, from http://www.census.gov/apsd/techdoc/cps/cpsmar08.pdf.

U.S. Census Bureau. (2000). Racial and ethnic classifications in Census 2000 and beyond. Retrieved December 19, 2006, from http://census.gov/population/www/socdemo/race/racefactcb.html.

U.S. Department of Education, National Center for Education Statistics. (2005). NAEP data explorer. Retrieved from http://nces.ed.gov/nationsreportcard.nde/.

U.S. Department of Education, National Center for Education Statistics. (2007). *The nation's report card: Reading 2007 (NCES 2007-496)*. Washington, DC: U.S. Government Printing Office.

U.S. Department of Education. (2008). *Public school principal, BIE school principal, and private school principal data files, 2007–2008*. Washington, DC: National Center for Education Statistics, Schools and Staffing Survey (SASS).

U.S. Department of Education. (2009). National Center for Education Statistics. Common Core of Data (CCD), Public Elementary/Secondary School Universe Survey, 2008–09.

U.S. Department of Health & Human Services. (2003). *School-Community partnerships: A guide*. Washington, DC: Author.

U.S. Department of Labor. (2008). *America's dynamic workforce*. Washington, DC: Author.

Uzzi, B., & Dunlap, S. (2005). How to build your network. *Harvard Business Review*, December, 1–8.

Valenzuela, A. (1999). *Subtractive schooling: U.S.-Mexican youth and the politics of caring*. Albany, NY: State University of New York Press.

Vanneman, A., Hamilton, L., Baldwin Anderson, J., & Rahman, T. (2009). *Achievement gaps: How black and white students in public schools perform in mathematics and reading on the national assessment of educational progress, (NCES 2009-455)*. Washington, DC: National Center for Education Statistics, Institute of Education Sciences, U.S. Department of Education.

Wheelright, J. (2005). Human, study thyself. *Discover*, March, 39–45.

Villegas, A.M., & Lucas, T. (2002). *Educating culturally responsive teachers*. Albany, NY: State University of New York Press.

Vogelgesang, L.J., Ikeda, E.K., Gilmartin, S.K., & Keup, J.R. (2002). Service-learning and the first-year experience: Outcomes related to learning and persistence. In E. Zlotkowski (Ed.), *Service-learning and the first-year experience: Preparing students for personal success and civic responsibility* (Monograph No. 34, pp. 15–26). Columbia, SC: University of South Carolina, National Resource Center for The First-Year Experience and Students in Transition.

Vygotsky, L. (1978). Interaction between learning and development. From Mind and Society, pp. 79-91. Cambridge, MA: Harvard University Press.

Wang, J. (1998). Opportunity to learn: The impacts and policy implications. *Educational Evaluation and Policy Analysis, 20*(3), 137–156.

Weinstein, C.E. (1994). Strategic learning/strategic teaching: Flip sides of a coin. In P.R. Pintrich, D.R. Brown, & C.E. Weinstein (Eds.), *Student motivation, cognition, and learning* (pp. 257–274). Hillsdale, NJ: Lawrence Erlbaum.

Welty, W. (1989). Discussion method teaching. *Change, 21*(4), 41–49.

White, E.M. (1985). *Teaching and assessing writing*. San Francisco: Jossey-Bass.

Whitt, E., Edison, M., Pascarella, E., Terenzini, P., & Nora, A. (2001). Influences on students' openness to diversity and challenge in the second and third years of college. *Journal of Higher Education, 72*, 172–204.

Weissglass, J. (2001). Racism and the achievement gap. *Education Week, 20*(43), 49–72.

Wieman, C.E. (2007). Why not try a scientific approach to science education? *Change, 39*(5).

Wiggan, G. (2008). From opposition to engagement: Lessons from high achieving African American students. *Urban Review, 40*(4), 317–349.

Wilder, D.A. (1984). Inter-group contact: The typical member and the exception to the rule. *Journal of Experimental Psychology, 20*, 177–194.

Wilkie, C.J., & Thompson, C.A. (1993). First-year reentry women's perceptions of their classroom experiences. *Journal of The Freshman Year Experience, 5*(2), 69–90.

Wilson, R.F. (1987). A perspective on evaluating administrative units in higher education. *New Directions for Institutional Research, 56*, 3–13.

Wilson, S.M., Floden, R., & Ferrini-Mundy, J. (2001). *Teacher preparation research: Current knowledge, gaps, and recommendations. Research report prepared for the U.S. Department of Education*. Seattle, WA: Center for the Study of Teaching and Policy, University of Washington.

Wlodkowski, R.J. (2008). *Enhancing adult motivation to learn: A comprehensive guide for teaching all adults* (3rd ed.). San Francisco: Wiley.

Wolvin, A.D., & Coakley, C.G. (1993). *Perspectives on listening*. Norwood, NJ: Ablex Publishing.

Wong-Fillmore, L. (1991). When learning a second language means losing the first. *Early Childhood Research Quarterly, 6,* 323–346.

Worchel, S. (1979). Cooperation and the reduction of intergroup conflict: Some determining factors. In W. Austin & S. Worchel (Eds.), *The social psychology of intergroup relations.* Monterey, CA: Brooks/Cole.

Wright, D.J. (Ed.). (1987). *Responding to the needs of today's minority students.* New Directions for Student Services, No. 38. San Francisco: Jossey-Bass.

Yan, W. (1999). Successful African American students: The role of parental involvement. *The Journal of Negro Education, 68,* 5–22.

Yosso, T.J. (2005). Whose culture has capital? A critical race theory discussion of community cultural wealth. *Race Ethnicity and Education, 8*(1), 69–91.

Zajonc, R.B. (1968). Attitudinal effects of mere exposure. *Journal of Personality and Social Psychology, 9,* Monongraph supplement No. 2, Part 2.

Zajonc, R.B. (1970). Brainwash: Familiarity breeds comfort. *Psychology Today,* February, 33–35, 60–62.

Zajonc, R.B. (2001). Mere exposure: A gateway to the subliminal. *Current Directions in Psychological Science, 10,* 224–228.

Zimmerman, B.J., & Kitsantas, A. (2005). Homework practices and academic achievement: The mediating role of self-efficacy and perceived responsibility beliefs. *Contemporary Educational Psychology, 30,* 397–417.

Zinsser, W. (1988). *Writing to learn.* New York: Harper & Row.

Index

A

Acceleration of learning, 27–30
Acceptance, 65–66
Acculturation, rates of, 122
Acknowledgment, 63–65
Action in personal development model, 66–68
Aesthetics, component of culture, 8
Ageism, 53
Allport, Gordon, 54
Anti-semitism, 52
Apartheid, 51
Assessment, 151–173
    expectations for students, 157–165
    feedback, 165–169
    self-assessment, 169–172
    self-awareness, 169–172
    timing of, 156–157
Association for Effective Schools, 88
Aurelius, Marcus, 113
Averaging student scores, 164
Awareness, 26–27, 61–63
Awareness of beliefs, 60

B

Background interest probes, 138
Background knowledge, 138
Backgrounds, diverse, meeting people from, 98–99
Bacon, Francis, 98
Beliefs
    awareness of, 60
    religious, human diversity, 1
Belongingness, 4
Bias, 45–72
    acceptance, 65–66
    acknowledgment, 63–65
    action, 66–68
    awareness, 61–63
    categorizing people, 56
    causes of, 54–59
    discrimination, 48–49
    group identity, 59
    membership, group, 59

    memory, selective, 55–56
    new experiences, comfort with, 54–55
    perception, 57–58
    personal development model, 60–68
    prejudice, 47–48, 54–59
    rationalizing, 58–59
    segregation, 49–53
    selective perception, 55–56
    self-esteem, 59
    stereotyping, 45–47
    unknown, comfort with, 54–55
Body type, human diversity, 1
Bok, Derek, 35, 40
Brennan, William J., 111
Brown v. Board of Education court case, 17
Bruner, Jerome, 7
Business-High-Education Forum, 34

C

Career preparation, 34–36, 41
Carnegie, Dale, 105, 108
Carter, Jimmy, 6
Case studies, 142–143
Categorizing people, 56
Causes of discrimination, 54–59
Causes of prejudice, 54–59
Citizenship, human diversity, 1
Class, social, diversity, 14–16
Classism, 52
Clemens, Samuel, 97
Cohen, Cheryl Bernstein, 4, 128
Comfort with unknown, 54–55
Communication, 97–117
    diverse backgrounds, meeting people from, 98–99
    human relations skills, 105–110
    interactions, 97–98
    interpersonal communication skills, 99–105
    leadership role, 110–115
    listening skills, 99–105
    speaking skills, 99–105
Community, creating sense of, 128–129
Community diversity, 80–81
Complexity of thought, 33

Concept map, 120
Conditionally phrased questions, 137
Conley, David, 26, 86
Context, 73–96
    community diversity, 80–81
    curriculum, 83–86
    family diversity, 77–79
    heroes, 83–84
    holidays, 83–84
    integration, 84
    leaders, 89–91
    mainstream curriculum, 83
    school diversity, 82–91
    structural reform, 84–86
    student diversity, 74–77
    teachers, 87–89
Cosmos, diversity from perspective of, 19–20
Council of Europe, 39
Course-student connection, 135–147
    future life-planning assignments, 147
    subject matter, 135–140
    writing-to-learn exercises, 140–147
Covey, Stephen, 101
Creative thinking, 34, 41
Critical thinking, 30–33, 41
Cultural competence, indicators of, 121–122
Cultural diversity, defined, 7–8
Cultural perspective, diversity from, 11–16
Cultural sensitivity, 68
Culturally aligned practices, 122
Culture, components of, 8
Curriculum, 83–86
    heroes, 83–84
    holidays, 83–84
    integration, 84
    mainstream, 83
    structural reform, 84–86
Cuseo, Joe, 6, 11, 13, 29, 48, 59–61, 66, 112, 124–125, 128, 134, 137, 171

D

Dees, Morris, 1
Delpit, Lisa, 62
Democracy, 39–40
DeMott, Dr. Benjamin, 124
Dewey, John, 39
Disability, human diversity, 1
Discrimination, 48–49, 51
    reduction in, 37–39

Distance, component of culture, 8
Diverse backgrounds, meeting people from, 98–99
Diversity, humanity, individuality, distinguished, 7
Diversity education, 25–43
    acceleration of learning, 27–30
    awareness, 26–27
    career preparation, 34–36
    creative thinking, 34
    critical thinking, 30–33
    democracy, 39–40
    discrimination, reduction in, 37–39
    emotional intelligence, 36–37
    insight, 26–27
    prejudice reduction, 37–39
    self-knowledge, 26–27
    social relationships, 36–37
Documentation, 158
Douglass, Frederick, 17
Drucker, Peter F., 102
Du Bois, W.E.B., 17
Dunston, Georgia, 5
Durability, 36, 86
Durant, Will, 124

E

EdChange Multicultural Pavilion, 120
EdChange Organization, 16
Education in diversity, 25–43
Education Trust, 83
Egocentricity, 102
Egoists, 102
Egotists, 102
Emotional development, 151
Emotional intelligence, 36–37
Empathy, 60
Environment, safety in, 90
Equality principle, 129
Ericksen, Stanford, 161
Esteem, 4
Ethical development, 133, 151
Ethnic diversity, defined, 9
Expectations for students, 157–165

F

Facial expressions, 3
Family, component of culture, 8
Family diversity, 77–79
Family guest speakers, 79
Family status, human diversity, 1

Feedback, 126, 166
Feedback to students, 165–169
Fight-or-flight reaction, 55
Finances, component of culture, 8
Fitzgerald, F. Scott, 63
Focused questions, 137
Forgiving grading system, 169
Frank, Anne, 5
Future life-planning assignments, 147

G

Gender, human diversity, 1
Generation, human diversity, 1
Genocide, 52
Global perspective, diversity from, 18–19
Group identity, 59
Group membership, 59
Guttman, Amy, 83

H

Hate crimes, 52
Hate groups, 52
Heterogeneous discussion groups, 133
Heterosexism, 53
Higher-order thinking questions, 137
Hill, Patrick J., 37
Holidays, 83–84
Home visits, 79
Homogeneous groups, 133
Homophobia, 53
Human diversity, 1
Human relations skills, 105–110
Humanity, diversity, individuality, distinguished, 7
Humor, 127

I

Ideology, political, human diversity, 1
Illness, human diversity, 1
Inclusion, climate of, 122
Inclusiveness, 119–149
    future life-planning assignments, 147
    peer connections, 128–130
    rapport with class, 123–128
    sense of community, 128–129
    small group learning, 129–135
    small group work, 129–130
    student-course connection, 135–147
    student-teacher connection, 123–128
    subject matter, 135–140
    writing-to-learn exercises, 140–147
Income, diversity in, 14–15
Individuality, diversity, humanity, distinguished, 7
Insight, 26–27
Institutional racism, 51
Instructional leadership, 90
Integration, 84
Intelligence, emotional, 36–37
International perspective, diversity from, 18
Interpersonal communication skills, 99–105

J

Jim Crow legislation, 51
Jingoism, 52
Jordan, Michael, 7
Jung, Carl, 67

K

Kierkegaard, Soren, 65
King, Martin Luther, Jr., 39, 50
Kluckholn, Clyde, 7

L

Language
    component of culture, 8
    native, human diversity, 1
Leaders within school, 89–91
Leadership for Student Success, 152
Leadership role, 110–115
Learning ability/disability, human diversity, 1
Learning assessment, 151–173
    expectations for students, 157–165
    feedback, 165–169
    self-assessment, 169–172
    self-awareness, 169–172
    timing of assessment, 156–157
Learning styles, human diversity, 1
Lippmann, Walter, 32
Listening skills, 99–105

M

Mainstream curriculum, 83
Mann, Horace, 83
Marital status, human diversity, 1
Maslow, Abraham, 4, 34
McIntosh, Peggy, 49
Memory, selective, 55–56
Mental ability/disability, human diversity, 1
Mental health/illness, human diversity, 1

Middle Eastern Americans, 12
Mission, school, 90
Model of personal development
    acceptance, 65–66
    acknowledgment, 63–65
    action, 66–68
    awareness, 61–63
Models of excellent work, 157

N

Names, remembering, strategies for, 105
National citizenship, human diversity, 1
National Council for Social Sciences, 135, 142
National Council for Social Studies, 30, 33, 46, 80–81, 84–85, 141
National origin, human diversity, 1
National perspective, diversity from, 16–17
National region, human diversity, 1
Native language, human diversity, 1
Nelson, Craig, 164
New experiences, comfort with, 54–55
Nietzsche, Friedrich, 33

O

Obama, Barack, 14
One-minute paper, 140
Open-ended questions, 137
Organization, 158
Orientation, sexual, human diversity, 1

P

Parent interview, 79
Parent newsletter, 79
Parental status, human diversity, 1
Pauses for reflection, 139
Peer connections, 128–130
    sense of community, 128–129
    small group work, 129–130
People skills, 105–110
Perception, 57–58
Personal development model, 60–68
Personalized feedback, 168
Personalized questions, 137
Persuasive feedback, 168
Philosophy, component of culture, 8
Physical ability/disability, human diversity, 1
Political ideology, human diversity, 1
Positive feedback, 168–169
Post-presentation strategies, 140

Practical feedback, 167–168
Pre-presentation strategies, 138–139
Pre-tests, 138
Precise feedback, 167
Prejudice, 47–48, 51
Prejudice reduction, 37–39
Presentation, 158
Proactive feedback, 167
Problem-solving presentations, 139
Public Service Enterprise Group, 2

R

Racial diversity, defined, 9–11
Racism, institutional, 51
Rapport with class, 123–128
Rationalizing discrimination, 58–59
Rationalizing prejudice, 58–59
Reflective thinking, 33
Reform of curriculum, 84–86
Region, national, human diversity, 1
Regionalism, 52
Relationship-building, 97–117
    diverse backgrounds, meeting people from, 98–99
    human relations skills, 105–110
    interactions, 97–98
    interpersonal communication skills, 99–105
    leadership role, 110–115
    listening skills, 99–105
    speaking skills, 99–105
Religion, component of culture, 8
Religious beliefs, human diversity, 1
Religious bigotry, 52
Remembering names, strategies for, 105
Responsive instruction, 119–149
    future life-planning assignments, 147
    peer connections, 128–130
    rapport with class, 123–128
    sense of community, 128–129
    small group learning, 129–135
    small group work, 129–130
    student-course connection, 135–147
    student-teacher connection, 123–128
    subject matter, 135–140
    writing-to-learn exercises, 140–147
Retrospection, 140
Rockefeller, David, 106
Rockefeller, John D., 99
Role playing exercises, 141

S

Safety, 4
Saks, Elyn, 2
School diversity, 82–91
   curriculum, 83–86
   holidays, 83–84
   integration, 84
   leaders, 89–91
   mainstream curriculum, 83
   structural reform, 84–86
   teachers, 87–89
School facilities, family use of, 79
School hotline, 79
School mission, 90
Science, component of culture, 8
Scott, Robert E., 157
Scripts, 141–142
Segregation, 49–53, 69
Selective perception, 55–56
Self-actualization, 4
Self-assessment, 169–172
Self-awareness, 40, 169–172
Self-esteem, 59
Self-knowledge, 26–27
Sense of community, 128–129
Sensitivity, cultural, 68
Sexism, 53
Sexual orientation, human diversity, 1
Shakespeare, William, 102
Shared presentation, 138
Simulations, 142
Simultaneity principle, 129
Slavery, 51
Small group learning, 129–135
Social class, diversity, 14–16
Social development, 41–42, 151
Social relationships, 36–37
Societal perspective, diversity from, 14–16
Socioeconomic status
   diversity, 14–16
   human diversity, 1
Socrates, 26
Speaking skills, 99–105
Spiritual beliefs, human diversity, 1
Status
   diversity, 14–16
   family, human diversity, 1
   human diversity, 1
   marital, human diversity, 1
   parental, human diversity, 1

Stereotypes, 45–72
   acceptance, 65–66
   acknowledgment, 63–65
   action, 66–68
   awareness, 61–63
   categorizing people, 56
   causes of, 54–59
   discrimination, 48–49
   group identity, 59
   membership, group, 59
   memory, selective, 55–56
   perception, 57–58
   personal development model, 60–68
   prejudice, 47–48, 54–59
   rationalizing, 58–59
   segregation, 49–53
   selective perception, 55–56
   self-esteem, 59
   unknown, comfort with, 54–55
Stereotyping, 45–47, 51, 69
Structural reform, curriculum, 84–86
Student-course connection, 135–147
   future life-planning assignments, 147
   subject matter, 135–140
   writing-to-learn exercises, 140–147
Student diversity, 74–77
Student journals, 127
Student-teacher connection, 123–128
   rapport with class, 123–128
Styles of learning, human diversity, 1
Subject matter, 135–140
Swinnerton, Frank, 107

T

Teacher-student connection, 123–128
Teamwork, 112–113
Technology, component of culture, 8
Terrorism, 52
Teton Lakota Indian saying, 128
Thinking complexity, 33
Thompson, Aaron, 5, 10, 15, 30, 46, 60–61, 64, 74, 78, 88, 151, 170–171
Thurber, James, 100
Time, component of culture, 8
Timing of assessments, 156–157
Tobe, Dorothy Echols, 157
Transferability, 36, 86

U

Universe, diversity from perspective, 19–20
Unknown, comfort with, 54–55

V
Verbal whips, 138

W
Wiggins, Grant, 166
Within-presentation strategies, 139–140

Writing-to-discuss, 139
Writing-to-learn exercises, 140–147

X
Xenophobia, 52